# We Keep a Light

N. Bar

Northern Beach

Little N.E. Pond

N.W. Bar

Salt Water Pond

Gunning Rocks

Woody Pond

Bar

Flag Pond

Swamp

Camp

Field

Garron's Cove

Kelp Cove

S. Bar

Fields

Cranberry Swamp

Slip

Boat House

Site of Breakwater

Red Bank

Wreck of ATLAS

Clearing

Wreck of WIN THE WAR

Baked Apple Swamp

Pool at Saddleback

Salt Rock

Fields

Gov't Property Line

BON PORTAGE ISLAND

Lighthouse

Boilers of SS EXPRESS

HEWSON

# We Keep a Light

Evelyn M. Richardson

Decorations by Winifred Fox

NIMBUS
PUBLISHING

Nimbus Publishing Limited
PO Box 9301, Station A
Halifax, NS  B3K 5N5
(902) 455-4286

Cover design: Arthur B. Carter, Halifax
Cover photo: Bob Brooks Illustrative Photography, Halifax
Printed and bound in Canada by Best Book Manufacturers Inc.

Canadian Cataloguing in Publication Data

Richardson, Evelyn M. (Evelyn May), 1902-1976.
We keep a light
(Nimbus classics)
ISBN 1-55109-114-3
1. Richardson, Evelyn M. (Evelyn May), 1902-1976.  2. Richardson family.
3. Lighthouse keepers—Nova Scotia—Biography.  I. Title.  II. Series.
PS8535.I32Z53  1995        387'.1'55 C95-950006-5
PR9199.3.R42Z478  1995

To My Favourite Lightkeeper
MORRILL

AND

His Assistants
ANNE, LAURIE

AND

BETTY JUNE
This Book
IS
Lovingly Dedicated.

I WISH to thank "Uncle Gilbert" Nickerson for information; various friends and relatives, especially my brother Harold, and Mr. Andrew Larkin of Shag Harbour, for snapshots; my cousin Annie Saunders for her help in securing a chart of the waters and islands near Bon Portage; and my friend Hazel Peveril for her trouble in procuring a typewriter without which I would never have had the courage to attempt this book.

# CONTENTS

*So whether the storm king whitens its shoals,*
*Or whether by soft winds fanned,*
*I love the sound of the sea as it rolls*
*In the hollow of God's hand;*
*For I was born within sound of its waves,*
*And it ever shall be to me*
*The song of all songs that I love the best,*
*The roar of the gray old sea, the laugh of the*
    *summer sea.*

# 1

## INTRODUCTORY

You will find our little Island of Bon Portage* on few maps. It lies off the south-west tip of Nova Scotia, and its northern end is within a mile of that part of the mainland known as the Great Bend, just where the coastline of the province turns easterly and westerly. The Island slants seaward in a southerly direction and away from the curve of the coast, so that its southern end where the lighthouse stands is more remote from the mainland and more exposed to sea and wind than any other portion.

The Island is about three miles long and very narrow, its width varying from approximately three-quarters of a mile at both ends to less than one-quarter of a mile in the

*Pronounced like "on shortage."

centre. Its area is between six and seven hundred acres. The whole Island is low-lying, at no place does it rise more than twenty feet above sea level, and the highest land is found on the southern and northern ends. The centre consists of low wet swamp, known in these parts as Savannah: much of it is below the level of the sea, protected from being flooded at abnormally high tides by a sea-wall of beach rocks which these same high tides have thrown up against their own depredations. Looking across this low centre one can easily imagine Bon Portage becoming two separate islands in the course of a few more years' encroachment by an ever-greedy sea. This was actually so for a short time during one exceptionally high tide, when the sea covered all the low centre and waves swept across from either side to meet in the middle of the Savannah.

The appearance of the Island from the mainland, or from the nearer vantage point of a boat's deck, leads no one into lyrics of rapture concerning its beauty. In fact, one friend tactlessly described it as "that God-forsaken strip of swamp and rock." That statement, however, does it somewhat less than justice, and it bears closer acquaintance more graciously than one might expect; it has even its spots of woodland beauty, in the shelter of the belts of fir and spruce that ring the Island and cover a good part of it. But all aspects of the Island itself pale beside the views it affords of the sea, stretching unbroken for hundreds of miles from the western beach, and breaking in unending, ever-changing splendour on the rocks and reefs that gird the shore.

Since this coast, typical of Nova Scotia's shoreline, is cut and eaten away by many arms of the sea—sounds, bays, coves, harbours and passages—there are a corresponding number of capes, small islands and points or headlands. The treacherous tides and rocky coast are dangerous to navigation, and to offset to some extent the hazards inherent in the swift tides among the reefs and shoals there are many buoys and lighthouses. Some of the latter, such as Cape Sable, are large and of importance to trans-atlantic shipping; some are small and serve mostly to guide belated local fishing boats to their home harbours. Our light is betwixt and between. This is true of its position and size as well as of its importance.

It often comes about that Morrill is not able to be home at sunset to "light up," and I act as substitute light-keeper. After the lamps have been lit, and the mechanism that revolves the light set in motion, I must stay for some time in the lantern, as we call the glass-and-metal enclosure that contains the light apparatus and through which the beams of the lamp are visible from the sea. This is to make certain that all is operating smoothly, since any flaw in the performance is most apt to appear when the mechanism starts.

This hour of "lighting up" is a time that I enjoy. I love to watch the beams of near-by lights take their places like friendly stars in the twilight. Though I know only one of the keepers, the lights themselves are old friends. Off there, about twelve miles to the west, is Seal Island's rather irregular beam; to the south-west is nothing but unbroken sea and sky, but eight miles to the south-east is Cape Sable's bright white flash; not so far away and almost due east glows West Head's warm red; while nearest to us, only two miles away, is the twinkling little harbour light of Emerald Isle. Then to the north, snug and protected by the outlying capes and islands, the small fixed light of Wood's Harbour glows redly.

On fine evenings these add to the beauty of sunset skies and placidly shimmering sea; but Oh! on stormy, wind-tossed nights, when the lighthouse rocks and the metal lantern vibrates like a taut wire under the rough searching fingers of the wind, they are the friendly smiles of comrades in the struggle against wind and sea, and as our lamps flash out through the murk, I am glad they are adding their bit to the forces that fight the darkness and storm. Even when fog or driving rain and snow shut away everything but the reflected beams of our own lamps, it is something to know that the other lights, like ours, still flash their messages from towers standing as sentinels, although I cannot see them.

While I watch the functioning of the light apparatus, I look seaward to the south where the whistle-buoy, a mile from the light, marks the out-lying reefs of the Island, for this, too, is under our supervision, and we must report to the Department of Transport if it shifts from its position, or fails to utter the dismal shrieks and moans that earn its local name of The Groaner.

So here I am, a lightkeeper's wife on a small island three miles from the mainland, isolated much of the year, and living under conditions that most of the country outgrew fifty years or more ago. When I stop to think of it I am as much surprised as you would be to find yourself in a similar situation, and I know Morrill often feels the same astonishment. Our three children do not share the slight sense of bewilderment that we sometimes feel. They have known no other life and are quite sure that they would want nothing different. To them, living on an island dependent on a small boat for the only communication with the rest of the world, going to school by letters and a correspondence course, exchanging most infrequent week-end visits and many letters with their little friends as their only companionship outside the family, providing their own amusement and sports, seems to them the most natural state of affairs in the world, and children who live otherwise are more to be pitied than blamed perhaps, but certainly not to be envied. Their chief worry is that we should be forced to change our place and mode of living.

While most children when learning to draw depict low, squat houses with a door, a window and smoke-billowing chimney, my children's first efforts at drawing a dwelling ran all to height. I was puzzled until I realized that to them home was a lighthouse, like ours small on the ground and running up four stories. When Anne and Laurie were tiny and we were returning from a walk or a boat-trip, their first glimpse of the lighthouse was greeted with joyous cries: from Anne who liked to repeat words, "Home-again-home," while Laurie was contented with a crooning "Homie-homie."

Perhaps the home in isolated exposed spots such as this is more beloved in spite of inconveniences and lack of facilities, because it is so patently a refuge, a shelter from the forces of the elements, so cosy in comparison with what lies outside it. The average city and town home shares its duty of providing shelter and warmth with office, school, theatre and restaurant, and one is seldom long exposed to the strength of the cold and the sweep of the storm. Our lighthouse is draughty, wind-swept and inconvenient to heat, but what comparative comfort it offers after a cold trip in an open boat, or a walk over icy, wind-swept fields! So if our children have missed a familiarity with some of the finer amenities of life, they have not missed a deep comprehension of the meanings that lie in "Home."

As for Morrill and me, although the Island is far from the paradise of fictional isles and many aspects of life here are hard and monotonous, I am sure we share a companion-ship and deep happiness that we never could have sur-passed, and might not have reached, elsewhere. I believe there is nothing that binds a man and woman more closely than mutual reliance and assistance and the knowledge of difficulties faced and overcome together. As a family we feel a sense of interdependence and a close community of interests that often must be sacrificed to the more widespread and diversified claims of modern life upon the different members of a family group.

## 2

## BEFORE BON PORTAGE

PERHAPS after all I should not be surprised to find myself in a lighthouse in this vicinity. One would never expect lightkeeping to run in families, as doctoring and seafaring seem to do, but on both sides of my family there have been lightkeepers. My father's great-grandfather was granted Cape Fourchu at Yarmouth, and the position of lightkeeper there as reward for his services as captain in the Royal Navy; his son succeeded him, and my grandfather was born in that light. I, myself, was born at Emerald Isle, only two miles from Bon Portage, where my mother's father, among other and varied activities, kept the light. As a child I often accompanied my grandfather on his short walk to the little harbour lighthouse when he went at sundown to light the lamps.  I remember climbing the steep ladder-like stairs, and the terrifyingly distorted face and hands of my grandfather as viewed through the thick round lenses.  I remember, too, the joy with which I caught the first faint gleam of the light through the swirling fog when one of my brothers and I were late returning from a visit to Shag Harbour, and the pressing folds of a curtain of black fog flattened and stretched the short mile journey over the well-known strip of sheltered water into what seemed to be an unending voyage upon unknown dangerous seas; and our small skiff was enveloped and lost in a strange grey world, only slightly less wet and cold than the water beneath us.  The little red light welcomed us, and in its diffused gleam we saw and felt the safety and warmth of the house-lights and the cosy kitchen fire waiting only a few minutes' row beyond us.

A lighthouse in the family also afforded us children a certain prestige among our contemporaries.  It was with great pride that we invited our young friends for a boat-trip to our grandfather's island; and when we escorted them to the points most likely to impress and interest them, you may be sure the lighthouse was never omitted.

However, lightkeeping never entered into my various childish daydreams.  Ever since I can remember my sole ambition was to be a teacher.  Since I adored my father and thought him the wisest and kindest of men, it was only natural that I should wish to follow his profession.

The first fifteen years of my life I spent in the fishing town of Clark's Harbour where my father was principal of the school, and my vacations at my grandparents' island home, so I was no stranger to the sea and its ways and had some idea of island life.  The chief difference between life at my grandfather's and our life here at Bon Portage has been that between the circumstances of a man who is established and successful in his business and the struggle of a young couple starting from scratch. This difference is not small.

When I was fifteen my father became principal of a Halifax school and we moved to the suburb of Bedford to live. I was very happy and made many dear friends there and at the old Halifax Academy. In due time I was graduated and realized my ambition to become a teacher. I loved the work, as I had thought I would, and had some success in my teaching.

In my daydreams and plans I had always thought of myself as "an old maid teacher"—how else to study and teach and travel? I had five brothers and our house was always bursting at the seams with boys, so I was not inclined to view the masculine sex with any undue romanticism.

Our children have always loved the story that their Daddy tells them:

"Once upon a time there was a Boy, who one evening when he was sixteen, went all unsuspecting to church as usual. And there was a New Girl, one he had never seen before. He thought she looked so pretty and nice, and she had on the cutest hat with daisies on it. Right away he said to himself, 'Now there's my Girl,' and this rather surprised him, since he had never thought that he wanted a girl at all. So when he went home he asked his sisters devious and complicated questions until he found out who this New Girl was. But it was almost a whole year before the poor Boy even got to meet the Girl."

(At this there are very accusing and indignant glances in my direction, to which I hasten to explain that the Boy was very shy, and that all the boys were strange to the Girl, so she didn't notice that Boy for some time.)

"Then after a while, the Boy got a car, a wonderful Ford that he made out of two old ones discarded at the factory where he worked. The Girl could not resist him then." (Great glee at this.) "So the Boy won the Girl and they got married and lived happily ever after." (Sighs of satisfaction.)

Actually our story was nearly as simple as the one Morrill tells, we were in love before we were twenty and married at twenty-four. Unfortunately, when we had just discovered our love, circumstances forced Morrill to find work, first in Quebec and then in the States, so that we saw each other only once or twice a year. Each of us was forced to fill the empty spaces left in our lives by the other's absence with different interests, and it seemed that if we were not to drift apart we should marry, although we had very little on which to set up housekeeping. Morrill had always contributed to his mother's support, and I had spent most of my savings on a year's study at Dalhousie and a piano. However, with all the high optimism which seems to go hand in hand with youthful love, I gave up my teaching and my hopes of finishing a college education to build a life with Morrill. I have never regretted my choice, or doubted its wisdom, although at times I have missed the companions in the world of schools and books with a longing that throbbed and ached as realistically as any physical pain.

For a year or so before our marriage, Morrill had been working in Worcester, Mass. We had decided that as soon as he had a steady job and a minimum salary on which we could be married I would join him there. Neither he nor I liked city life, and we hated to think of spending our future pent in a city, so far from friends and families. Then, too, Canada meant a great deal to us, and we wanted our children to be Canadians; so we hoped and planned to save enough to come back to Nova Scotia and buy a farm before we were too old.

It was while I, proudly wearing my newly acquired engagement ring, was discussing our plans for the future with my oldest brother, that Bon Portage first entered into them. Ashford had married and gone to live with our grandfather at the old home at Emerald Isle, and I was visiting him and Jean, his little new wife, during Christmas vacation. He suggested that Morrill buy Bon Portage Island, apply for the position of lightkeeper there when it became vacant, as he believed it would shortly, and with the salary of lightkeeper as mainstay, we could do mixed farming as a side-line. Ashford pointed out, as we had realized in our hearts, how hard it is to live on a small salary, while saving to make a start at a new life, and farming requires a large capital investment and a long wait for returns.

I wasn't sure just what I thought of this proposition, but I promised to write Morrill about it and I did. If I had been undecided as to whether or not the idea of light-keeping appealed to me, Morrill did not share my uncertainty. He wrote almost immediately that he had got in touch with Cousin Winnie, who owned the Island, and had practically decided to buy, the owner taking a mortgage on it. I didn't know whether I was glad or sorry to learn this; an imaginary farm of the future was quite different from an actual lighthouse, and the whole thing brought me out of my rosy day-dreams to solid earth with quite a jolt. I was amazed that Morrill should have purchased the Island so quickly, "sight unseen." As a matter of fact, I, myself, had only seen the lighthouse from Emerald Isle, two miles away, and had no clearer idea than Morrill had of conditions there, although my mother had visited the Island when she was a girl, and her friends the Wraytons were lightkeepers there.

Morrill and I were married at Emerald Isle in August, 1926, and returned to Worcester until a vacancy should occur at Bon Portage, when we hoped to receive the appointment as lightkeeper there. Morrill had only one day to spend at Emerald Isle, and the thickest of thick fogs shrouded everything beyond the distance of a few feet, so Bon Portage might have been on a different continent as far as catching a glimpse of it was concerned. Morrill returned to the States with no more knowledge than before of the land he had bought, and the spot where we planned to make our future home.

Of course we were happy in Worcester, together after many long separations, but we were not contented. I was lonely in furnished rooms all day and was not able to find a job; a business training rather than one for teaching would have stood me in good stead. Morrill's work was difficult, he became terribly thin during the hot weather and caught bad colds easily at other seasons.

On hot summer evenings we spent much of our time in a park near our apartment. This park had a lake with a tiny island and as we sat beside it we would compare it in size and shape with what we knew of our Island and its surrounding waters, and I would describe to Morrill the crisp salt breezes that swept across Emerald Isle and doubt-less across Bon Portage too; and every little detail I could remember of life on an island. We tried to imagine our-selves on a cool island shore instead of in the sweltering city, and busy in our garden and fields. It was just a game of make-believe, a modest version of Castles in Spain.

When the evenings became longer and cooler we spent many of them poring over the deed, and a blue-print of the government property and lighthouse that Cousin Winnie had sent us: trying to visualize from these scant details every aspect of the Island we had bought and hoped to use. Then Jean sent us a number of snaps she had taken for us of the lighthouse, the pond, and the path, and these spurred our imaginations anew. We borrowed books from the

Public Library on subjects we thought would prove useful to us when we started lighthouse-farming and especially on sheep husbandry. From these we made notes, and remembered more, that helped us when we really started sheep-raising.

During our stay in Worcester we made several fine friends, and enjoyed an occasional good movie, but neither of us was meant for a city-dweller, and from the first our minds and hearts were fixed on returning to Nova Scotia and starting life on the Island. When we had been married a year and a half Anne Gordon joined us. She was, it goes without saying, the most wonderful baby in the world, and our loneliness vanished. We hoped we would not be forced to rear her in a city on our modest means and found the hot summers trying for all of us.

Later Morrill changed his work to Boston and we obtained a flat in a suburb that was very like the country, but before many months Morrill's office was closed, a vacancy at Bon Portage Light appeared, and we came to my folks in Bedford to stay until it was filled—we hoped by us.

No words can describe our joy when the appointment at last came through. But we found it hard to content ourselves from that day in February that brought the long-awaited news from Ottawa until the day at the end of May that I with baby Anne left Halifax on the plodding Halifax and South-Western train to join Morrill at Bon Portage. He had preceded us by a week to learn his duties from the resigning lightkeeper and to have our furniture moved and installed before my arrival.

## 3

## ARRIVAL

SHAG HARBOUR is a little fishing village looking to the sea
across its shallow, island-dotted harbour, its neat houses
set squarely down amid huge grey granite boulders,
deposited by the edge of the receding ice-cap that covered
this part of the land ages and ages ago. My four-year-old
niece gave her impression of the place when someone spoke
of the houses of Shag Harbour, "Not *houses*," she said,
"*wharves* in Shag Harbour." Wharves and boats and fish
do seem to dominate the village and the men spend nearly
as much time on the water as they do on the land. Here
we get and send our mail, buy our supplies, and have what
little contact with the "Mainland" as our being so tied
to the lighthouse and its duties allow. Morrill probably

14

averages a trip a week to Shag Harbour, I average one or two a year, so that he is better known there than I. The women have been friendly, and I have had neighbourly visits with some of them, but so far I have not had the opportunity to accept many of their kind invitations, and few of them will face the boat trip and the water to call on me.

I have known the place and its inhabitants slightly since I was a child and spent my vacations at Emerald Isle. At that time we children knew it simply as "The Main," since our grandparents spoke always of "going to the Main," or "off on the Main." My mother's childhood home is in the centre of the village and my father taught the school there when he was a young man. Still I knew few of the people of the place when I arrived there one windy, overcast day in the spring of 1929.

Ashford met me in his car at the station of Shag Harbour, with his grin and a big hug, and took me and baby Anne to the wharf. I could see it was blowing "quite a breeze," and after a consultation with the man who was to take us to Bon Portage in his boat, it was decided the sea was so rough as to make landing on our Island impracticable for a woman and baby, so I said we would spend the night at Ashford's, and he would "set me on" (as they say hereabouts) when the tide was suitable in the afternoon of the following day.

Since I had last been to Emerald Isle, Ashford and Jean had built themselves a little new home in which they were living. My grandfather was still in the old home with (Bless your heart!) a bride of twenty-odd. Ashford was the same easy-going, lovable big brother. Poor Jean was very miserable, in bed under the doctor's orders, but chipper and happy as could be because she was to have the baby she wanted so much.

Ashford was taken and amused by Morrill's energy and keenness to get at things on Bon Portage. "You'd better take yourself a piece of ice to cool that fella of yours off. When I was on the other day, he said he already had work laid out for the next ten years! Make him take it easy."

Alas! He little knew Morrill. I have never yet been able to make him take it easy.

That evening the wind went down, and I stood at the kitchen window watching the flash of the Bon Portage Light and wondering what Morrill might be doing on there all alone.

"Morrill was doing the same thing the first night he was here," Ashford said, "And Dayson Kendrick told him, 'You're wishing you were on there now. Many a night you'll stand on there and wish you were off here.'"

Shag Harbour generally was decidedly sceptical of our staying in such a remote, lonely spot, especially after coming from Boston, the Mecca of their dreams to so many of them. Probably few would believe us if we told them we had been far lonelier in the cities than we ever were on the Island.

One of our luckiest breaks was to have Ashford and Jean as our nearest neighbours those first four years. We were able to visit back and forth occasionally, and it was so comforting to have someone of our own to whom we could turn, if the need should arise. They left Emerald Isle during our fifth year here, and we have never ceased to miss them. Jean, like me, loved the island life, the boats and water, and even the inconveniences, although she and Ashford were not as isolated or tied to their job as we are. Ashford, like Morrill, did some mixed farming, but he depended on buying and selling lobsters as his main source of income. The business was not good at the time of our arrival and soon deteriorated even more; this slump was a contributing factor in their decision to leave Emerald Isle, which they both loved and still love, and to which they return for a short but happy stay each summer.

When I stopped at Emerald Isle on my way to Bon Portage I had not seen Ashford and Jean for over a year, so we had many things to talk over, and soon it was time for bed. I was so excited at the thoughts of all the next day held that I slept little, but lay trying to imagine what I should find when at last I reached the Island that had been the centre of all our dreams and plans for three years,

The sea was blue, that deep bright blue that is the ocean's most beautiful vesture, and a crisp breeze had whipped up a small white-tipped chop that slapped merrily at the sides of the boat and sent showers of spray across us. Days like this are our most exhilarating. Sea and sky, clouds and rocks, grass and trees all sparkle and dance. Though you gulp it down in great lungfuls, you can never get enough of the salt-tanged, sun-sweetened air, and the old trite comparison of air and wine seems fresh and inevitable. To me, after years in the city, it all seemed clear and heady beyond words.

The motor-boat, aptly named *Ricketty Ann* by Jean, would have made dirty weather of a real blow, but found this jolly breeze much to her liking and bounced and tossed merrily across the two-mile strip of water that separates Bon Portage from Shag Harbour and Emerald Isle.

Ashford had Mike, his hired man, along to help land us in the skiff, now dancing in our wake at the end of a taut painter. Good old Mike, always ready to help out, and as handy with children as if he were the father of ten! Since I had been away from the sea and boats so long, and was awkward about keeping my balance on the lobster-crate that consistently serves as a seat in the fishing boats, Mike soon took the baby and held her in his arms until we reached within fifty yards of the shore. At this point it is necessary for those in a motor-boat to drop anchor and transfer to a dory or skiff, and row the remaining distance to the beach. This transferring is a frightening business to anyone unaccustomed to boats and the sea, and is one of the chief reasons why my women visitors are few and far between. The small dory bounces and bobs alongside the larger boat, and it seems it must pound itself to pieces or fling into the sea anyone foolhardy enough to attempt to step into it from the big boat. Actually the change is more easily and safely accomplished than appears possible, since both boats pitch and toss more or less together, and the men who handle them are so expert. Their every movement flows with that of the sea rather than against it and are timed exactly. Fortunately, on this, my first landing, the wind and sea were so that the water near the shore lay calm and smooth and no seas were breaking on the beach.

Once in the small boat I could see nothing of the shore we were approaching but a sea-wall some eight feet above the water's level, formed of large rocks which have been smoothed and rounded by incessant tumblings and rollings in the wash of the sea; and above this wall showed the dark tips of the trees that grew some yards behind it.

The eastern shore of the Island faces the mainland and is less exposed than the western side to the full force of the seas. Along this eastern side, when the tide has ebbed half-way or more, can be seen several narrow "landings." These were lanes leading through the rocks that form the beach, from the point of lowest ebb to high water mark. From them the larger rocks have been removed and piled on either side, forming a passage-way with slightly greater depth of water and a smoother bottom upon which to ground and haul up a small craft. Some of these landings were made by early settlers of the Island, and some by fishermen who lived here during the fishing seasons in the early years of the present century, before the coming of the motor-boat lessened the importance of having fishing stations as near as possible to the waters where fish were plentiful. The sea has heaved rocks across and completely filled in the upper parts of these landings, but the lower portions remain open, although narrowing year by year. Never wider than would accommodate a trawl-dory they now afford scant passage to a small skiff. It was one of these landings that the resigning keeper had been using and into which we rowed.

Thirty yards to the south of us lay the breakwater, a small jetty-like affair of wooden crib work and rocks, put up by the government to afford safety in landing when heavy seas were running up the shore. It was never a great help in bad storms, however, as it had not been carried out sufficiently far, and the breakers merely rounded the end and struck with undiminished force on the shore and in the landings. A few years after we came here the sea began to tear away the breakwater. This was during the depression years of the early thirties, and by the time the question of repairs had been bandied back and forth between different departments of the government, the sea had finished with it and there was nothing left to repair. Only a few jagged stumps of the larger piles now show where once the breakwater attempted to lessen the fury of the in-sweeping surf, and the sea is at present in the process of tearing down the miniature headland of rocks that had been thrown up in its assaults upon the breakwater, so that soon there will be nothing left of another effort to divert the inexorable movement of the sea.

The breakwater was still standing peaceably intact, however, on that bright spring day when I first stepped ashore at Bon Portage. The tide was not low, so I was spared the long slippery scramble over rock-weeded stones that so often awaits the hapless voyager that steps upon our shores. I walked eagerly over the crest of the beach to see what lay beyond. It would have been easy to

imagine myself on a desert island.   Not a soul was to be
seen, and there were few signs to show that anyone had
ever been near the spot.   A complete silence lay over
everything, there was not even the roar of surf on the
shores and this is seldom absent here as I afterward learned.
The dark softwood trees came within fifty feet of the shore,
and nearer yet they were fringed by a narrow belt of
alders just beginning to put forth their delicate new leaves
and golden drooping catkins; the strip of sod that lay
between them and the clean grey beach was bright with
that tender green of early June.   The mingled scent of
woods and sea was almost overwhelmingly sweet yet
bracing.   A roadway of small well-packed beach rocks in
which the odd daisy and wild strawberry plant had taken
root led from the top of the landing in a southerly direction.

At the head of the landing was a small winch, a drum-
like round of wood, with an iron crank, for use in pulling
up a small boat over the rocks.   This had been supplied
years before by the Department of Transport for the use
of the lightkeeper, and after changes and repairs it is still
in use.

To the south about thirty yards, and at the head of the
breakwater was the boathouse, a plain white-washed
building, about twenty-five feet long and fifteen feet
wide, with a pitched roof and a wide red rolling door facing
the sea.   In it are stored the oil and supplies from the
government steamer when they are landed, and any oars
and boat supplies that need to be kept under cover.   It lay
still and glistening in the bright blue day.

We turned southward and started along the path that
leads to the lighthouse.   One of our greatest disadvantages
and time-wasters here is the more than half-mile distance
that separates the lighthouse from the landing-place.
The heavy surf and rocky shore make any nearer point
impracticable for landing, except in the smoothest weather

and in a small boat, and these conditions present a difficulty we have not been able to overcome. But I enjoyed every step of the way and thought I had never seen a lovelier little road, as it wound through the woods and then opened out to the sea before turning again to the shelter of the trees. Softwoods and alders lined the sides of the path, with here the delicate lacy white of an Indian pear and there the blaze of rhodora. The end of the path near the boathouse had been newly constructed and was of reddish yellow clay, held in place by huge logs on either side; the rest of the way was carpeted by greensward, and along the sides grew the sharp green swords of blue iris, not yet in bloom but the clusters spaced and grouped as by some clever landscape gardener. Low bushes and soft luxuriant ferns bordered the walk while small fir and spruce crowded close above them, each branch proudly extending its tender buds of spring green. The trees and bushes seemed alive with birds, the bright coats of the Yellow Warblers predominating over the more sober hues of the others, and all singing their hearts out to welcome us—or perhaps just because it was such a gorgeous day. I had never seen so many birds in so small a space, and the numerous birds on the Island have continued to be one of our chief joys here.

Only once did the path break through the woods to a view of the sea, and this spot we call the Clearing, since a small strip of land, now grown over in blueberry bushes and furze, but which had evidently once been cleared for a garden, here lies between the path and the shore.

I am sorry to have to admit that this path has lost much of its untouched beauty in the years we have been here, although it is still a lovely walk. Morrill has driven an ox and cart to haul oil and supplies, hay and wood over it, whereas the former keepers had used no vehicle but a wheelbarrow and conveyed only the necessary supplies for the Light. Now the soft, rich greensward has been broken and rutted and the holes filled with beach rocks. The surf has eaten away a great deal of depth from the belt of trees that protected the path from seaward, and in spots the remaining trees grow bare and ragged. At a few places the high seas break over at every bad storm and leave the path and its bordering trees and bushes most untidily strewn with sea-weed and broken driftwood. The newer clay part is sinking into the lower swamp that borders it, the log sides have collapsed, and Morrill has been forced to fill in parts of it with loads of rocks from the beach. The spruce and fir have crowded out much of the small bush, and now have to be trimmed back at some places to allow the cart to go through freely. Formerly the government maintained the upkeep of this road, but since we have been here it has been left entirely to Morrill's care, and he finds it an impossible task for one man.

But fourteen years ago the little path wound along, all unaware as I was, of the changes the years would bring; and our small group, little Anne in Mike's or Ashford's arms, wound our leisurely way along, too. Soon we reached the top of the slight rise (which we flatter by calling it the Hill) that lies just back of the lighthouse field, where the trees end and the lighthouse comes into full view.

From this point I could see all our new home and its surroundings, and I thought the view one of the loveliest I had ever seen; on a fine day I still catch my breath as I come upon sight of it. The intensity and clear vividness of the colours are most striking, yet these colours are so few, so simple and obvious one would expect them to have nothing but a garish effect; but because they are Nature's and applied in her own way they are beautiful and perfectly fitting. The blue and white of the sea and little pond, the red and white of the buildings, and the yellow-flecked green of the fields under the bright clear sky are so exactly as they should be that they draw an exclamation of delight from most beholders. On darker days and in other lights the view lacks appeal to many and only we who love it might consider it pleasing.

As my eyes drank in the picture before me, my heart said, "Home. I have come to my home. Here Morrill and I can feel settled, as we never have since our marriage. We can put down roots and grow and build, and make a home that we and our children can cherish, where loved ones and friends will come to lay aside their cares and share with us its peace and steadfastness in spite of storms. Here we may help others. We must try to be truly keepers 'of a light along the shore.'"

On this southern tip of Bon Portage across which I was gazing are about five acres of land which is government property, and on which are built the lighthouse and smaller outbuildings belonging to the Department of Transport. The field is rough and uneven, with many rocks just below the surface, but covered with a thick close sod that grows wild grasses and weeds abundantly. There are few rocks to be seen, in great contrast to the adjacent fields on the mainland and Emerald Isle, and the field has a deceptively smooth appearance to the casual glance. At the extreme southerly tip of the Island, now only twenty-five feet from the lap of the waves, although some fifteen additional feet separated the two at the time of our arrival, stands the lighthouse. It is very similar to most lighthouses along the shore but I imagine it is one of the oldest. The tower, with its slanting walls, four stories or forty-nine feet in height faces the sea; on the landward side is a story-and-a-half addition; these two parts formed the original building, but back of it again, sort of thrown on as an afterthought by one of the early keepers, is a second story-and-a-half end, with a porch jutting off from it on either side. The whole building covers little ground. It is small and looks it; as a dwelling it leaves much to be desired, but it has an attraction of its own, and of course, it is now as Laurie used to say, "Homie-homie," and by us loved as such.

The out-buildings that clustered close to the lighthouse consisted of an oil-shed, a small one-story structure built to house the oil for the lamps of the Light; a cow-shed; a roofed over pig-pen; and off by itself to the westward a small hen-house with a yard covered by an old fishing net, according to local custom. Also standing aloof and looking like nothing I had ever seen but a sentinel-box, was a tall narrow building that proved to be the outside toilet: though why, in this spot of gales and winds, it should have been constructed and placed so as to catch the full sweep of every breeze, and fastened to earth so insecurely, is a question I often had reason to ponder but never succeeded in solving.

To the west of the lighthouse, only some seventy yards away, lay a triangular pond, blue and sparkling under the sun; its apex lying nearest the Light, and its longest side, which has a length of about a hundred yards, bordering a high seawall, almost white in the clear sunlight, but composed mostly of grey granite stones; the base and other side of the triangle spreading over into a swampland, dotted with low spruce and bushes. This shallow little pond and its beach later proved to be a wonderful playground for our children and all the young visitors we have had; there are boats and rafts and fishing (for eels) in the summer, and skating and sliding and sailing with burlap wings in the winter.

I saw lighthouse and buildings, field, pond and beach as I stood looking across the Point, and beyond it to the sea which stretched unbroken to the horizon and its meeting with the sky.

It is quite beyond me to give you an impression of the sense of remoteness and isolation that the little clearing between the woods and the sea gave. Morrill said he felt he had reached the end of nowhere when he arrived. Though three miles of wooded island lay behind me to the north only the narrow Point with its tiny group of buildings was between me and the sea whose deep blue stretched unendingly east and south and west. The former light-keeper and his family, although he had three growing children, had left little imprint of his six years here; it almost seemed as if we were the Island's first inhabitants, although we knew we were not, by any means.

But there is Morrill! And now Anne and I are in his arms and our little family is united again. Ashford and Mike are saying "So long!" and starting off on their return trip, and Morrill with Anne Gordon happy in Daddy's arms once more, is leading me to the house and our new life as lightkeepers.

## 4

## THE LIGHTHOUSE AS A HOME

I HAD been pleased with all I saw of the Island, and had
had a continuing sense of coming home to familiar and
loved scenes as I followed the winding path from the boathouse to the Point, and certainly I had been greatly charmed
by the picture the lighthouse and its surroundings had
presented to me. Inside the house it was quite a different
story. My heart sank as I crossed the threshold into the
kitchen; and as I went from room to room, my feeling of
disappointment deepened. The rooms were dark and
gloomy, and what was worse, they looked unloved and
unlived in as a home. Plaster was loosening from the
walls in patches and sifted continually to the floor from
behind wallpaper that had become unstuck and stood
slightly away from the wall in several places. Some

rooms and one chimney showed signs of leaks. The floors were of soft wood, and that of the living-room disgracefully rough and uneven with wide cracks that had been filled in with rope, and worn spots that showed splinters through the poor grey paint that did nothing to hide its defects.

I had time for only a hasty look around, as it was now late afternoon and there were many things to be done. Morrill had the stove put up and had even cooked some supper for us, but the water from the well that was then in use was of a decidedly reddish tinge and gave the food an unappetizing appearance, so that the first meal in my new home was not greatly enjoyed.

Our furniture, which had sufficed for a small three-room apartment looked pitifully inadequate spread out in more and larger rooms. My tiredness from the long train trip of the day before with a fifteen-months-old baby, from the unaccustomed boat-trip and walk, in addition to the strain of the baby who was soon to be born, hit me all of a sudden and I could have set me down and wept. And yet, I had the enduring sense of coming home at last; this was the home I knew I would love in spite of its bedraggled appearance, but because I knew it was surely mine and I loved it, I resented the fact that it had been neglected and was not at its best.

Later, when Anne was contentedly asleep, but before the long summer twilight had completely left the sky, we prepared for rest after what had been for me an exceptionally hard day. As I stood near the bedroom window looking out at the sea that seemed to be breaking among the rocks almost beneath my feet, a sudden doleful whoop made me jump in consternation. "What in the world . . ." I gasped.

Then Morrill explained to me about the Groaner, or whistle-buoy, a mile or so off shore. General Laurie, when M.P.P. for Shelburne County had had it placed there.

Morrill was born on General Laurie's estate in Oakfield and so gets the first part of his name "Laurie Morrill"; we were pleased with this slender link to his past.

Once I was in bed the sea began to whisper its welcome to me. It lapped so gently and evenly, so softly and musically among the rocks outside my window, that it seemed to be consciously trying to sing me to sleep. I yielded myself wholly to its song and the wonderfully fresh seabreeze through our open windows, so in no time at all I was in the deep rest of slumber.

Things looked better, of course, in the bright sunshine of a new day, but it would have taken more than a good night's sleep and a beautiful morning to alter the hard fact that the lighthouse, as a home, was inconvenient, gloomy and very much in need of repairs, and that mountains of work lay ahead of us, both indoors and out. This was Sunday, so we spent much of the day inspecting the fields and out-buildings, and in taking stock of what we had and where we stood.

Financially we were in a decidedly poor position. The Island mortgage of $600.00 still stood, and the interest on it represented quite a sum when our income was so small; our little reserve of cash had completely disappeared while we waited for the appointment to the Light. The many unavoidable expenses of moving a family had forced Morrill to borrow a hundred dollars, and to get the bare necessities with which to work in such an isolated spot, we had gone in debt for two hundred dollars' worth of feed for cow and hens, staple foods for ourselves, farming tools, and utensils for the house such as a churn, small cream separator and wash-tubs. These were advanced to us by the owner of the general store in Shag Harbour, who waited patiently until the bill was paid, a few dollars monthly as our cheques arrived. Altogether, we started here about a thousand dollars in debt—that is not a great sum, but considered in the light of a salary of sixty-odd dollars monthly, with which to keep a family of four, and at least part of the year a hired man, its relative size mounts considerably. For many years every available cent went into stock and equipment and there were no cash returns from our outlay and work, so that our debts were reduced surely, but Oh! so slowly.

We possessed one cow, Amaryllis, and what a blessing that was. She had been given to us when a calf as a wedding gift from Ashford and Jean, and was now, most timely, producing milk. Unfortunately she did not have sturdy calves, so we never succeeded in raising any to increase our "herd," but she gave us beautiful rich Jersey milk and enough cream for all our butter. We have found by the process of trial and error that, due to the difficulties of making hayland and the impossibility of selling anything but cream, three cows are the limit of a profitable herd here, and we gradually built up to that number, with an ox, a young bull, and often a young heifer coming along to replace an older cow.

Morrill had bought a small pig, and although it was not large by fall, it gave us our first winter's pork. Now we find it pays us to keep two pigs to kill in the fall and another for the spring. They and the hens utilize our excess milk. We sugar-cure the hams, shoulders and bacons for our own use and sell what we do not need for family consumption. No meat we buy or raise "goes as far" or is more enjoyed by family and visitors than our home-cured pork. However, during the first years here we had neither money to buy the little pigs and their feed nor suitable quarters in which to raise them.

Our half-dozen hens and rooster provided us with eggs, and even gave us some chickens the following spring. We have never attempted to keep a large number of hens, but are satisfied with a small flock that supplies us with enough eggs for our own use. The difficulties of transporting feed and the lack of a dependable near-by market closed to us that sideline that supplies so many farm wives with a little extra cash.

There was not a cart or a sled, or a tool or utensil with which to work on the place. Morrill had already purchased some tools and had put in a small garden, but since the former keeper had not bothered to plant, and there was no time to clear a large plot, our returns that first year were mostly lettuce and a few summer vegetables.

About three acres of the government field were then being used as hayland and the cow was turned outside the field to forage feed. There was ample grass for several cows close by, but cows are notoriously cantankerous critters, so nothing appealed to Amaryllis but the feed on the very northern end of the Island. Consequently, Morrill, after a hard day's work, faced the prospect of walking three miles to get his cow and a like distance returning. Then, too, Amaryllis resented being led or driven and on the homeward journey would suddenly decide to take a jaunt into the swamps or thick brush that bordered the way. She could run like a deer and twist and turn as lightly. Many times that summer I saw Morrill kick off his rubber boots and tear through the swamps or over the beach rocks to circumvent Amaryllis. Another trick she had and which she taught the other cows (or it is a trait inherent to the cross-grained nature of the animals) was to go on foggy nights into the densest of woods just off the path, and stand perfectly still so that no faintest tinkle of her bell betrayed her, and wait until her frantic searcher was well beyond hearing. The wear and tear on Morrill's time, energy and disposition were enormous, and one of the first improvements he attempted was to fence off pasture land for his cows. That was a few years later, and for the first summer Amaryllis had things very much her own way.

We had a seventeen-foot boat built in Shag Harbour and fitted with an outboard motor, and also with a thwart for rowing and a place for the sail which I soon manufactured out of cotton feed bags. The rough shore and poor landing facilities made it impossible to handle a large boat at the time, but this one was hardly seaworthy enough for the strip of water between us and the mainland. The former keepers had all made use of a small skiff, or the trawl dory supplied by the government and travelled only on fine days; but these men had grown up about the water and rowing came to them as naturally as walking. Morrill frankly admitted he was no oarsman, and more, he had no intention of rowing if he could travel by any other means, and he thought the little motor a great improvement over oars.

Although the resigning keeper had cut his wood free from our woodland for three years, he left us not a single stick at the woodpile, so that Morrill was hard put to it that first summer to find fuel, and in the fall we bought coal for winter use, although we have not had to do so since, as the trees on the Island provide us with ample fuel for our needs. There is always driftwood along our beaches, but the salts and acids in it eat away stove linings and metal. We are eagerly awaiting the time when we can have a fireplace and utilize some of this beachwood, as it makes the most colourful of open fires.

We had no ox or draught animal, so that first summer Morrill made himself a small two-wheeled cart and dragged his meagre cut of hay into the shedlike barn. Later, when he had an ox, he bought wheels and made, first a dump-cart that served many purposes, and then, a hayrack and sleds for hauling wood.

That first summer I was not able to help Morrill out-of-doors as I did in succeeding years, so I do not remember the difficulties that faced him as well as I do my own inside

the house.  I have mentioned how disappointed I was in
the appearance of the rooms and closer acquaintance did
not heighten their appeal, although "our own things,"
pictures, curtains and furniture, made them less bare
and more home-like.

Most of the inside painting was done in battleship
grey, which apparently was a very popular colour with
the former keepers.  It is not the most cheerful colour
under any circumstances, and on foggy days and sombre
winter afternoons it did little to dispel the gloom.  Other
rooms were finished in the dark-grained effects so common
when the lighthouse was built.  The plastered ceilings had
some years previous to our coming been covered by dark
sheathing, made yet more deeply stained by the smoke of
the years that had since passed.

All our paper and paint show the darkening effects of
the stove smoke soon after we have freshened our rooms.
The lighthouse tower, so many feet above the tops of the
dwelling chimneys, affects both stoves.  When the wind
is from the north the heat stove in the living-room smokes
back and refuses to burn well.  Its performance pales into
insignificance, however, in comparison with what the
kitchen stove can do when the wind veers a few points east
or west of south, baffles around the tower and down upon
the kitchen chimney.  Flame and smoke billow out into
the room, and we are forced to open both kitchen doors,
then after flinging the burning sticks from the stove out
into the field we take refuge in the living-room until the
worst is over.  I have a single plate kerosene stove for such
emergencies and on it we make tea and heat canned food,
but I have never found any solution to the problem of
what to do with the baking of bread that always seems to
be ready for the oven just as the wind strikes down the
chimney and forces us to retreat.  I have learned to keep
pilot biscuits always on hand.  Such windy spells seldom

last more than twenty-four hours and it is with great joy we find the wind has hauled in and we can have a fire once more. Each of these sessions leaves its deposit of smoke on my walls and ceilings and makes keeping the rooms fresh and clean more difficult. Morrill has tried several devices to overcome this trouble but the force of the wind has proved too great for all of them.

The kitchen was, and is, our poorest room. It was added to the original building as a summer kitchen and is three steps below the level of the rest of the lighthouse. (These steps, so often found in old houses, my grandmother called "woman killers.") The kitchen, exposed on three sides, is built directly on the ground and is bitterly cold in winter. The pantry, to add to the general inconvenience, is up the three steps and at the end of a small cloak room, so that it is practically useless as an adjunct to the kitchen but serves as a storeroom for bulk supplies.

The Department had installed a pump and a kitchen sink some years before our arrival. Though the pump was "left-handed" it was a great improvement over the method of getting water that formerly prevailed. It seems that when the lighthouse was built, many wells were sunk in a vain attempt to obtain clear water; always it was darkly tinged with red. Then the lightkeeper asked for permission to try his luck and sank a well only six feet from the back steps. He got an abundant supply of clear water; unfortunately it is extremely hard and has a brackish taste but it is the best we have. Then the next keeper added his summer kitchen, so that it covered the well, and he cut a trap-door in his kitchen floor to give access to his water supply. When water was needed the trap-door was lifted, the cry, "All away! the trap-door's up!" was raised and the water pulled up by bucket and rope.

We were warned against using this well for drinking purposes and all the first year we carried water from the

well in the field, which we now use for the cattle only.   I
could never overcome my dislike for its red colour and
was glad when Morrill found time to clean and lime the
well under the kitchen.   At the bottom he found a mis-
cellany of old boots, sticks and tin cans, knowledge of
which may have prejudiced the former keeper against
its use.

A few years later some of the rocks about its top
collapsed into the well, and we had to have it cleaned and
the rocks cemented into place.   If you have never had a
well bailed out, cement mixed and applied all from your
kitchen floor, you have missed quite an experience.   (But
don't feel envious.)   I can still see the ungodly conglomeration of rocks, water and cement, and the two men in the
midst of it struggling to repair the walls of the well in the
darkness below the trap-door.   I served dinner outdoors
on the grass.

The kitchen, though poorly built, has an advantage
over the rest of the house —its walls are straight.   When
you step up into the lighthouse proper you notice that the
walls have a decided slant and large squared timbers that
run the height of the building project one face about four
inches into the rooms.   The slant, necessary for the
reflection of the light's rays from the white outside walls,
presents various difficulties in the interior; it increases the
task of papering the irregular beamed walls and limits the
number and arrangement of pictures.

The rooms on the ground floor are three large ones
(kitchen, living-room and bedroom), with four smaller ones
(two porches, a cloakroom and a pantry).   The bedroom
is really a very pleasant room, with two windows looking
out to sea, one of them offering the only southern exposure
we have.   The living-room is cosy but marred by the steep
enclosed stairway and none too fully lighted by a single
window in each of the two outside walls.

On the second floor are two small bedrooms, originally one; and a hallway. There is also a small unfinished attic called "The Dog Room." Don't think we keep our dogs there, although you could find almost everything else among its accumulated discards. When the children were small and Laurie had to pass the low swinging door of this rather dark little catch-all, naughty Anne used to frighten her smaller brother by insisting there were dogs in it, just waiting to pounce out upon him. As they became bigger and his fear a joke, the little attic was known by no other name than "The Dog Room."

On the third floor is the light-room, where Morrill keeps the cleansers, polishes and small supplies for servicing the light. Here are a work bench, extra plate-glass windows for the lantern, oil-carriers, extra lamps and chimneys, and in one corner a barrel of sand to be used in case of fire. There is also a small bedroom on the third floor, which was not in use when we came, but which we cleaned and painted for the hired man.

Atop of all is the Lantern, with its lamps and revolving mechanism. It is decagonal in shape; each of the sides consists of heavy iron-plate for the lower two and a half feet, above this a plate-glass window thirty inches by thirty-six inches set in narrow metal sashes topped by six inches of metal.

The metal parts are painted a vivid vermilion and the window frames are white. Also white is the peaked ceiling, with an inverted saucer-like round of metal that is placed directly above the Light apparatus, and about a foot lower than the peak of the roof, with ample space between its edge and the roof at every point to allow the air from the Lantern to pass into the ventilator above it. In the centre of the roof, and above the metal plate, is an opening, and this is topped by the ventilator, very like an elbow of six-inch stove piping, with a vane on top of it, which causes the mouth of the ventilator to swing away from the wind and weather.

In the northern side of the Lantern, set in the metal part, and only a few inches above the floor, is a small door, just large enough to allow a man to pass through and out on the Lantern deck. This is a square flat flooring all around the outside of the Lantern for a width of about three feet, and is railed off by four corner posts joined by two wooden bars along each side. The deck is slightly sloping to shed rain and affords precarious footing in windy, icy weather. I never venture out on it at such times, but often Morrill must go out to clean snow and sleet from the outside of the windows, so that the light beams may shine undimmed. Lashed to one side of the railing is a short flag-pole, this we fasten to one of the corner-posts, and attach the flag to it, when it becomes necessary to fly the flag as a signal for the doctor.

The floor of the Lantern is painted dark green. Along its southern part is a metal trap-door, two feet long and a foot and a half wide, through which we enter and leave the Lantern. Below it is a flight of steep stairs leading down into the Lightroom on the third floor.

In the centre of the small Lantern floor is the Light apparatus itself, really a very unimposing piece of machinery, set on a small wooden stand. When we came to Bon Portage the Light was still one fixed lamp, set in a thick lens, and the flashes were produced by revolving bars of metal a few inches wide, that, passing around the lamp, shut out its beam at regular intervals. We had been here only a year or two when that Light was changed for the one now in use, which is said to throw a brighter beam and is a much cheaper apparatus.

The same two springs that revolved the old Light serve also for this, and are encased in a squat metal cylinder, and, attached to the springs with gears, is a crank by which we wind them.

Above the spring-case is a shallow, circular, pan-like trough, twenty-four inches in diameter and about three inches deep. This is filled with mercury, and on this mercury bath revolves a float that is connected to the springs by clock gears. The float is a circle of metal that fits over the pan of mercury, and is buoyed up by it. The purpose of the mercury bath is to neutralize the shaking of the whole Lantern structure in heavy winds and keep the lamps themselves steady and unaffected by the vibration of the tower. It also acts as a bearing for the revolving lamps.

On the float, and attached to it, are two lamps, quite like the ordinary house lamps in common use at the turn of the century, and still our means of illumination. Each of these lamps is backed by a silver-plated reflector, twenty-six inches in diameter. Small metal oil-reservoirs, one set back of each reflector, feed the lamps by gravity. As the Light revolves, anyone within the radius of its rays sees the flash of a beam, then the beam disappears as the lamp is replaced by the dark back of the reflector, and no beam is visible until the companion lamp swings into view.

The Light revolves once in thirty seconds, giving four flashes and alternate dark periods every minute. Morrill times it regularly and makes any slight adjustments that may become necessary.

No doubt I have made this all sound very complicated, but it is actually an extraordinarily simple apparatus, and the only part that ever causes any difficulty are the springs. These sometimes break. Then we have fun! The Light must be turned by hand until a new spring can be installed. Former lightkeepers used to send to the Department for a new spring and a man to install it, but when the Inspector found that Morrill was repairing the broken spring and replacing it, he left a spare spring here. The next time both springs broke!

The first time we had a spring break, there were two men here to lend a hand, and one turned the Light while the other helped Morrill at the repairs. The next time the hired man stayed with the Light while I helped Morrill with the spring. It was a large one, well packed in axle-grease, and I was not accustomed to wrestling with such things. We worked on the kitchen floor by lamplight, and when Morrill had finished heating and riveting together the two broken ends of the spring, he and I and the kitchen floor had acquired almost the entire amount of axle-grease that had once covered the coils of the spring. I am always amazed at the cute little smudges of grease the girl mechanics of rotogravures get on their faces. Somehow when we are through a tussle with the greasy spring we both resemble members of a minstrel show, only decidedly more dishevelled and far less debonair.

I got a very bad scare the time the spring broke when I was winding the Light. Betty June was only four and I had allowed her to accompany me to the Lantern as I lit the lamps; she loved to watch the Light revolving, and to get from the Lantern window a bird's-eye view of the familiar surroundings. The lamps were lit when the spring broke and the whole Light apparatus jumped and shook from the recoil. I saw a fine spray flung all over Betty June, I took it to be kerosene. I believed a lamp had exploded, and I thought for a terrified few seconds of what would happen to her oil-drenched clothing if and when the flame from the lamp reached her. So I grabbed her quickly to thrust her below the trap-door to safety. Then I saw that the fine spray was mercury from the shallow bath, and that the lamps were still burning, unaffected by the jolt of the breaking spring.

These breaking springs are bad enough at any time, but the last one that broke chose the middle of the winter and a cold windy night to let go. No one could stand to turn the Light uninterruptedly in the cold draughty Lantern, so Laurie and I took alternate shifts of one hour, in which one of us turned the Light and the other helped Morrill in the kitchen, with the aid of the hot coffee we kept on the stove all night. I optimistically went up for my first turn at the Light without putting on enough extra socks, and my feet and legs were nearly paralysed from the cold metal floor before Laurie came to relieve me at the end of the hour. Once I had taken over from him there had been no leaving my post to dress more warmly, and I found it a very long hour as the turning of the apparatus is done so slowly that it affords little exercise and is no help in keeping warm. You may be sure I was well bundled up before starting my second shift. By one o'clock Morrill had the spring repaired and the Light revolving under its own power once more, so we could thankfully tumble into warm beds. So much for the Lantern and its contents —really, of course, the nucleus of our job here.

Each of the three flights of stairs in the lighthouse are steep steps, similar to the companion-ways of ships, and are very difficult to navigate, especially if both hands are not free. I was often terrified for the children when they were small, but none of them got bad tumbles. I used to notice, when they were visiting Grandma in Bedford, how they loved to walk up and down, up and down, the lovely broad and easy steps of her stairs.

In the dwelling part of the Lighthouse there are many flaws that we have not been able to overcome, but we have made a great many changes and improvements. We were unfortunate in having the depression hit our Department in Saint John, along with the rest of the world, just as we took over here, so that the amount of materials for repairs

and the supplies were curtailed, but we found our Inspector
willing to cooperate with us in any improvements that we
wished to make, in so far as it lay within his power to do
so. However the final word as to any expenditure lay
with Ottawa, and we sometimes wonder (as others have
before us) just how clear a conception Ottawa may have
as to the conditions prevailing at isolated Light-stations.
Our dealings with the Inspectors and agents at Saint John
have been most pleasant, and I am sure they do everything
possible to improve living conditions here, but the lighthouse is old and worn now. Seventy years is a long time
for a small wooden building to stand erect against the
winds that sweep unhindered across miles of stormy water
to strike it as the first challenge that has dared to oppose
its puny strength against their might. No wonder they
scream and shriek in derision as they tear past. The
wonder is that the tower still stands in patient defiance.

It seems to us from our experience here that it would be
much better for both Light-tower and dwelling if the two
were separated, as they are in some (but not all, I notice)
of the newer lighthouses. The dwelling would then be
more easily kept clean, and more cheaply heated, and in
cold weather the Lantern would be spared the excess
condensation on walls and windows that is caused by the
warm moist air that rises from the rooms of the dwelling.

When the Inspector found that Morrill could and would
do the work necessary in making repairs and improvements
(although we notice from old records that this kind of work
was formerly done by outside help and paid for by the
Department), he did all he could to supply us with materials
to use.

All the rooms on the ground floor have been beaverboarded and papered in gay light colours, the ceilings
which were dark-stained sheathing and the dark woodwork
have been painted cream or—in the kitchen—a light grey.

This means I must do more cleaning and painting, but it also makes a surprising difference in the appearance of the rooms, they are light and bright now.  The two bedrooms on the second floor are papered and painted, but need beaverboarding before I again paper them.  The slanted walls and windows and odd stairways make beaverboarding and papering jobs that require considerable ingenuity in fitting and cutting.  Last summer as I was struggling to put ceiling paper in Betty June's room, and she was trying to help me, I remarked in disgust, "No wonder Hitler is crazy!"

"Mummy," returned Betty June in a very small worried voice, "do you think *one* little room would do it?" Sometimes I think one of our rooms would be plenty.

Originally this Light had been operated by a chain and weight that ran down through the three flights from Lantern to cellar, and were enclosed by a foot-square wooden shaft.  Though this system had been discontinued for many years before we came, the wooden shaft still remained.  We obtained permission and removed the shaft, which made the bedrooms seem much larger and less cluttered.

New shelves have been put in the beaverboarded pantry, now painted a fresh blue and white, and a cupboard put up in the kitchen for small quantities of cooking staples.  The back porch, which was of unfinished lumber, has been sheathed and painted cream and brown.  In it are my washer and wash-day equipment, and across one end are the separator and milk bench.

The greatest accomplishment in my eyes is our final success in having a supply of soft rain-water always on hand, and running hot soft water at the sink.  As I have mentioned, the water in the house well is exceptionally hard.  It is almost impossible to obtain a suds in it; it gave our clothes "that tattle-tale grey," and "dishpan hands" were smooth and lily-white compared to mine after a spell of using our well water. The appearance of my hands I could have ignored, I had little time those first busy years to be conscious of such things, but when my hands cracked and bled in spite of all the care I could give them, that was something else again.

Our first effort to overcome this trouble was to catch rain water from the kitchen roof in a puncheon. This was a big help at times, but during dry spells we had no reserve, and through the winter the puncheon froze and burst, so that it had to be emptied before freezing weather.

Next, Morrill bought four puncheons, connected and covered them, and fitted the centre one with a low faucet, so that I did not have to lift heavy buckets of water from inside the puncheon. This was an improvement over what we had had, but the water in the barrels still froze in spite of Morrill's banking them with sea-weed or sawdust. This was partly due to the fact that the construction of the lighthouse made the northern end the only possible spot where we could collect any quantity of rain, and this was exposed to our coldest winds. So still throughout most of the winter we were forced to use the hard well water, or what rain water we could collect and use when the weather was mild. Often the children would fill pails, kettles and wash-boiler with freshly fallen snow, and I would melt this to obtain a little precious soft water; even enough to wash the dishes from a meal seemed to caress my poor sore hands.

While we were still depending on the row of casks under the rain spout, Morrill succeeded in locating and buying a second-hand force-pump, which he attached to the puncheons and had water piped into a tank in the kitchen through rubber hose. The tank was an empty fifty-gallon gasoline drum that Morrill had salvaged after a storm. A hot-water front had been with the stove we bought in Worcester; now Morrill bought a few feet of piping, and with the help of a diagram in our old stand-by, *The Family Herald*, he connected the tank, pipes and stove front, and put a faucet at the sink for hot water. What luxury! And with its bright new coat of aluminum paint, the drum, while it might have been said to lack graceful lines, looked clean and bright.

You may wonder how Morrill, pumping away at the outside puncheon, could tell when the inside tank was full. He couldn't. I stood by the tank in the house, with a slender stick down an opening in the top of the tank, and by pulling out the stick and noticing the water level on it I could judge when the tank was full. Then I thumped vigorously on the wall between us, Morrill would sing out, "O.K.," and stop pumping. It didn't do for my mind to wander during this operation.

One lovely summer evening my friend Mildred and I had just finished a tremendous ironing, then taken an old rug out on the front steps to rest and cool ourselves. Morrill decided to pump the tank but when I offered to watch it as usual he waved me down and assured me he could manage. Nothing loath, I settled back in comfort again. Morrill pumped a while, then we heard him go into the kitchen by the other door and in a few moments resume his pumping. I knew he had been in to ascertain the water level in the tank so I rested serene. What I didn't know was that the water in the tank had been right up to the metal top and exactly the same temperature of Morrill's finger, so that he thought he hadn't touched water whereas the tank was already filled to its utmost capacity. The first stream that gushed from the tank didn't arouse me, but the cascade that followed did! Mildred and I rushed into the kitchen to see the water spurting over the sides of the drum, and already forming pools on the floor. Morrill, quite sure that the tank would hold considerable more water, kept blithely pumping in spite of our yells.

Finally we convinced him that enough was really enough. Since we always kept our wood-box beside the tank, and had shoes drying on top of it, there was considerable straightening away and mopping up to be done, so a pleasant evening was had by all.

Even last winter with our new tank and years of experience behind us, we had another such accident. Two friends had just arrived for a few days' gunning. Laurie went down to pump up the tank, while we proudly explained to one of them (on his first visit here) how our system worked, but forgot to watch it. Just as the friend turned the faucet at the sink, a geyser of water shot from the top of the tank and down over its sides to the floor. We shouted and Lo immediately stopped pumping, but the water already on its way continued to pour down and force more out. So more mopping up, and this time Morrill officiated.

"Well," said our friend, as the excitement died down and the waters subsided, "*I thought* that was a funny way for the faucet to work."

But this was later. After we found that the puncheons were not a success, the Inspector sent us cement, and Morrill put a cement cistern in the cellar, and new rain-gutters leading to it. The same force-pump still serves us. The cistern holds about fifteen hundred gallons of water and keeps us well supplied with soft water although I do not use it during the summer months as lavishly as do our visitors who are accustomed to town and city water supplies. Our latest improvement in our water system was the purchase of a second-hand copper tank that had sprung a leak, and so was no longer serviceable under pressure but quite usable for us. It is much neater and takes up less room than our old drum, but Morrill bemoans the loss of the flat top of the old tank, "It was such a grand place to dry and warm my heavy boots!"

## 5

## THE FIRST SUMMER AND FALL

NEVER since have we enjoyed such glorious weather as we had that first summer here. Each morning the sun rose clear and trailed its glory across a sky arched above its perfect reflection in a motionless sea. The days were fine and warm but always made comfortable by a light sea-breeze, and the evening sky repeated in deeper and more vivid colours the beauty of the morning. When we stepped out the kitchen door we invariably paused to gaze anew at the wide expanse of blue sea and sky just beyond our field, which that summer was yellow with the golden tips of waving buttercups. The sea stayed calm, and the small waves as they broke lazily along the shore formed the little semi-circular scallops that Betty June in one of her poems calls "a frill on the dress of the sea."

The sun, it seemed to us, rose unnecessarily early—
4.15 a.m. is an ungodly hour for even the sun to get up!
Since the light must be extinguished at sunrise, Morrill
also got up at that time, but because I was not feeling so
spry, I was allowed to stay in bed until baby Anne wakened,
once or twice until six o'clock! By dusk we were glad to
tumble into bed and sleep the deep dreamless sleep of
physical exhaustion.

There was little fog, a blessing which we didn't completely realize and appreciate at the time, not knowing
what an added strain foggy weather brings to an already
crowded day, when one of us must always be within easy
reach of the fog-horn, and everyone goes about with one
ear cocked for the sound of a boat's horn. Bon Portage
has not an automatic fog-alarm as its neighbours Seal
Island and Cape Sable have, but depends on a small hand-
horn which is blown by the lightkeeper in reply to the horn
of passing boats. The ultimate exasperation is, I think,
to sit on the fog-horn beside the lighthouse and give the
necessary answering "toots" to some sailing vessel tacking
back and forth outside the Point, in an almost complete
calm, while dinner gets cold or housework goes undone for
hours. At other times, when the fog presses down against
a surf smashing angrily amongst the cruel rocks, I am glad
to blow with all my might, or wait indefinitely in the
numbing wet wind, thinking I may be of help in keeping
some boat and its crew outside that greedy maw. Men
have told me of their great relief when they have "picked
up" our horn, or seen against the fog the faint reflection
of the beam from our Light. That makes us feel good—
as if we were serving a real purpose—and repays us for
much of the monotonous repetition from which we never
see or hear results.

Each noon, that first summer, we lay for an hour in the
clear, fresh sunshine, and feasted our eyes on the sky and

sea. I remember seeing several fantastic "looms" as the mirages across the sea are called, and these are only seen on the finest of summer days. Baby Anne we stripped and she stumbled about with uncertain steps or tumbled and rolled in the grass like a puppy. I could not undertake any great changes or do any heavy cleaning until after my new baby should have been born, so I had a little free time after my day's housework was done; and that is the only summer of which I can say as much.

I discovered wild strawberries on the hill beyond the field, and I often took Anne Gordon with me and gathered enough for Morrill's and my supper. Wild strawberries and rich Jersey cream; the smell of the grass and the flowers mixed with the tang of the sea; the sound of the waves whispering among the rocks; all welcomed me with the scents and sounds I had loved in childhood, and gave me a sense of being home again at last. I was happy with a deep contentment.

One day we all went fishing. Our boat was not finished, and Clayton Sears of Shag Harbour, whom Morrill had met, had lent us his skiff to use until we should have our own boat. (This was but the first of many favours we were to receive at his hands, for he proved to be a kind true friend, always ready to do us a good turn.) The morning was silky calm, and we thought we would try our hand at catching a few small fish, cunners or frost fish, so we went out in the skiff with our lines. I remember the unmarred loveliness of the sea, the crystal clearness of the water, almost indiscernible between us and the rocks and sand on the bottom, with their graceful adornments of kelp and rock-weed and strange mosses, so beautiful in form and colour, there in the lovely garden of the sea; so different from the limp unattractive strings that lie along the shore after a storm has cruelly plucked them and then tossed them carelessly aside to wither. I couldn't give too much attention to the beauties about me, however; I didn't dare loosen for a moment my firm grip on Anne Gordon's dress, she loved to play in the water and was determined to climb over the side of the skiff to do so. Inches or fathoms, water was water to Anne, and was meant for a little girl to play in.

I remember all that lovely morning perfectly, except that it completely escapes my mind whether or not we caught any fish—probably we didn't.

Very little of our time, however, was spent lying in the sun or lazily fishing. Morrill was tremendously busy, with new tasks and demands for time and efforts facing him every time he turned around. For my part I learned to make bread, to churn and make butter, care for milk-pails and separator, fill and clean oil-lamps, and do the many extra things that never enter housekeeping in a town or city.

I learned, too, to clean and fill and care for the Light, in case Morrill should be detained or absent at lighting time. I learned when fog was about to be always listening for the sound of a boat's horn, and to run out-doors and give an answering blast on the hand-horn; to notice when the fog shut in and when it cleared, and to enter this information in our records; to notice the weather conditions at sunset (the state of the sky, and the direction and force of the wind) and record them; to help with the monthly and quarterly reports that are sent to the Department at Saint John. These are Morrill's duties, but I learned to act as substitute, if and when necessary.

Fortunately the lighthouse did not have to be painted that summer, as it is done every third year only, and there were no materials on hand with which to make repairs; so with little fog to contend with, our duties were not as numerous as they have been almost consistently since that time.

The morning of July 17th dawned in all the beauty that the rising sun spreads across the silver sky and water, but before the mist in the eastern sky had reddened I knew it was not going to be another easy care-free day for me. Although it was two weeks before his expected arrival, we were fortunately able to have both doctor and nurse on hand to greet Laurie Morrill. At sunrise a fisherman, out hauling an early morning net off the Point, was hailed by Morrill and took a message to Ashford. Within a few hours he arrived with doctor and nurse. Anne Gordon had been born in a hospital with what amelioration modern science can supply, but Laurie was born late that night, not easily and without benefit of anæsthetics. He was a lovely boy, weighing eight pounds, and started right in being my best baby.

When Jean saw him a few days later she exclaimed in glee, "Oh! A bald-headed baby; I do love bald-headed babies."

But as I indignantly informed her, he was not bald-headed; his hair was such a light-coloured down that it did not show. Laurie is blonde like his Daddy, while the girls have medium-dark colouring like mine.

The greatest excitement that day and what the nurse remembers most clearly was provided by Amaryllis the cow. Dr. Wilson, out for a breath of fresh air, came rushing in to the kitchen exclaiming that the cow had somehow got tangled in her rope, was flat on her back and choking to death. Whereupon the nurse, a local woman and familiar with cows and their ways, snatched a carving knife and ran to the rescue. Between her and the doctor they managed to cut the rope that was choking her and so saved Amaryllis from an untimely death. Morrill had had to be away for a time, and knowing that if Amaryllis were left at liberty she would immediately hike to the

farther end of the Island and necessitate his following her
there, he had tied her in a corner of the mowing field,
hoping the excellent grass would keep her contented until
his return. Not Amaryllis! Though she couldn't have
known there would be a doctor and nurse in attendance
if she got into difficulties.

It was just as well that Laurie was a good baby, because
after I had been up for a day or so, I developed a touch of
septicemia and was quite ill for a time. The day I became
sick Mother and Dad arrived most opportunely with a
friend who was a practical nurse, so although my nurse had
left, I was well cared for and soon was able to be up around
again.

The doctor told me it would be a year before I was over
the effects of my illness, and how right he was! I remember
I made a record for myself during the next March when I
stayed out of a sick bed for two whole weeks, the longest
continuous stretch since Laurie's birth. All fall and winter
I had nauseated or dizzy spells, or would be seized by a
vice-like cramp across my back; either type of misery would
send me helpless to bed. While I was kept in bed, Morrill
would do the absolute necessities about the house, but so
many things outside were crying for attention, that he felt
he could spare little time for household chores. Of course,
all that Morrill couldn't handle piled up while I lay in bed
gathering strength for the next round in a battle that see-
sawed, first on the side of the accumulated tasks, then on
mine, as I somehow found strength to conquer most of
them before they put me flat on my back again. When I
was out of bed I kept the babies clean and well fed, and
meals prepared for Morrill, myself and the hired man; but
the house was probably never so neglected since it was
built, and as it is a hard house to keep clean, and was
even more so then in its unrepaired state, it was in a
shameful condition much of the time. I was glad that

few of the excellent housekeepers of Shag Harbour had occasion to see it.

The two women callers I had saw it at its worst. Every fall we buy enough supplies in October to do us throughout the winter, and Morrill had brought our winter's groceries, several large cartons of them, into the kitchen and left them for me to unpack and check, while he and the hired man went to Shag Harbour to get the winter's feed for the cattle and hens. Our kitchen is small, so nothing else could be done until those cartons were out of the way, and I tackled the job. I had no experience in handling quantities of groceries, and no system yet worked out, so that the kitchen was a clutter of cartons, packaged goods, stuff in paper bags, string and wrapping paper, when to my utter amazement I heard a knock, and looking out the window beheld two ladies. Of course, any housekeeper knows that the chances of unexpected visitors are in inverse ratio to the preparedness of home and hostess to receive them. I have found this holds true even on an isolated island, and over-rides weather conditions that might be expected to give the poor housewife a break!

These ladies had kindly come to keep the house and children so that I could go to vote. Morrill had blandly assured them that I would be glad to leave if someone would stay with the children. Just like a man! I have often wondered if they weren't shocked at the state of my house, but they stayed and I went off to vote. However, their trouble and mine was all in vain, as we hadn't been residing in this district long enough to be entered on the voting list.

The fishing boat that brought my visitors on, took me off, and I returned in Ashford's large boat that was bringing the feed for Morrill, as our boat was too small for the heavy load. As it was calm, we landed at the Point to save hauling the feed from the boathouse. Mike had been lent us for the day to run the big boat and help handle the heavy bags of feed. When it came time for me to go ashore, the tide was at its lowest ebb and I begged Morrill to go get my rubber-boots, so I could wade through the puddles and over the slippery, sea-weeded rocks. But Morrill decided he was going to carry me ashore; so he picked me and slung me up over his shoulder as he had the bags of feed. I held my breath as he slipped and slid among the rocks, expecting every moment we would both fall, or he would drop me head-first into the pools beneath my shuddering eyes. The water here is not warm at any time and this was a bleak overcast day in October. Mike shouted a helpful suggestion, to which Morrill replied,

"Never mind, Mike. I'd never have married her if I couldn't handle her."

This tickled Mike immensely but didn't increase my confidence to any great extent. Nevertheless, handle me he did, depositing me, after a few nerve-racking minutes, safely on a rock above the wet sea-weed whence I was able to make my own way.

A few minutes later I had reached the house, and I hustled about and cooked a roast duck dinner for my guests, hoping to make up in hospitality what I lacked in housekeeping qualifications.

The children throve and were never sick. Laurie took his daytime naps outdoors all winter, the head of his carriage covered by an old fur jacket to keep out the wind and snow. The temperature here is seldom low, although the winds are searching and chill, and keeping the baby warm was mostly a question of finding a spot out of the wind for his carriage.

Some time during that first October, Lem, our hired man, arrived. He was a tall young fellow of twenty-one, with a thin pale face and a blonde moustache. His family had belonged to Shag Harbour, but had been living for a few years in East Boston. His mother had died but recently, Lem still wore the black mourning band on his sleeve, and the home had been broken up. The city is not kind to the Lemuels of the world, and he had decided to come back to his old home vicinity. Lem was Mike's brother and we heard of him as a possible hired man for the winter through Mike.

The folks along the shore are an independent lot, and resent above all else the assumption that they might not be "as good as any living man," and Lem surely shared this democratic idea. He told us he, like so many of our young men at that time, had been employed on a yacht out of Boston the previous summer. I judged not everything about this job had his approval.

"Once me'n Manus was standing by the rail talkin' when the bosun come along an' told us to go over to the other side o' the boat. The owner was aboard, and coming out of his cabin fer a walk. Jest as if," said Lem indignantly, "we wasn't as good as him. We wasn't goin' to stop him takin' a walk. They was lotsa room."

Another time, Lem was one of a crew sent to row the owner and some of his friends ashore for a picnic. Lem watched all the good things being unpacked, and then—

"Them fellers set there, not twenty feet from where we was, and et all them things, and never offered us a bite. I call that bein' right tight with their grub."

Then there was something about raising and lowering the flag, which Lem "never could fathom out" and of which I got no clear conception from his accounts. The upshot of all this was that "they never signed me on fer next season. I dunno why not."

If Lem considered himself as good as any living man, he also declared his independence of feminine domination. Soon after his arrival here, he remarked of some poor hen-pecked soul that his wife forced him to shave *every other day!* "I wouldn't," declared Lem with an air of serving notice, "shave oftener than twice a week for *any* woman." So far as I know he never did.

Hereabouts hired help is treated as one of the family, and so we treated Lem and all our help. This is fair enough and the only possible course to follow situated as we are, but there were times when I wished we could have our growing impressionable children to ourselves.

One of Lem's recommendations was that he didn't share the fears and superstitions prevalent in Shag Harbour about life on the islands, and which is a contributing factor to our difficulty in getting help, when helping necessitates a stay of any duration on the Island. Or if Lem could not forget all he had heard and was perturbed by any of it, he hid his feelings well, and scoffed at the various "yarns" that friends told him of mysterious noises at Bon Portage Light, and Wrayton's ghost that cries and moans at night until you leave out a generous chew of tobacco for him. It was Lem who gave us our first inkling that the lighthouse was supposed to be haunted, and of the queer things that were rumoured to have happened here. I am afraid I showed some impatience and intolerance with such stories, and so never heard any full accounts of the mysterious ghost yarns that are told about the islands—Bon Portage and Emerald Isle.

Some years ago we had a visit from a lovely little lady from Detroit. She had been one of the Wrayton girls, and lived here as a child when her father was keeper of the Light. She told me her father was still hale and hearty, though in his eighties. Of course, no hard stupid fact like that of his being still alive would suffice to lay a popular ghost, and the Wraytons would provide excellent material for such stories; they did not belong to the district and were different—unforgivable faults in small closely knit communities, doubly so in the isolation prevalent fifty years ago.

Though ghosts do not constitute one of the drawbacks of Island life for us, the current stories have affected some of our visitors from near by. One summer Morrill and I went to Shag Harbour to vote and took the children with us. The boat that came to take us off left two boys of about twelve to keep the Light, for although we left in the middle of the day and expected to be back in an hour or so, we are not supposed to leave the lighthouse untended. As I left the shore I called to the lads that I had prepared a lunch for them, and told them where to find it. While we were away, the wind freshened from the south-west as it sometimes does in summer, and when we returned the two boys were at the water's edge, waiting to leave, and lost no time in getting away. At the house I found the lunch untouched, most unusual I thought with boys of that age about; but I decided they had been too shy to eat, or hadn't fancied what I had set out for them. Two years ago Morrill was away for a few days' deer-hunting, and one of these lads, now a tall young man, came on to help me and to get in a few days at duck-shooting. While he was here the wind went again to the south-west and I learnt why my lunch had gone uneaten. A south-west wind blows into our back porch, even when the outer door is closed, so strongly and in such a way that it opens the back door to the kitchen, which is fastened merely by a latch that drops into a slot and fits none too snugly. The two youngsters had spent a terror-stricken afternoon closing that back door and watching it open, each time to reveal a complete absence of any human opener! Melvin laughed as he told me they had been too scared to eat anything, and how, to make matters worse, the first thing one of them had done was to trip the cantankerous old pump, which released its water with terrifying moans and shrieks and left them with no means of moistening their parched throats or washing their hearts back into place with a good long drink.

They had remembered all the rumours and half-statements regarding queer "going-ons" at the lighthouse, and had resolved if they ever got off the Island, they would never set foot on it again!

I must admit I have seen no supernatural manifestations, much as I should like to have a ghost or two to boast of to visitors.  But for years Betty June had a most companionable ghost for a friend.  One day she heard Mike and me laughing about some unaccountable incident and deciding to lay the blame on Wrayton's ghost, since we could think of no reasonable explanation.  When I went to get a chocolate-frosted cake for supper, and found the marks of two little fingers drawn through the frosting, I had only to glance at Betty June to hear, "Mummy, it must have been Wrayton goat."

So Wrayton goat did all the mischief, mislaid all the tools, and was accountable for all the annoying incidents that took place from that time forward.  Then from a scapegoat he developed into a companionable friendly sort of ghost, who could assume almost any characteristics, and had many interesting accomplishments.  While he was still a new-comer to the family Betty June used to put cabbage leaves (I never could find out why cabbage leaves, they seemed odd fare for a ghost) for him under the mat by the back door; they were always gone when she looked later—Mike saw to that.  Later Wrayton goat became purely a fictitious character, and Betty June sat on Mike's lap and related the most exaggerated adventures that she and Wrayton goat had shared, with Mike asking leading questions and enjoying all her impossible yarns to the utmost.  Mike left before Betty June was five and with him went her interest in Wrayton goat.  So we had a ghost in the family for a while, but Betty June is ten now and has long outgrown such childish things; she prefers not to mention her erstwhile companion, "Wrayton goat."

We didn't have the company of Wrayton goat that first winter, however, but Lem stayed with us until spring. He and Morrill cut firewood, and hauled it home with Broad, our first steer, then scarcely more than a calf. They managed to cut and haul from the woods enough fuel for the next year, and since that time we have depended on our own wood for all our fuel. This wood alone has repaid us for the money we spent to buy the Island.

Lem was very good about staying with the babies, so that occasionally on a fine Sunday I was able to go for a walk with Morrill, though it was difficult to find many free moments.

Lem also liked to sit in the kitchen as I worked and recount to me the plots and counterplots of the Western films ("Them's the only kind I like") he had seen while in Boston. "Indians was all bad," he'd say, "but them *Red* Indians, them's the worst kind!" Or he would tell me of the time he was hired man for one of the fishermen. He became tangled in the rope of a pot that had been tossed back into the sea, and only saved himself by clutching the bar that runs across the stern of the boat and holding on for dear life until he could make the other man hear his cries above the noise of the engine.

"It's funny," he'd say, "they's places in the water has names same as on the land. They's a place they call Woody Pond becuz their pot-lines get tangled in old stumps and such after a storm, and they's Cameron's Shoal, only I ain't never heard why, and they must be a place called Brawny Deep becuz Willie said that day he almost lost me in the Brawny Deep."

As soon as the duck season opened, which was on October first in those years, both Morrill and Lem started gunning. This was a source of great pleasure to them, especially Morrill, who had missed the rabbit shooting and occasional deer-hunting that he had enjoyed as a young

man in Bedford.   I was glad to see him enjoying the sport,
but I felt there should be reason in all things, and Morrill
wouldn't even forego his shooting on Sunday, which
almost broke my heart and still tinges unhappily my
memories of the first winter here.   Ever since we had
been married Sunday had been our one day of the week
together, and at my own home Sunday was observed as a
quiet family day with Sunday school and church for us
younger ones.  So it was at Morrill's home, too, but
Morrill had gone to work at fourteen and missed the games
and sports of boyhood, so that when he found himself in a
duck-hunter's paradise nothing could hold him.  He
would have been glad to take me along, but I didn't approve
of hunting on Sunday (since he could go any day and every
day during the week), even if I could have left the children,
and he couldn't bring himself to be content with a quiet
Sunday at home while there were ducks waiting to be shot
up the Island.  I think he felt, being so far from church
and public opinion, that ethics didn't enter into the question at all.  It was our first radical difference of opinion
after three and a half years of marriage, and my Sundays
from being the happiest days of the week became miserable
and lonesome, as long as the gunning season lasted.  I had
read of women who became so engrossed in their children
that they had no place in their lives for their husbands,
but though I loved my two little ones devotedly, I never
succeeded in replacing Morrill's companionship by theirs.
I tried to establish new interests to fill the day and in time
succeeded fairly well.  A few years afterward Morrill was
forced to observe strictly all the gunning laws, including
that of Sunday shooting, but we never recovered the
special, happy-family, Sunday feeling that once we shared.

In December of that year Jean's and Ashford's baby
was born at the hospital at Yarmouth, and after long
months of worry for us all while Jean was very ill, she and

the baby arrived back at Emerald Isle. It was great to have them home again as we had missed their companionship and the exchange of visits.

Much of this sounds as if that first winter was pretty grim, and so it was in many ways; but I remember lots of fun together, too, some beautiful walks, two adored and adorable babies; our first Island Christmas and an entranced Anne Gordon. One of my fondest memories is of Morrill in the old wicker rocker, a baby on either knee, rocking in time and singing lustily,

> "Away we go on Laurie's little po,
> And away, and away, and away we go!"

It was so utterly ridiculous, and the children so innocently enthralled with it, that I have to smile as I remember.

Providence still tempered the wind for us—if not shorn lambs at least very inexperienced ones. Our first winter was mild and had few bad storms, so that we were not out of communication with the mainland for more than a week or so at any time. As I have mentioned, we took no chances on the weather and laid in sufficient supplies early in October to last us throughout the winter. Even when we have "travelling weather" during the winter, it is much better not to be bringing on any quantity of groceries when the boat trip is apt to be sloppy and wet.

Fresh meat was one of our greatest lacks during the first few years, as we had no animals of our own to slaughter, except a small pig, and Morrill never seemed to connect with the meat-cart that went through Shag Harbour once a week. Ducks furnished by far the greatest part of our fresh meat, and we enjoyed them to the full. Nothing could be more delicious. We have never tired of them and prefer roast black-duck to any other fowl we have ever tasted.

In spite of not being well the first summer, I had managed to can and preserve several bottles of berries, particularly raspberries, which grew in great abundance along the path to the boathouse. Morrill and I would put both babies in the carriage and wheel them to the berry patch, where even keeping an eye on them we could fill a water-bucket in a short time. Another berry which was plentiful that summer, but upon which there is no depending as the crops vary greatly from season to season, was the luscious swamp berry which we call the baked apple. I could not go to pick these as they grew some distance from the lighthouse and in swampy places where we could not take the babies, even if we had not feared the mosquitoes would carry them off bodily; but Morrill gathered the baked apples and I canned many of them.

I have seen an explanation of the name of these berries as being Bakyt apples, after a man of that name, but I am of the opinion that the name derives solely from their appearance. When these berries first open from the centre of their surrounding green sepals they look like small, hard, green apples, although instead of being a single round as an apple is they are formed of several rounded sections, somewhat like a raspberry except that the sections are larger and fewer. Then the berry grows and looks like a red-cheeked Gravenstein, and when they become fully ripe they have the transparent juicy look of a good baked apple, with a slightly more orange cast. We consider them the most delicious berry that grows, though many folks whose judgment in other matters we respect do not care for them at all. It seems, too, that they are one of those things about which there is no happy medium, you like them, or you don't—emphatically.

Later in the fall we had gathered a plentiful supply of cranberries, which at that time grew abundantly in almost every swamp on the Island, but which seem to have now almost entirely disappeared.   All the berries were a great help in our supplies for the winter, as we could not have afforded to buy much fruit even if we had had access to a market.

We had followed the example of the other keepers and did not remove the storm windows that first summer and so they did not have to be replaced in the fall, although each succeeding year we removed them during the warm weather.   The house, however, had to be banked against the winter storms, and for this Morrill used eel-grass that lay in dry windrows along the shore.   After a few years the eel-grass disappeared from all the Atlantic coast, and we tried rock-weed as a substitute.   This was not very satisfactory as it dried and shrank apart before the winter was over and left us little protection against the driving March winds.   We now use sawdust.

We took every precaution we could think of for the hard weather ahead, and as the storms and fate were kind, came safely through our first winter on the Island.

6

## A WALK AROUND THE ISLAND

IT WAS not until spring that I made the walk around the Island with Morrill and saw all our domain. It is an interesting walk, though the six miles over beach rocks and through swampy stretches make hard going. We went up the western shore and home along the eastern side, perhaps on the principle of getting the harder part over first, as the western shore is much the rougher and seems considerably longer.

Though I have walked the shoreline of the Island many times since, the walk never ceases to provide interest and unexpected beauties as the changing seasons, the varying weather conditions, and above all the restless winds and beneath them the never-constant sea with the added diversities that different phases of the tides emphasize, all lend infinite variety to every part of the walk.

The flat dull-wet sand beach blurring into the cold grey fog, with the almost human shrieks of the wraith-like gulls rising above the hiss of the waves on the nearer beach and the thunder of surf on the outer bars, present a picture of desolation, utter and complete. But in contrast, around the bend of the Island, where the sun is breaking through the fog, a distant group of white sheep peacefully feeding in the bright grass against the blue of a thicket of spruce and the tender green of alders is perfectly reflected across the unmarked waters of the pond, and might be a pastoral scene from the heart of a farming district miles from the pounding sea, and the distant sound of the bell-buoy could come from the bell of another peaceful flock beyond the mist.

The way is long and rough, the uneven beach rocks punish unaccustomed feet, but if you like wild seascapes or spots of sheltered beauty, won't you come for a walk around our Island?

We pass the lighthouse pond as we leave the field at the point and follow the high beach that lies between the pond and the sea. This beach used to be carpeted by a beautiful creeping plant with a frosty green leaf and tiny amethyst and blue blooms; the contrast between its fragile beauty and the rough grey rocks on which it grows is most entrancing, and when silver-green plants and dew-darkened rocks were reflected in the pond on a still morning, I beheld from my kitchen window a picture beyond price. Our sheep now prevent these plants from reaching their former luxuriant growth and I miss their beauty.

Just beyond the pond is one of the few spots on the Island where wild strawberries grow plentifully. It is fringed by the bare limbs of trees, stripped and blackened by the fire that once passed through them, but now beginning to show a soft silver.

The first spot we reach that bears a definite name is Salt Rock, a lonely sentinel, rising above the level of the low rocks that surround it, and providing an almost perpetual delight as the surf, rolling in unhindered over the gradual slope of the beach, strikes the rock and is flung upward some forty feet to fall back into the smother of foam at its base. The rock gets its name from a salt-laden ship that was once wrecked near this spot.

The next strip of shore is known as "The Graveyard." But no bodies lie buried here. The name refers to the hundreds of lobster-traps that have been lost along this shore, and whose battered and twisted skeletons lie scattered atop the beach and inland to the fringe of the trees. Many lobsters have been caught off this strip of shore, but looking at the cluttered fragments of traps, I would say they had been dearly bought.

Then begins a belt of woods and a strip of high land called the Red Bank, because of the appearance its red clay side presents to passing boats. The trees here come almost to the edge of the shore, sloping inward and upward from the outermost, whose branches twist and crawl in tortured shapes close above and through the moss. The trees inside these can rear a short trunk and raise their limbs slightly above the ground, while those which they in turn shelter rise less crookedly and still higher, until, some twenty yards from the shore, the trees are straight and natural. To me, there is a beauty in the twisted forms of those trees whose struggle and deformity allow their sheltered fellows to grow tall and graceful. These thickets form an almost impenetrable wall; I have seen our children run up over the matted branches as they might up the sides of a sloping wall; and it would be impossible to force a way through them. They afford excellent shelter for our sheep.

Not long ago I read an article regarding the Bird Sanctuary on Grand Manan. I am afraid someone pulled the author's leg, for he wrote of trees, bent and twisted by the weight of the birds (presumably ducks) which alight on them. That sounds to me like a "gunner's yarn," something the men about here would love to tell and chuckle about afterward, especially if it had been credited. I think likely those trees, like ours, were bent and twisted by the sea-winds blowing unceasingly across them and pressing them always in the same direction.

The wild beauty of the western shore draws my friend Mildred as it does me, and we have had many companionable walks along its rough ways. There the blue sea stretches unbroken to the horizon, and the gulls' weird wild screams rise above the wash and splutter of the summer sea among the reefs and boulders beneath us as we stride along the Red Bank, with the sloping green wall of aromatic spruce hemming us to the narrow rough footpath that twists along the shore. The scent of spruce and sun-soaked turf mingled with the breeze that has slipped across the crests and hollows of hundreds of miles of sparkling waves is as exhilarating as the view before us. Occasionally, when we reach the point where a long smooth out-cropping of rock lies exposed by the receding tide and looks invitingly dry and warm, we scramble down over the rocks and boulders and stretch ourselves in the hot sun. We lie there for perhaps half an hour, silent and relaxed, lulled by the soft whisper of the rockweed around the base of the ledge as it washes gently in and out to the almost imperceptible swell that murmurs and gurgles among the crevices gutted and smoothed by the innumerable tides that have risen and fallen along this portion of the rocky spine of the Island. I leave many petty cares and small irritations there in the sun-warmed crannies of the patient rock for the incoming tide to dissolve and obliterate, before the pressing memory of duties waiting at home force me to my feet and the return walk,

Beyond the Red Bank are two clearings, separated by a narrow neck of trees. These are now mostly overgrown with furze and low shrubs but they were once the sites of early homesteads on the Island. Pathetic little piles of loose stones, collected from the rocky surface of their fields, tiny partly caved-in cellars, and an occasional rock-lined well are still to be seen scattered along the outer portions of the Island, as Bon Portage supported several families in the days of the early settlement of this district. Rather, I should say the surrounding sea supported them, as the land never could have done so, nor would the settlers have expected it, their thoughts would have been on the harvests of the ocean.

Beyond these clearings and about half-way up the Island on the western side lies the Kelp Cove. There is no need to explain its name; although at some seasons no kelp is seen there and the cove lies glistening with its silver sands stretching in a slight crescent for a quarter of a mile, at other times the kelp and sea-weeds are piled in banks many feet high and lie there rotting in the sun and seepage from the swamp behind the beach. The sand is beautiful when it is clean and we have had a few wonderful swims at the Kelp Cove, but the tides there are treacherous, with a terrific undertow, so we have gone swimming only at slack water on the high tide, and are careful to swim along the shore, never out into the current. The Kelp Cove is also a favourite spot for ducks—and for duck-shooters. From the northern end of the Kelp Cove westward runs a bar, a narrow ridge of rock, exposed at low water and marked by a line of white breakers at high tide. At the Kelp Cove the Island is narrowest and lowest, and standing on the beach here, we can see Shag Harbour and Emerald Isle across the narrow width of treeless Savannah between us and the eastern shore of the Island.

Inside the beach at the northern end of the Kelp Cove lies Flag Pond. Although it must have been named for the Blue Flag, or Iris, that grows so abundantly in all our low land, none are found about it now, but a wild swamp hay and tall rushes grow lushly along its inland edge. The crisp fall sun across the pond and grasses, with their background of dark fir and spruce, accentuates an unsurpassed combination of colours and textures. Flag Pond is the favourite haunt of the Island black-ducks. Often in late summer or early fall we have crawled from the shore up to the tip of the beach to watch hundreds of ducks lazily swimming and preening themselves, or dozing with head tucked cosily under a wing, while the shores of the pond and much of its surface are white with cast-off feathers. The pond is small and it would seem it could not accommodate another duck, yet those in possession obligingly "move over" for new-comers as they scale down to join their comrades already enjoying the calm warm waters.

A hundred and fifty yards of slightly higher ground lies between Flag and Woody Pond. This is the prettiest and most sheltered of our ponds, the beach rises steeply before it and the trees come directly down to it on the opposite side. It is not large, and stumps of trees projecting from its waters and lining its shores no doubt provide its name. The seaward tide of the beach here has the most beautiful pebbles found anywhere on the Island; they are round and smooth as eggs and slightly smaller. They form a symmetrically rounded shelf between the sand of low tide and the heavier rocks that form the high-water line.

Off to the westward a mile or so from here lies a tiny islet known as Duck Island. Though it is scarcely more than a reef now, and is marked by a raised wooden structure to enable boats to sight and avoid it more readily, it was considerably larger not many years ago. I can remember when the fishermen from Cape Sable Island had a fishing

shanty there and lived in it during the lobster season.
The little shanty showed clearly from Emerald Isle as it
ranged across the low Savannah of Bon Portage, and I
looked at it with interest after I heard how one of the
fishermen had spent a long stormy night astride its ridge-
pole, as heavy seas pounded across the island and threatened
to wash shanty and man into the ocean.   I have heard my
grandfather speak of spreading the sails of his fishing
schooner to dry on the greensward of Duck Island when
he was following the sea, but no soil now tops the sea and
wind-swept rocks.   The island forms a good lee in some
winds, but in bad storms the seas break clear across it.
It lies between us and Seal Island, which cannot always be
seen from here but is plainly discernible under other
weather conditions.   Apart from these islands, nothing
breaks the sea rolling between us and the coast of New
England, two hundred miles or so distant.

Beyond Woody Pond we come upon a strip of trees,
shrubs, swamp grasses and a tangled growth of gooseberry
bushes.   In lucky years, these last yield us a bounteous
crop of the most delicious berries.   People who should
know tell me they are not the wild gooseberry, but may
be a cultivated variety run wild.   Whether they started
from seeds dropped by birds, or whether a ship with fruit-
bearing shrubs was wrecked on the shore as I have heard,
I shall probably never know.   The best of these berries
are as large as the cultivated ones and of a superior taste
and texture.   Of course, they *would* be at the point of the
Island farthest from the Light and the devil's own job to
pick from the tangled and matted bushes.   We are days
getting all the thorns out of our fingers after a gooseberry-
picking expedition, but the jam and jelly thus provided
are well worth the inconveniences of gathering and "nibbling" them.   This "nibbling" is one job at which any

visitors who chance to be here at the time are encouraged—
they may feel "coerced" is a more adequate word—to
take part.

The gooseberry patch lies next to the extreme end of
the Island and the Salt Water Pond.   This is a stretch of
shallow water a third of a mile long and a quarter of a mile
wide.   At times it is completely enclosed by the land
and a high sea-wall; at other times the sea smashes through
the beach and leaves a wide opening through which the
pond fills and empties with the tide.   Then the sea tires
of this and fills the cut again by tossing rocks into and across
it.   The beach was closed at our coming, it was opened
again a few years later and remained so for some years,
but it is now almost completely closed.   One of the fishermen took his thirty-five-foot motor-boat into the Salt
Water Pond through the Gap when it was widest, just to
be able to say later that he had done so.   My friend,
Mildred, and I had a grand swim across that part of the
pond where the tides had deepened a channel, but the water
had been warmed by the sun; ordinarily the water is too
shallow and stagnant for swimming.   We can walk the
high sea-wall along the outer edge of the pond, or take the
shorter route along the inner side through the sedge grass
and wild swamp hay.   The Salt Water Pond makes a
wonderful feeding ground for the ducks, and every year
an old shell-duck raises a brood and teaches them to swim
in its sheltered water.

At the farther end of the Salt Water Pond is a high
ridge, treed for some distance but cleared at the extreme
end where once was a home and its little stone cellar still
remains.   From this ridge one can look west, north and
east across the ocean that laps the shores of the Island.
To the south the length of the Island stretches, beginning
with half an acre of wild rosebushes, a beautiful sight when
they are in bloom.   To the north a continuation of the ridge

extends into the sea towards the upper islands and the
mainland of which Bon Portage was no doubt once a
part, and this rocky extension is known as the Northern
Bar. The tide here is very strong and the water wicked
after a storm. Although I have never seen it I have heard
described an awesome sight that is beheld occasionally at
this bar: the seas after a heavy rough run up both sides of
the Island, swing inward at its tip, and meet over the bar
with a thunderous crash that jars the adjacent bedrock
of the Island, and sends water and spray seventy feet into
the air! Because the Northern Bar is dangerous, it is
marked by a light-buoy on the east, and a sweet-toned
bell-buoy on the west.

From the northern ridge we make a half-turn and start
down the eastern side of the Island; and here just as we
swing about is the best beach we have, with white sand
running out a mile or so under the water. As the tide
flows in over this shallow water and hot sand it becomes
warm in comparison to the icy water found at the Point
and most other places along the shore. Mildred and I first
discovered the swimming possibilities of the beach; we had
an exhilarating swim and went home enthusiastic. We
persuaded Morrill to take us all in the boat for a swim the
following day. Morrill loves a good swim but loathes
having to wade in, and prefers to dive from something
if at all possible. He was first in, diving from the boat.
He was in and out and over the gunwale into the boat all
in one movement! We were just a little late and the icy
water from the western side had been flowing for some time
across the Bar, so that the water at our much-lauded beach
was no warmer than at any other part of the shore. Morrill
felt he had been duped.

Then there was George—but George really had it
coming to him. He was Morrill's nephew from Ontario
and he was spending a year with us. He was young and

confident and not overly receptive to the ideas of others. As he looked across to Emerald Isle one day he remarked, "Why, a fellow could easily swim that!" It is two miles from Light to Light.

"The distance mightn't bother you," I said, "but the water here is so cold, you probably couldn't stand the chill unless you spent some time building up the necessary resistance."

Whereupon George gave us a lengthy dissertation on the cold water in the lakes near his home, and on how he and his brothers set it at naught.

Next June Morrill's sisters were visiting us and a picnic being in order, we decided the tide should be about right for the season's first swim and we'd have it at the northern end.

The children were already ankle deep in the water when I was ready to step in and felt the water burn before it numbed my feet. Half the children's enjoyment of our swims comes, I think, from the shrieks I utter and the roars Morrill emits when we are forced to wade into the cold water. We found when the children were tiny, that they became enormously brave and cold-defying when they heard the disgraceful fusses Morrill and I made, so we've always carried on this performance. This day, I remembered George, undressing behind the sea-wall, so I was disappointingly stoical, and made sign to the children not to reveal the temperature of the water. So when George appeared at the top of the beach we were all apparently enjoying ourselves near the shore, though in reality we were clenching our teeth to keep them from chattering. George, with long arms and legs flying, came tearing across the sand and into the water. He had good headway on, and it carried him well out into a depth above his waist. By that time he had recovered his breath, and with an ear-splitting yell he rushed out of the water, back over the beach and into his clothes. We never mentioned the comparative temperatures of Ontario's lakes and Nova Scotia's Labrador current, nor did he again suggest swimming to Emerald Isle.

Here, too, Mildred and I had a near adventure when I had been here only a year and Mildred came for the first of many visits. We decided to go clamming at the northern end. We picked a foggy day, when Morrill must stay close to the hand-horn and so could keep an eye on tiny Anne and Lo, and off we set with clam-fork and buckets. When we arrived at the spot where I was certain Morrill and I had dug clams the previous fall, there were no clams—not even a beach that remotely resembled the kind clams prefer. How could I suspect, being still new on the Island, that the heavy seas during the preceding winter had changed the whole shore line here, and buried the clam beach under many feet of gravel and rock?

As we tramped back and forth in a vain search for the missing clam-flat, we came upon footprints in the sand. At that part of the Island and on that sort of day they surprised us as greatly as Friday's did Crusoe. We had left our shoes on the greensward above tide-line, and these prints were several sizes larger than ours would have been. We decided they had been made by men's rubber-boots and while we were wondering why anyone should have been ashore on this end of the Island, suddenly out of the off-shore fog close at hand came the muffled roar of a starting boat engine and indistinct words shouted in a voice that carried above the noise of the motor, but distorted beyond recognition by the fog. The boat ran a short distance, stopped, drifted silently a bit, and repeated this several times before the sound of voice and engine were lost completely in the grey wool of the fog. Then we came to a place where several pairs of foot-prints crossed and recrossed a trampled stretch of sand. We decided it was all most mysterious. By this time the tide had covered any possible clams and we started home with empty buckets and very tired feet.

A few weeks later we heard there had been a cargo, or part cargo, of liquor cached at the northern end that week-end and picked up later. These were the days of rum-running along this coast and the story ran that a Cape Island boat had found itself in a tight spot and forced to get rid of its cargo before entering harbour. Knowing that the northern end of this Island had been little frequented for several years, the crew had picked it as a likely spot, unloaded in the thick fog and hid their cargo among the trees and bushes, planning to return at a safer time. This they apparently did. Mildred and I have often wondered what would have happened if we had stepped out of the fog a few minutes earlier and come upon them unloading.

As I have said, the eastern side of the Island is the more sheltered and has the prettier spots and calmer views, although I prefer the wild seascapes of the western side. From the eastern side the mainland and Emerald Isle are much nearer and it is more readily seen how our Island is the outer side of a large basin; and how "Bon Portage" or "Good Harbour" is a suitable name for the anchorage that it, along with the mainland and Emerald Isle, forms.

On the eastern side there is one small pond, known simply as the North-East Pond, and it is the favourite haunt of a flock of blue-winged teal, to me the most appealing in appearance of all our ducks, they always have such a neat, tucked-in look. This is where Ted, our first little dog, fell victim to the wiles of a mother black-duck. Mildred and I had taken Ted along for a walk, and as we passed this pond, out flew a duck, flapping her wings, and barely able to clear the water. Ted naturally gave chase, while Mildred, so sensitive to any pain or suffering, cried,

"Evelyn! Stop him! Oh, you must stop him! Your dog's going to hurt that poor little duck!"

I made a useless attempt to call Ted to heel, but I soon realized what was happening. The duck flapped piteously to the farther end of the pond, uttering frightened cries and apparently unable to lift her injured wing. Then, as Mildred continued to cry out, and Ted thought she was about to grab herself a duck, it rose gracefully over the beach and settled down on the water about twenty-five yards off-shore. From this vantage point, it complacently watched the crestfallen Ted join us and move along, totally unaware of the ducklings, now securely hidden in the tall swamp grass or under the old stumps that line the little pond.

The sheltered eastern side was favoured by the early settlers, and on our way home we pass five clearings with their tiny cellars and abandoned wells. Each would provide a lovely spot for a home if only beautiful surroundings and a wonderful view need be considered. All these old fields could easily be made into excellent pasture land by dressing them with the sea-weed that lies along the near shore. However, one man can do only so much, and thus far Morrill has been able to make use of only one of these fields, the one which is about half-way up the Island and is known as "Garron's."

Between Garron's and the boathouse we follow a small wood road cut by Morrill during his first few winters here; it is now thickly bordered with blackberry and raspberry bushes, interspersed with the sweet-smelling bayberry bushes. We reach the boathouse field, and take the path through the woods to the lighthouse—Home-Again-Home.

## 7

## A BIT OF HISTORY

LONG BEFORE the white man knew these shores, the Indians in their war-canoes were rounding Cape Sable and skirting outlying islands to what is now Yarmouth; and legend has it that certain Indians from the Fundy shore carried their dead to an island near Cape Sable for burial. Before Port Royal was many years old, the French had set up a trading post in what we call Shag Harbour, and Indians from along the shores came into the little harbour to barter their furs. On calm summer days and more especially on still evenings, I can readily picture one or more of the big canoes moving noiselessly past the Point, and across the opalescent waters to the entrance of Shag Harbour, where the point of Inner Island would shut them from my view.

If the Runic Stone at Yarmouth and the stone remains of what was apparently a building of Norse construction found near Tusket are accepted as proof of a visit by Leif Ericson, then without a doubt he passed close to Bon Portage as he followed his questing prow along the unknown coast. I like to think he did.

Wherever Leif sailed or didn't sail, Champlain left records to show that he stopped here in 1604. He called it "Ile aux Cormorants" probably because of the presence of those same shags which afterward gave their name to the little harbour near by. He stopped here at least long enough to gather a boatload of birds' eggs, either those of the wild ducks or of the gulls; the latter are still considered a great delicacy by many people along the shore although it is unlawful now to gather them. Champlain sailed on, found and named the Seal Islands, and continued on his way to make at Port Royal the following year the first white settlement on this continent, north of Florida. But history had brushed in passing this tiny sea-girt Isle.

The early French navigators, whether bound for Port Royal or nearer Pubnico, gave the Island and the anchorage of which it forms the outer breakwater, the name of Bon Portage. The strip of water above the northern end of our Island they called Cockawee Pass (now Cockerwit), from the Indian name for the small black-and-white water-fowl which we know as Old Squaws. Mr. H. L. d'Entremont of Pubnico, who is an authority on Acadian history, could tell me nothing more of how the Island got its name, but found it thus named on old French maps. Old English maps of 1850 have it marked as Hope Island, while in the old Proprietors' Records of 1785 at Barrington it is called merely Shag Harbour's Outermost Island, and it is still known locally as Outer Island.

In 1785, shortly after Barrington was settled and its settlers had in turn moved to Shag Harbour and other neighbouring districts, the mainland at Shag Harbour and Wood's Harbour were re-divided, and with them the adjoining islands. "The Outermost Island" was divided into seven shares ("shears" the old record says), by the Committee Men. The first owners of these "shears" apparently made no use of them, no doubt they had ample land on the mainland, and it was not until about 1840 that some families built homes on the Island.

Before the Island was settled history was to touch it lightly again.

During the early part of the War of 1812 American privateers were numerous along this shore, and often visited the harbours and little settlements where they helped themselves to whatever struck their fancy, and their fancies were rather inclusive. For a small self-dependent and isolated settlement to be stripped of its supplies and stock was to cause its inhabitants great hardships indeed, and the men along the shore were not inclined to take such treatment submissively. At the larger places these unwelcome visits were planned for when the men of the village were away on their fishing voyages, but I suppose at the smaller settlements the privateers felt confident of easily overcoming any resistance that might be offered.

Be that as it may, the time came when news reached Shag Harbour that a privateer had been raiding the Argyles, only forty miles or so to the westward, and was expected to pay her next call at Shag Harbour. The village prepared to welcome her. Word was passed among the local men to be on the alert and ready for trouble. Not many days later a suspicious-looking vessel was sighted, and the summons went forth for the men of Upper Shag Harbour to be ready to oppose a landing if the vessel approached the harbour and attempted to send men ashore. Some of the village men took a small boat and rowed across the Sound to the northern end of "Outer Island," where they landed. Then with their old flint-and-steel muskets they marched down the eastern side of the Island, keeping out of sight behind the high beach or in the shelter of the woods until they reached a point near the southern end of the Island, where the beach rose ten feet or more above the low land behind it, and where a boat might be expected to land for water, as a little brook trickled through the beach close at hand.

Soon the watchers on shore saw the vessel round the Point and pull up along the shore for an anchorage. The anchors were dropped not far from the spot chosen by the Shag Harbour men, and soon a boat was put out. The ambushed men watched the small boat and when it had closely approached the spot where they lay hidden, one of them hailed her, and at this the startled coxswain gave the order, "Pull the bow oar!" This brought the boat broadside on, and the leader of the Shag Harbour men gave the order to fire. A volley of shots burst forth and the surprised men in the small boat dropped below the gunwale, some of them doubtless killed or wounded. All had not been hit, however, as one man, lying below the protecting gunwale, managed to skull the boat back to the vessel with only his hand and arm exposed. The boat rounded the vessel's stern and reached safety.

In a few moments came a cannon shot from the vessel's gun, but this succeeded only in striking the sea-wall and scattering beach rocks over the heads of the concealed men. The privateer had not relished the Shag Harbour welcome, and in a few moments got under way and headed for the open sea; while the Shag Harbour men returned to their homes, glad to be able to tell the village that it was safe from pillage for some time at least.

From a story I loved as a child I believe another privateer fared little better on its trip to Shag Harbour.

Abigail Bradford, a matron of the place, lived on Inner Island, very near the mainland at Shag Harbour. One day she was surprised to see a privateer anchor off the Island and a small boat prepare to come ashore. The men-folk were all away fishing, but "Aunt Nabby," nothing daunted, prepared to defend her property. She loaded two guns, fastened pots and pans among the trees and shrubs with strings leading to where she lay hidden in the bushes that faced the cove in which the boat must land. When the boat drew near she fired her two guns and manipulated the strings leading to her noise-makers in the trees so as to make as much noise as possible. It must have sounded convincingly like a number of men preparing to resist an attempt to land, since the boat pulled away and made no further effort to come ashore.

This same Abigail Bradford had a tragic adventure off the Northern Bar of Bon Portage. The dory she was in became caught in the tide and surf of this dangerous point and capsized. "Aunt Nabby," the only woman in the boat, was the sole survivor; she lost father, husband and son in that dread few moments. She managed to manœuvre the dory ashore, and there she got branches by which she paddled the heavy dory back to the mainland. She later re-married and "reformed her husband to sobriety by her self-sacrifice, fortitude and energy."* Quite a woman, Aunt Nabby.

When the Island came to be settled, no doubt those who first made their homes here were fishermen who sensed the advantages of easy access to the fishing grounds in those days of sail and oar. Since most travelling in these parts was then by boat, or by a rough footpath along the shore, the inhabitants of the islands were not much more remote from other settlements than were their friends and relatives on the mainland. It was not until the little

*Quotation from Edwin Crowell's *History of Barrington Township*.

villages of Shag Harbour and Wood's Harbour had progressed to a school, a church, a general store, and roads to facilitate communication with neighbouring districts that the disadvantages of island life became apparent, and the families left one by one. A fisherman, who once chanced in at the lighthouse, told me that his mother, then an old lady, had been born in one of the first houses erected on the Island, and that her family had been the last of the original settlers to depart for the mainland.

The landings along the eastern shore, fields still sodded but rapidly growing up in furze and bush and losing ground year by year to the encroaching fir and spruce, the little piles of rocks cleared from the fields, and an occasional cellar and well, remind us that here and there lived men and their families. Men who scanned the sea and sky to judge what the morrow might bring, who basked in the warm sun on the smiling sea or braced themselves against the howling nor'westers and strove to keep their homes secure and warm against its driving chill. Other women, like me, watched the fog and surf and strove to calm their hearts as their men were long delayed in returning home, and the sea wore a cruel gloating look and chuckled derisively at their helplessness. Other children played among the sun-warmed rocks and came running to show Mother the pretty pebbles or shells, or the delicate beach blooms they had found. Perhaps other little boys painfully picked the first wild roses and brought them in a hot scratched little fist, because he sensed Mother missed the flowers she had known in a less wind-swept home.

The chain of human life unrolls as limitless as the waves in the sea that laps all shores; it is good to know of those who went this way before and to think of those who will come after. The spots of earth we call our own, as we take our place in the life continuity, never actually belong to any of us; what are really ours are the eyes and the ears to see and hear, and the soul to love and understand the beauties around us. Though Morrill holds a title to the Island of Bon Portage, who could sell or buy the sea among the rocks, the winds rippling the fields of grass, the moon's lustrous path across the surging water, or the star-studded bowl of the night sky? They are without price, and priceless, and will be here for those who follow us. Then the work of our hands, those insignificant scratches on the face of the earth, may serve to remind others of our passing, as the tiny heaps of stones, laboriously gathered a hundred years ago, bring to our minds those who preceded us at this tiny speck in time and place.

When the families that had been making their homes here moved from Bon Portage, their shares in the Island were bought by Michael Wrayton, who had already purchased the shares of Emerald Isle and had made his home there. He was an Irishman, shipwrecked on this coast as a young man, and it was he who had the name of his island home changed to Emerald Isle in place of the former Stoddart's Island. There are innumerable tales told of him and his family, in fact they have become legendary in these parts, as witness "Wrayton's ghost." Michael Wrayton himself never lived on this Island, but when the lighthouse was erected about 1870, his son Arthur was appointed the first Keeper of the Light. Arthur brought his bride here to the little new lighthouse, standing in its clearing that had recently been cut from the midst of the thickly wooded point. Mrs. Wrayton told my grandmother that the years spent on Bon Portage were the happiest of her life. After a few years she went to the Wrayton homestead on Emerald Isle, and trouble and sorrow seemed to join her there. She was a proud woman, and her domestic unhappiness added to her reserve, so that she rebuffed any friendliness that might have been shown her in spite of her vast difference in manner and training from the people of the place. Her unhappy taciturnity and the suspicion of strangers found all too often in small isolated places, finally resulted in her being tried for murder when a poor idiot helper-about-the-place perished in a cruel snow storm, while returning from the Emerald Isle lighthouse to the house. Her husband was absent, and she had her small children whom she daren't leave alone in the house to attempt to rescue poor "Billy." She was acquitted at the trial, but those who knew her said she never recovered from the ordeal. Her husband was tragically drowned shortly after that, and the unhappy woman returned to her former home in Halifax, where she died a few years later. I like to think that Bon Portage was kind to her, and that she had those first happy years here with her young loving husband and her small children.

I once talked with an old gentleman of Shag Harbour, who as a boy visited the Point the summer the lighthouse was built. No family had previously settled at this spot, as the rough seas and rugged shore made fishing from this point impossible, so this end of the Island had remained thickly wooded. When the government had selected the site for the lighthouse, a clearing was chopped out of the woods, but a wide belt of trees was left surrounding it as a windbreak. (Don't we often wish it were still here!) The old gentleman said the brush and limbs of trees had been left lying on the ground, and he remembered scrambling over them and the jagged stumps with difficulty.

When we came all that remained of the sheltering belt of trees were three or four small gnarled spruce on the bank to the south of the Light, and a similar bunch on the eastern bank, while two or three larger old trees stood on a small knoll between the Light and the pond. The sea had eaten away shore and trees along the outer edge, while indolent lightkeepers had chopped down those on the landward side for firewood; we could see the large stumps along the path. At the Point, the sea has never ceased to gain in its age-old struggle against the land. It batters and eats away the trees and soil that holds the large boulders, then it drops these which it cannot so swiftly and effortlessly destroy, and passes around and over them, grinding and wearing them away little by little, year by year. The land between the lighthouse is rapidly diminishing, and the last old tree on the southern bank is kept from being washed away only because it is fastened to a heavy post that holds my clothes-line. This helps to keep it in position, but the sea has eaten deeply under it and its roots are exposed along almost their entire length. The next storm, like many we have had, would wash it away completely.

There have been many keepers of the Bon Portage Light, but few of them stayed long. I think we probably hold the record with our fifteen years of service here, unless Will Wrayton, brother and successor of the first keeper, stayed a year or two longer. Most of the keepers, or their families, found the life too lonely. One, who was contented here, was forced to resign on account of ill-health.

Even after the people who had made their homes on the Island had left for an easier existence on the mainland, there were still a few men who lived here during the fishing seasons. They built their shanty at what had been Connell's field, and what we now call the boathouse field, the most southerly of the old clearings. About that time the government put up near by a boathouse, slip and breakwater for the lightkeeper. The slip was planked over, and usually the fishermen gave assistance to those coming ashore; several men would grab the sides of the boat and run it up the smooth slip to the door of the boathouse where passengers and freight would be unloaded. A flat-bottomed dory would be the type of craft used for landing, a larger boat, like a sailing sloop, would have to be anchored and a transfer made to a lighter craft. Now some twenty feet of beach and sod lie between the boat-house door and the top of the slip, as the beach built itself out into the sea under the protection of the break-water. The sea has already begun to narrow this strip since its destruction of the breakwater, and doubtless in a few years will have reduced the shoreline to its former position just in front of the boathouse. Occasionally a heavy storm will toss aside the boulders that ordinarily cover that portion of the shore and part of the old slip can be seen, well preserved under the salt water.

The fishermen did not make great use of the slip and breakwater, each boat and its crew had its own private landing nearer the shanty, and it is these we see when the tide is down.

These men lived a bachelor existence during the week in their "cook-house" or shanty—no doubt like those I have seen, with a cook-stove and long plain-board table in the centre, and at least two side-walls lined with tiers of bunks. Perhaps they took turns at the cooking and chores, a large group would hire cook and cookee. Saturday after-noon they would hoist the sails on their trawl-dories and with a rock or two laid in for ballast, go skimming off to Shag Harbour—to homes and families and "civilization." I suppose there were Saturdays when they had head winds and a long arduous row, but the picture I see in my mind is of the little fleet, all sails spread and a fresh following sou'west breeze.

When gasoline boats made their appearance, the advantages that their greater proximity to the fishing grounds had given these men were now offset by the speed of the motor-boats and their independence from the vagaries of the wind; and as the larger boats could not be pulled up and down the Island landings, the fishermen deserted their shanty, and the Island was left to the light-keeper alone.

History, but so recent as scarcely to be history yet, again skirted these shores when President Roosevelt, on a vacation cruise, twice sailed close by to anchor for the night in the excellent harbourage off the point at Emerald Isle. We had noticed the smudges of smoke to the westward, but busy about getting the last load of hay to the barn, we had thought the indistinct hulls on the horizon were merely the customary tug with some scows in tow. They were close in before we saw what a decidedly unusual flotilla was approaching and rounding the Point.

First came the graceful yacht, her spars tall and slenderly regal, her sails barely filled and soon to be lowered. A person, whom we took to be the President, sat casually relaxed in the stern, while another figure in a striped sweater moved energetically about the deck. Him we thought to be the President's son. These were plainly seen, as the yacht rounded the Point close to shore, but the ships of greater draught made a wider sweep and kept a greater distance. There was a swift low destroyer, a coastguard boat with pennants aflutter, and a beautiful big steam-yacht, her white paint and brass work glistening blindingly in the westering sun. Trailing some distance behind came the press boat, a former Gloucester fishing schooner, her drab black hull and dingy sails looking decidedly disreputable in comparison with the spit-and-polish of the more resplendent craft.

Nothing like this flotilla had ever before entered Bon Portage Sound, unless it had been long ago, when a squadron of the Royal Navy occasionally anchored here, and some of the young officers went ashore to dance with the bevy of beautiful Wrayton girls. Needless to say the Shag Harbour boats were out in full force and circled and recircled the visiting ships. Among them was our little boat, for Morrill had taken Mildred and our children to see the beautiful craft and to share the excitement. Even from the shore they presented a lovely picture with their hulls waveringly reflected and their lights twinkling across the iridescence of the sunset sea. On their return trip from Shelburne the boats again anchored in the harbour and Walter being here to keep the Light, Morrill was able to take me on a similar short excursion on an equally lovely evening. We were kept at some distance from the President's yacht, but moved close beside the other boats, and I remember vividly the row of smiling Filipino stewards in their spotless white coats lining the sides of the other boats as we went by.

Most of the facts in this chapter that deal with days gone by I learned from "Uncle Gilbert" Nickerson, the old chairmaker of Shag Harbour, whose knowledge of and interest in local history is equalled by his friendliness and kindness to all.

## 8

## THE SECOND SUMMER AND INCIDENTALS

WHEN the spring of our second year at Bon Portage arrived we felt we must manage the work by ourselves and let Lem go, not because we no longer needed his help, but still in debt and lacking so many necessities, we knew we must economize on even the small salary we paid him and the cost of his board.

I remember that spring mostly for the clothes problem it brought with it. During the previous summer we had worn what garments we had on hand, but now most of these were worn out, especially every-day and work clothes. Morrill's good suit had scarcely been worn, but I had not been so fortunate, the printed silk dress I had bought expecting it to last some time for dress-up occasions had

gone to pieces in a most unexplainable manner. The
children, too, were growing and needed more and larger
clothes. The spring brings many demands for money to
buy seeds and equipment for planting, as well as for the
thousand and one things ordinarily needed for a family
and home. Well, we had little money, so we made shift
somehow without it.

I had on hand a few clothes too small for me now, and
some ends of print Mother had sent me for quilt-pieces,
and out of these I fashioned the children's spring wardrobe.
I had never before used a sewing-machine, and my hand
sewing had been limited to the fine things I had made for
my Hope Chest. We had been given the sewing-machine
of Morrill's mother, well-used but serviceable still, and I
began to try my hand at dress-making. There was no one
to whom I could turn for help and advice, what I could I
learned from the printed patterns, the rest I did "by guess
and by gosh." The first results were decidedly crude.
They served the purposes of cover and warmth, and that is
about all that could be said for them.

Left over from days before my marriage were two pairs
of sport breeches, and to save much-needed cash Morrill
decided to wear these out, as I had put on weight after
Laurie's birth and could no longer wear them in comfort.
Too, it seemed to me then that I should never again have
time to do anything but cook and wash and scrub and tend
babies. So Morrill used them and also wore out two
heavy roll-neck sweaters of mine before the next winter
was over. So those things helped out on his wardrobe.

For myself I bought a piece of blue broadcloth, and
using a pattern Mother had given me, made a dress—I
remember it cost seventy-two cents and the cost of the
thread! This was my *only* dress for some weeks; when it
was too dirty I washed it at night and ironed it next
morning before breakfast, while I wore an old dressing-

gown. It bothered me to think that if I should be called home by illness in the family I would of necessity have to travel in that ill-fitting cotton garment.

During that year, and for several succeeding ones, I had a close and continuous acquaintance with the possibilities inherent in cotton feed-bags, and the varieties of garments and household articles that can be fashioned from them. We used them for every imaginable necessity, from sails for the boat to little suits for Laurie. I also learned the numerous uses to which factory cotton, dyed or natural, can be put.

That spring we reached rock bottom financially; sometimes we were forced to rob the kiddies' penny banks in order to mail a letter, and to wait until our next monthly cheque to repay them. I don't remember things ever being quite so stringent afterward. Since few people saw us and we were young and full of high hopes for the future, we passed through this period quite unaffected, though certainly we didn't look the same. It was hardest to see the little ones, who in our eyes at least were pretty babies, do without the adorably cunning garments that graced the offspring of friends and relatives with a little more money to spend on their children. However, I realized that the children themselves felt no sense of neglect or of missed opportunities to shine, and it was merely to gratify my pride in them that I wished them more attractively dressed.

My sewing gradually improved with practice and now passes muster, but sewing does not come easily to me, and I would never do it for pleasure or relaxation. We have been fortunate in having many clothes given me and the children; friends send us better things than we could afford to buy; I accept them gladly and make the most of them. I seem to have no pride.

While we need few garments for "dress-up" occasions, the life here, particularly for Morrill and Laurie, is very hard on clothes.  Boots and socks suffer most.  Rubber boots are worn from necessity almost all year round; even the girls and I must have rubber boots or lumbermen's rubbers if we are to venture beyond the doorsteps, except on fine summer days, and even then they are often necessary, as much of our land is low and wet, and in foggy weather the moisture-laden grass and bushes demand that we go rubber shod.

The men (since Laurie is now as tall as his Daddy, I consider that I have two men) must have innumerable sweaters and socks.  It is not unusual for me to have a dozen pairs of socks for them in the weekly wash, most of them with their heels completely chewed out from walking in their rubber boots.  I knit their sweaters and socks out of white and grey yarn from the woollen mill at Barrington. This yarn is not soft or fine, but it wears exceptionally well, and garments knit from it can be laundered weekly in the washer with as little fuss as any cotton piece.  The men like their socks long enough to turn down below the knees of their breeches, so that means plenty of knitting in each leg.  I never catch up on my knitting and it seems I always have a sock, or sweater, or mitten in the making for "pick-up" work.

The temperature here seldom drops below zero, but the wind goes through clothes like a hot knife through butter. So Morrill and Laurie each wear a leather jacket outside sweaters or coat if it is windy, and for the boat they must have high rubber boots, oilskins and sou'westers.

To watch Morrill and his friend Walter dress for gunning on a cold winter's day brings a revelation as to how much clothing can be piled on the human frame.  To start, Walter always pulls on an extra pair of heavy pants; Morrill need not do this since he already has inside his outer trousers a pair of shorts that I made him out of pieces of chamois, and he claims these are the best yet to break the wind against that unprotected part of his leg that comes between his jacket and the uppers of his rubber boots. Two or three pairs of extra socks go on next, and then their rubber boots. Three sweaters, or two sweaters and a wind-breaker are none too many, and these are topped by an oilskin or rubber jacket "to break the wind." If there is snow down an old white sweater goes outside this so it doesn't show against the whitened beach. I knit a special shawl collar for each of Morrill's gunning sweaters, so this comes well up about his neck to prevent chafing by the oilskin collar, and stops the wind from blowing down the back of his neck when he is prone. Caps were for a time a great problem. A dark one shows against the snow; a white one shows against the rocks and sea-weed if he's crawling among them when the tide is out. I solved this weighty perplexity by knitting Morrill a double cap, white on one side, brown on the other, and he can turn it to suit circumstances. That does for Morrill's headgear, but Walter "minds the cold" on his head, so he must have something, he doesn't know just what, inside his cap for extra protection, and I search for linings, kerchiefs, or squares of warm flannel. I have seen him sally forth with one of the children's woollen mufflers over his head, and the ends tied perkily under his chin. Now a pair of mittens for Morrill, who is very likely to toss them aside and forget them if the shooting proves exciting, and as Walter has brought two pairs of his own, they appear about ready to start. This they do, after putting their guns up to sight and declaring that they can never in their bundled state move quickly enough to shoot anything, anyway! They look as round and shapeless as snowmen as they set out, but I know if they lie long waiting for ducks they will soon be wishing they had put on another sweater or an extra pair of socks.

Even in the summer we wear more clothes than we would inland. The winds, and especially the fog-breezes, are cool, and a sweater is almost always welcome. Rubber boots for the wet land demand woollen socks; and the path to the boathouse and the way along the beach tops is too rough for lighter footwear, even when the weather is dry.

My usual vestment is a housedress. I seldom have occasion to wear anything more elaborate except on my very infrequent visits to Shag Harbour, and my still less frequent trips to my old home at Bedford. When I work in the garden or silo I wear overalls, or if a cold wind is blowing I put on woollen breeches even in the summer. I am forced to don warm breeches for about the house on cold days in the winter, as the kitchen is particularly draughty and hard to heat. My feet are usually numb with the cold when I work about the kitchen, and Morrill is long-suffering as a bedfellow.

One Christmas my brother Doug's wife sent me a hot-water bottle and a few days later a blow-torch arrived from Doug for Morrill. He had wanted one for ages to use on odd soldering jobs, and to singe ducks. But as he held it off and beamed with pleasure, this is what I heard, and I had no misapprehension as to what he meant:

"Gee! Doug certainly means me to have comfort this winter. Nights that the hot-water bottle won't do the trick, I can apply the blow-torch."

But my feet haven't been quite so icy since I found a pair or two of the men's long woollen stockings in an out-grown pair of Laurie's shoes were a help. I shiver just to imagine silk stockings and slippers, which I once considered ample for winter house wear.

I do not wear my winter ensemble of outsize shoes, coarse grey hand-knit stockings, and worn shapeless breeches and sweater for its chic, as you may have gathered. I imagine few weirder combinations have been seen than my

large white aprons above the garments I have described.
Mike always said he didn't have to step outside to see
what the weather was like, when he came downstairs in
the morning and found me preparing breakfast in my
"cold weather rig" he knew the temperature had fallen,
or the wind was blowing strongly from the north-west.

The girls wear light sweaters and ski-pants indoors
most of the winter, although I think they do not always
need them but are too indolent to change even when the
house is comfortably warm, as the living-room almost
always is. They have heavy jackets for outdoors, and
extra coats for the boat. Anne often "iles up," that is,
dons Laurie's oilskins and sou'wester, in wet weather or
for a sloppy trip in the boat. In the summer they wear
light dresses occasionally, but more often shorts, slacks or
overalls.

My wardrobe, or lack of one, is a constant worry to
Mildred. She would like to see me well-dressed and
modish, since she is sincerely fond of me and remembers
me as I was when we taught school together. I cannot
convince her that I am happier in clothes meant to stand
the wear and tear of the work I do, much of it heavy and
dirty when I am helping Morrill, and that I cannot find
time to change and "pretty up" except on rare occasions,
but a wash and a fresh dress has to serve the purpose.
If we were where Morrill and the children saw me in
contrast with smartly dressed women, then certainly I
would feel that presenting a similar appearance warranted
extra time and care on my part, but here it seems more
essential that I be suitably dressed to participate in their
work and play.

I remember one spring when the children were small,
Morrill was ill for some time, and when it came time to
plant the potatoes he was not strong enough to do it
alone, and we had no hired man. So we all helped him,

that is, Anne and Laurie, aged eight and seven, and I helped while Betty June played at the edge of the field. Since Morrill had had a hired man for several springs previously I had not been helping him and thus did not have suitable clothes for the purpose. I put on an old pair of Morrill's pants, torn off below the knees, and a shirt he had used for whitewashing, these I topped with an old sweater of my own, equally disreputable. Morrill usually concentrates completely on the job at hand, so I was greatly surprised when after a short while I found him close beside me, and then felt his arms around me. He held me close while he shook with quiet laughter, and,

"Dear— Oh, Honey, I can't help it. You—you are the *darndest* looking thing!"

Without a doubt I was; but somehow I never felt more certain of how much I meant to him.

Of course, we do at times "get all dressed up" and the children are quite thrilled, being still at the ages when they think Daddy and Mother very special persons. I am under no illusions as to their not noticing our appearances. A few years ago I was ill for a spell and when I was able to be up and around again, my mirror showed me looking very grey and haggard. So for the sake of morale, I appeared one day with lip-stick. Betty June pretended to be amazed.

"Why, Ma," she gasped, "*busting out in glamour!*"

("Ma," I may add, is only used on the occasions of similar wise-cracks or in an attempt to tease me.)

Making or otherwise obtaining our clothes is only the start in keeping a family presentable: then come washing, ironing and mending. For the past six years I have had a washer driven by an engine. We were expecting my brother, who had been ill, to spend the winter with us, and as we had a hired man, Morrill decided he must do something to lighten the work of the family wash. He had bought an old hauling engine, the kind the fishermen used to haul their traps before car-engines became the customary power in their boats, and this he had been using to saw firewood and to charge our radio battery. Now, he "figgered out" a way to connect a wooden washer to the engine, by putting a shaft through the wall of the back porch where I washed. This does all the hard work of washing for me. Although it is not, of course, in the same class as a modern electric washer, it is much superior to a washboard and elbow grease. It is also much noisier.

During the second summer Morrill enlarged his garden and we tackled hay-making on our own; the first year Morrill had had help with the mowing. We had only a few tons of hay, but it had to be made without benefit of machinery, and Morrill had never mowed with a hand scythe. He had all the chores to do besides going so far for Amaryllis each evening, so he found no unoccupied time on his hands. I helped all I could, but two small children took much of my attention. We had more fog than during the previous summer, and it bothered Morrill, who had never been accustomed to it and who feared some slight unknowing negligence on his part might result in a wreck or loss of life, so that he worked under a mental strain much of the time. The prevalence of fog, too, caused hay-making to become a long-drawn-out process, during which we hopefully spread our hay when the fog lifted and restacked it as the fog shut in again.

Morrill's sister was the first of the many relatives and friends who have come to spend vacations with us, and she was doubly welcome after our first winter here. Winters were rather lonely during the early years at the Light, but always we have had hosts of visitors in the summers, and in spite of that being our busiest season we manage somehow to enjoy them all immensely. Both Morrill and I are members of large families and have many friends; our visitors hail from as far apart as Shawinigan Falls and New York. All whom the weather favours are delighted with the beauties of the sea and the freedom and spaciousness of the Island and its surrounding waters.

More unfortunate, and less favourably impressed, are those whose visits coincide with a foggy spell. Some visitors to the Island have never seen more than a few yards to either side of them, and since most guests, for some unfathomable reason, arrive at dead low water, their conception of the Island must be of cold grey fog, colder and greyer water and equally cold and wet weed-covered rocks that seem to stretch interminably not only into the fog on either hand but before them as well; and over these they must clamber to reach the path with its trees and bushes dripping cold and wet fog on both sides, and drenching any but rubber-booted feet and legs. I love the fog: its cold moisture condensing on my face and hair, the sense of mystery it always brings with its distortion of familiar sights and sounds, even its rank smell as it rolls in over the sea and the banks of kelp and rock-weed, but I can understand that for many it lacks appeal. Those who enjoy the fog and those who do not are equally chilled by it, and so I plan to have ready a cup of hot tea, or better still a hot meal by the cosy kitchen fire, to welcome guests after their boat trip across the cold water.

The lighthouse is small; it seems to me that with only the family we have not an unused inch of space, but we continually put up "gangs" of people, without apparent extra crowding. We have cots that are easily put up and taken down and the children early learned to "double up" for the pleasure they get from company. We eat most of our meals outdoors, and everyone pitches in to help and makes the least fuss and the most fun over any difficulties and inconveniences. Last summer we set a record when for a week there were nineteen of us! We had a grand time, with the younger fry sleeping in two tents and one family retiring to the haymow after evenings of fun and singing.

Nearly every summer, until their illness prevented, my father and mother spent a week or so with us, and how we loved having them!  The Island life brought back to Mother her days as a girl and young wife at Emerald Isle and memories of visits to Bon Portage when the Wraytons were keeping the Light.  She enjoyed picking berries and helping with the hay, while Dad was unfailingly interested in whatever plans and projects we might have in mind. The children adored their grandparents, followed Grandpa everywhere and showed him all their secret places and treasures.  They enlisted his moral support on the question of cats.  Even I felt that three cats were too many in our small house, in spite of the argument the children put up, "Three cats are exactly the right number for three kids. Now, Mum, how could you divide two cats or one cat among the three of us?  She couldn't, could she, Grandpa?" And Dad would agree that he didn't see how we could get along with any fewer cats "under existing circumstances."

That second summer we also started "pic-pics," to quote Anne Gordon, who loved them, and they have continued to be one of the pleasantest phases of our life here.  A "pic-pic," may I explain, is any meal, consisting of whatever our larder provides at the moment, eaten any-where outdoors, but preferably where we can have a fire. In fine summer weather breakfast is the only meal we eat indoors, and the children often take even that out on the front steps.  If we are busy and rushed for time we have our picnic on the leeward side of the lighthouse.  Everyone helps to carry out dishes and food and to bring them back after the meal is over.  If we can spare a little time we pack everything necessary for an outdoor meal in an old square wash-tub which is easily carried between two of us, and go down the path to a spot near the shore, or over the hill to a sheltered nook by the woods. Morrill or Laurie make a fire, if only to boil a cup of coffee for the grown-ups. Once in a great while we manage to find time to take a half day and go to the northern end or the Kelp Cove. A few times we have gone to Emerald Isle or Shag Harbour to picnic with friends there.

When a pig is slaughtered in the fall, I make a big pot of head-cheese and can it with future picnics in mind. Similarly, I can a few bottles of lobster in season (for special picnic occasions), and if we are killing off old fowl in the fall, the meatier pieces are canned while the rest makes soup. So I am usually able to find the wherewithal for sandwiches. Sometimes we take fresh fish or meat and cook a meal over our picnic fire, but as I said, anything makes a picnic, just so long as it is eaten out-of-doors and with the proper gusto.

We never had any trouble from disturbing the children's routine if we took them with us to work or for a picnic. When they were tiny, Anne and Lo took their afternoon naps wherever we chanced to be; we folded a heavy blanket on the ground under a tree or in the shade of a building, and put another blanket over them; they lay quietly and soon dropped off to sleep. When Betty June joined the family we carried her, with bottle and "spares" in a large meat-basket, and fixed an old red umbrella over it for protection from the sun; we warmed her bottle for her "pic-pic" and she slept in her basket. I could never detect any ill-effects on the children from these outings, and they gave me a change from the kitchen and my house work, even though we could seldom travel far afield.

That summer, besides berries, I had also a few quarts of peas to can. Peas are slow developing here, but perhaps because of that, or because of something in the soil, they have an especially sweet flavour and we found our home-canned peas delicious when we tried them the following winter. We now can between fifty and seventy quarts of them each summer. I concocted that summer my special brand of raspberry dumpling, which is still our favourite dessert. And it was during that haying season that I established the routine whereby I dropped my rake or fork at eleven sharp, made a fire, cooked dinner and had little faces and hands cleaned so we all sat down to dinner at twelve. I didn't waste a minute or a movement— especially on raspberry-dumpling days.

Many friends visited us, and before we could realize it the summer was gone; it was time to prepare for autumn, and Lem arrived to be with us for the winter months. We felt it would be too dangerous for one man to be handling the boat on and off the shore, and if Morrill left for the necessary trips to Shag Harbour, I must remain alone on the Island with two small children, and should he be storm-stayed, it would be difficult for me to manage cattle, Light and all the chores. Besides this, since we had no phone, I would have no means of knowing whether he were safe on the mainland, or had been lost trying to return to us. Lem was accustomed to boats and the water, and need not run any great risk to return to the Island, so we decided he would do most of the travelling during the winter.

# A TRYING EXPERIENCE

It was during the following February that I put in the most worried hours of our years on Bon Portage.

Lem went to Shag Harbour to carry our mail and to get that at the post office, and to buy what few groceries we may have required. Usually he arrived back at noon or shortly after, but on this day he did not return when expected. His brother Mike was working for Ashford on Emerald Isle, and we had been somewhat annoyed at Lem because he had been seizing every opportunity to stop with Mike for meals and even overnight. This, we felt, and believed Ashford and Jean felt, was imposing on their hospitality, so we had asked Lem not to stop there long, unless forced to do so by an unexpected storm.

Morrill came to the house at half-past three, just as the wind began to spring up, and the first snow-squalls drove across the Point. I asked if he had seen any sign of Lem.

"You won't see Lem today; he'd never start over in this storm, so he'll stay at Ashford's. I only hope it doesn't storm for two or three days and he's stuck off there for Jean to look after."

I said I hoped not, and Morrill went on, "I'm going to take the ox, and get another load of wood. I'll be back for supper at five. It looks like a dirty night; keep track of the weather." He was away.

"Keeping track of the weather," by the way, means to notice when snow or fog lessens visibility to five-eighths of a mile or less, and enter this in our records, also the time when visibility increases beyond that limit. Since I am most often where the clock and books are, this duty usually falls to me.

The storm worsened throughout the afternoon, till the snow clung whitely to the windows and the wind moaned in the chimneys and swirled around the corners of the lighthouse in angry gusts. By the time I began to watch for Morrill's return, it was indeed a "dirty" night, as he had predicted.

Five o'clock came and no Morrill. That was not greatly out of the ordinary, very often he stopped later than he had planned to do some extra work and I never depended on his being home at any specified time. But I wondered when it became dark enough for the Light to be lit, as he had not asked me to do this and I knew he preferred for me not to have the care of the Light on cold wild nights like this one. I went to the Lantern, wound the spring and lit the lamps. While I waited in the cold, windy Lantern to see that all was functioning smoothly, I kept an anxious eye on the gate through which Morrill and the ox should appear. I was decidedly worried when I still saw no sign of him as I finally descended the three flights of stairs to the kitchen again. I wished Lem were home so that I could send him to find out what was detaining Morrill.

I gave the children their suppers and prepared them for bed, hoping every second to hear the welcome sound of Morrill stamping the snow from his feet as he came through the porch. I tried not to communicate my apprehension to the children, but I had decided I must go look for Morrill if he did not soon return. I felt it unlikely that he had cut himself, since he had taken the ox to haul, but I feared a log had rolled or fallen on him, and injured him so that he could not get on the sleds and so reach home. It was not hard to imagine any number of things that could have happened.

Once the children were ready for bed, I put them both into Laurie's crib, which had a side I could fasten securely and so prevent any chance of them getting out of bed and into danger while I should be gone, perhaps for several hours. Anne Gordon took this all very calmly, but Laurie sensed something was wrong and began to cry. I took time to talk to him quietly and gently, telling him to "cuddle doon," a little phrase he loved and invariably obeyed, but he would have none of it. He cried and cried, and when I could stay by him no longer, he pulled himself up by the bars of his crib and clung there, crying broken-heartedly. This added to my feeling of worry, and of fear for the safety of the children.

Getting ready to set out was like the preparations in a nightmare; my dread of leaving the children and my sense of urgency towards finding Morrill also had a nightmarish quality, and seemed to be pulling me in opposite directions. Both fires must be put out, I had let them down in readiness and the house was already becoming cold. There was the cat, she must go out. I must get and fill the hand-lantern. It might blow out in the wind. Get matches and a piece of sandpaper to scratch them on. Wrap them in a piece of waxed paper and put them in an inside pocket. I must dress warmly since I would be exposed to the sweeping wind much of the way. I knew of nothing I could take for Morrill. My only prayer was to find him, and that the ox had stayed near enough that I could get him on the sleds, and then drive or lead the ox home. I rejected the idea of trying to carry blankets to him through the wind, but at least I could make a fire and prevent him from perishing in the cold.

I extinguished all house lamps, my greatest fear was of the children being trapped by fire. The last thing I heard as I closed the door behind me was Laurie's heart-rending cries; so pitiful in the dark, cold house. I had never before in their short lives left the children alone in the house more than a few minutes. When we returned we found Laurie fallen exhausted in a huddle at the bottom of his bed, his little hands still clutching the bars of his crib.

When I stepped out into the night the wind and snow closed around me immediately. The easterly wind, cold and evil, sweeps across the Point with ugly force; that night it brought snow with it, picked up what lay on the field and drove it into my face and through every tiniest opening in my clothes. It howled and shrieked, "What can you do on a night like this? Look. How far can you see? Turn and face the lighthouse where you have left your babies alone. You can scarcely discern the beam of the Light only a few yards away. See, I can shut it out completely with this effortless swirl. Suppose the Lantern catches fire as it did in the Light at Baccaro? Suppose you fall? It might well be days and nights before the absence of the light is noticed. What will become of your children fastened in their crib? Your chance of helping Morrill? You fool yourself."

As the snow swirled blindingly between me and the indistinct outline of the lighthouse, I paused. Perhaps my first duty lay with the two little ones, helpless there in the cold, wind-battered bedroom. But Morrill—he must need me. So with one more look and a quick prayer to God to guard them and to help me in what I had decided to attempt, I turned again towards where I felt Morrill awaited my coming.

Once up the slight hill and in the shelter of the trees, the force of the wind was less and the snow, though still blinding, no longer cut into my face nor choked my breath as I hurried on. Once I thought I saw sled-marks in the eddying snow before my feet, if so the ox must have returned alone to the barn. But I refused to entertain that thought. All my hopes of helping Morrill lay in the ox having stayed near him, so that I could get him home, since the wood-cutting where he was working was a mile or more from the lighthouse.

A great deal of snow had not yet fallen, or had mostly blown clear, for the drifts were not high enough to seriously impede my way, so through the more sheltered parts of the path I made good progress, the fear for Morrill's safety that choked me lent speed to my feet. At no time was I sensible of the cold.

"When I reach the boathouse," I thought, "I will be more than half-way."

But when I turned out of the woods at the boathouse, my heart stopped for gladness as I heard Morrill's vigorous hail, and as I ran forward he shouted reassuringly, "O.K., dear."

My first surge of happy relief was followed quickly by bewilderment. What was Morrill doing at the landing this hour of the night? And why? And there was Lem.

There was no time for explanations. Both were safe, and pausing only long enough to put a few things under cover in the boathouse, Morrill and I made all possible haste back to our babies at the lighthouse. Lem followed close behind. The children were both safe, and it was with an overflowing heart that I made up the fires, got dry clothes for Morrill (Lem was not wet), and made a cup of coffee around. Then Morrill had to see that the ox was safe, those *had* been fresh sled-marks I had seen, and Morrill found the ox near the barn with his sleds tangled in a tree.

Finally I heard the story of the night's adventures. How good for Morrill to be safe and sound at home, and to hear the even tones of his voice, after the hours of worry and dread.

Lem had got as far as Emerald Isle on his return trip from Shag Harbour and then had delayed setting out on the last part of his journey until the storm was almost upon him. Then he left for Bon Portage, but when he neared the shores of the Island he found a band of ice-cakes some two hundred yards through, which the storm had collected and packed against our shore. Looking at the line of ice blurred and distorted by the snow-squalls, he decided it did not appear formidable, so he attempted to row through it. Then, when he had worked the boat well into the grip of the ice-cakes, he became afraid he had underestimated their size and extent, so he tried frantically to turn the boat, upon which it jammed in the ice and would move neither way. Had the bow of the boat been left pointing into the ice, the force of the wind astern would have helped to push her bow into the cracks between the cakes and slowly edge her towards the shore. Broadside on, with her deep keel below the ice, she was helpless.

No doubt Lem was frightened; he told us, "I thought my time had come." And well he might be afraid. Everyone along the shore has heard of the cruel strength of the drift ice, and how it sweeps all with it out to sea with the ebb-tide; the cold wind and the driving snow would have made it a terrible night to be adrift in an open boat. He knew the thick snow-squalls would prevent our seeing him if he were carried past the lighthouse, or if by a remote chance we caught sight of him, we could neither help him ourselves or get word to Shag Harbour for aid, since he was in our boat.

I've no doubt that Lem put in a bad half-hour or so, and when Morrill appeared around the boathouse I imagine he was a most welcome sight. It was fortunate for Lem that Morrill decided to get that last load of wood in spite of the storm, and that the storm was not then, at four o'clock, thick enough to blot man and boat out of sight from the shore. It was typical of Lem, that in such dire straits, he was not working with oar and every ounce of energy that he could muster to gain an inch or two nearer shore, but was dispiritedly flapping his arms across his chest in a vain effort to keep warm.

Lem had now been sighted, but by no means rescued. He had our boat; the only other craft was a trawl-dory, nineteen feet long, with a beam of about five feet, and sides at least two and a half feet high. This had been put here by the government for use by the keepers, and was under cover in the boathouse. Here Broad, the ox, played his part, for he pulled the awkward heavy dory from the boathouse to the water's edge. Morrill had put into it two pairs of oars with thole-pins, a large sweep, and several coils of pot-line in hopes of getting a rope to Lem's boat.

Then began a three-hour struggle to work the big dory out through the ice-cakes and against the strong wind to where Lem lay imprisoned in the ice. At first, Morrill used the sweep as a pole; placing one end on bottom and the other against his stomach and exerting all his strength he would force the boat forward a foot or less at a time.

Soon the water became too deep for this method of progress. It was impossible to row, as oars could not find water between the packed cakes. The trawl-dory, with its broad flat bottom, sat upon the ice-cakes, rather than amongst them, so Morrill would get out on a large cake that looked as if it would bear his weight, and push the dory along, inch by inch. A slip would have meant certain death under the ice-cakes, which would have opened to let his body down through their cruel pack, but would never have allowed it to reach the surface again. But the unwieldy weight and height of the trawl-dory, so disadvantageous in many ways, were safeguards in this respect and when an ice-cake broke beneath him, Morrill held to the sides of the boat and clambered back in with nothing worse than wet feet. But soon he began to fear his feet would freeze. Again he would step out, and using his weight at the stern to lift the bow clear and above the ice, would then change his position to the side of the boat and once more inch the dory forward.

It took him three hours of this heart-breaking labour to cover the less than two hundred yards that separated him from Lem. The wind fortunately held in the same quarter, else he might have been carried out to sea beyond the Point. The blinding snow-squalls as night began to blacken over the surly water snarling among the ice-cakes must have made his task much more difficult, and if he had paused to look about him might well have caused him to give up in despair. But at last he reached the other boat, and Lem stepped into the trawl-dory.

Morrill had hoped to save his boat by fastening a line to her, paying it out as he worked his way back to shore, and securing it when he reached there; but in the dark and snow some of the coils of rope had become covered by his discarded oilskins and he failed to locate them, so he was forced to leave his little boat to the mercy of ice and storm.

With two of them to work the dory in and its high sides almost as serviceable as sails in the east wind, they made much better time on the return trip. They had just landed and pulled up the dory when I made my appearance. Morrill had known I would be terribly worried, and had caught glimpses of my lantern as I struggled along the path.

Never were two people more thankful than Morrill and I as we revelled in the warmth and security of fires and home—unless it might be Lem! Morrill's feet, though touched with frost, were not seriously frozen, but he was completely exhausted. Ashford used to tease him about never pausing a moment but going to another job as soon as one was finished. The day after his struggle in the ice, Morrill, for once, just *sat*. Several times he pulled himself out of his chair with the idea of attempting some chore, but each time he settled back again, too worn out to move.

The next morning was fine and clear and when the flood tide came in, we saw our little boat miles away to the southward. The wind was too strong for Morrill to attempt to get her even if he had felt equal to rowing; so we watched her drift away with the ebb, and thought sadly that we had seen the last of her, and wondered how we would make out with no boat for a while, and where to find money for a new one. The ebb tides here are strong and usually sweep what they clutch out and around Cape Sable and thence to oblivion, but this time the high wind that blew on shore countered the tide and held our boat inside the Cape, so that the next flood brought her in and deposited her safe and sound on near-by Bear Point; from there we recovered her by paying a little to the boy who found her.

Lem was sent off to Shag Harbour to bring the boat back on the Island, and our friend Clayton was there to help him push off. He laughed as he told us how Lem, with a rush, pushed the boat off and jumped gaily aboard— without his oars! Clayton had to pull him back and give him his oars. "I never," Clayton used to say, shaking his head, "saw the beat of him."

It was the following winter that Lem froze his ears. He had come to the house and been in the warm kitchen for some time, looking at them in the mirror, before I, busy with the final touches to dinner, noticed anything unusual about his appearance. After they thawed out, huge water-blisters formed across the surface of them, and seemed to drag them outward and forward, so that he looked "to have all sails set." Since the weather did not permit him to get to a doctor, Morrill finally opened the blisters with a sterile needle and drained them; they healed with no apparent ill effects.

Lem spent three winters with us before he went to Emerald Isle. Morrill used to cut his hair, as there was no barber in Shag Harbour at the time. Once Laurie, seeing the small curly bits of hair falling, and accustomed to seeing ducks picked, came running.

"Mummy, come quick. See! Daddy's taking the feavers off of Lem!"

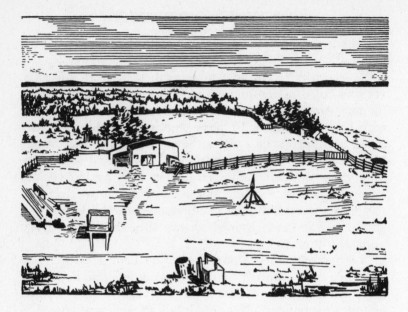

10

# A TEN YEAR PLAN

It was during our third spring here that Morrill took the first steps towards clearing a plot of land in addition to and adjoining the government field, which the sea was gradually eating away and continually littering with debris at every storm. We needed more cattle and so more hayland. We called our plan to clear and bring into hay four acres of land, to stock the Island with sheep and increase our cattle to three cows, an ox and a few young animals, our "Ten Year Plan." It has taken us the full ten years to get the land cleared and growing grasses of sorts, and some of it still needs further attention. It has been a long struggle, and at times Morrill has become discouraged at the slow progress and meagre returns, but it is very satisfying now to look out over four acres of hayland and know it has all been wrested from its primitive condition and a reluctant soil. We know a little of what pioneers must have felt as they saw their fields take shape in the midst of virgin forests.

We were fortunate in having banks of sea-weed fertilizer within hauling distance of our fields, as this, while it is not a balanced dressing, does well for the first few years. The soil is very light and rooty and practically the whole four acres had to be broken by hand. As the Agricultural Representative exclaimed in surprise as he picked up a handful of soil after viewing Morrill's excellent stand of clover and grass, "Why, man! The Lord never meant this land to grow grass." No doubt he was right, but it was the only land available, so grow grass it does—though Morrill had no suspicion as he struggled with it that he was flouting Providence.

As soon as our hayland came into bearing we found we had to have a new barn and this Morrill put up on our own land, first a small building to which he added as soon as possible, the final piece being a cement manure pit. The old shed that served as a barn now is a woodshed which makes another convenience.

Of all the outdoor activities to which I lend a hand when my household duties are not too pressing, the one at which I am most eagerly welcomed and the one I most enjoy is hay-making.

When my brothers and sister and I were children spending our summer vacations at Emerald Isle we were all expected to take part in the hay-making. The fields there, as here, were not suited for the use of machinery and the long spells of fog made drying difficult, so we spent nearly every fine day of our vacation in the hayfield.

My grandfather, who until he was fifty captained a fishing schooner to the Grand Banks, was not the most

patient teacher for small children learning to make hay,
though I think the boys always took his roared commands
and salty criticisms far more casually than I ever could.
I usually escaped much of his impatience by sticking close
to my uncle, a silent kindly man, who taught by example
and seldom spoke to me as we worked along together but
who sometimes boasted in my flattered hearing that I was
as good as a man!

Although we all worked hard we had some fun and sky-
larking, especially as we tramped the sweet hay down in
the hayrack and bumped about over the rocky field.
The long rides back to the barn on the loaded rack were
sheer joy.

And if, as I remember, I found some of Grandfather's
bellowed roars terrifying, being accustomed to my own
gentle-voiced father, I never dreamt there was anything
incongruous in making hay with an ox-cart and such
commands as "Stow her down aft there, boys!" or "Get
f'r'd," shouted in the same tones that had been used to
carry orders along the windswept decks of a schooner. Nor
did I imagine that "the starb'r'd wheels," "the bow" and
"the stern" of the cart were ever called anything different.

All these memories with their innumerable clear and
intimate details rush back to me with the first smell of newly
cut grass, or the first ring of whetstone on scythe. So
when we came to Bon Portage and Morrill started to make
hay I really had more conception than he of hay-making
under the conditions that prevail here, as his experience
had been gained on an inland farm. It is usually pleasant
for an adult to resume a childhood occupation, and any
task that took me out into the bright summer days and
at the same time provided amusement and a playground
for the children could not help but appeal to me.

While we often wish for more heat to dry our hay, it is
pleasant never to be uncomfortably warm, and there is

almost invariably a crisp little breeze to keep us cool as we work along.

For several years Morrill and the hired man used hand-scythes, but we now have a mowing-machine which the ox pulls. Of course, I never mowed and seldom pitched from the cart, but at all the lighter parts of hay-making I have done my share, and the children learned to shake and rake while they were still small. We have always enjoyed working along as a family at jobs like making hay.

There is a rhythm and pulse to shaking, turning and raking hay, that in the warm sun and cool breezes is most invigorating after muscles throw off the neglect of a long house-bound winter. Then, from any of our fields I have only to lift my eyes to view the magnificent summer sea, with green field or vivid bush in the foreground to point a contrast. Gulls wheel and bank above us, and there is no more unutterably beautiful sight than the perfection of a gull overhead, its dazzling white wings tipped with jet, outlined for an instant's motionless grace against the deep blue concavity of the sky. Sometimes we are forced to haul hay to the beach for a final drying; there the sun's rays on the rocks crisp the hay while the still damp fields would steam it. Here we work with the sea splashing only a few feet away, and if there is a surf running it is difficult to keep our minds on our work; we call to one another to watch some particularly large and splendid breaker as it roars thunderously in, flinging itself over the outer boulders in a light-hearted smother of spray to dissolve in creaming wavelets at our feet.

However, there are two sides to hay-making as to most things. The more time I spend in the hayfields, the less there is to put to my house work, and it often means a terrific rush to get meals prepared and chores done when a threatened change of weather demands that every available moment be spent at getting the hay stacked or under cover.

When a choice must be made it is the house work rather than the hay which suffers neglect, since inside work can be done in wet or foggy weather.  Often, too, we must forgo a swim or some equally enticing diversion, because hay-making takes priority.  In foggy summers getting the hay becomes almost a nightmare, in which we handle and rehandle the same lot, trying to take advantage of every hour of precious sun, and often have to watch a good cut deteriorate for lack of drying weather, while inland a mile or so hay is being put into barns under a hot sun.  Usually we are all too tired after a day in the hayfield to do more than tumble into bed after the necessary chores are done, and papers and magazines go unread for weeks.

As hay-making is so uncertain and often such a long-drawn-out undertaking, Morrill was very interested in the possibilities of grass silage as soon as he read about it, and we tried it first in 1939.  Our small quantity of grass does not warrant buying a cutter and blower as most farmers use for this method, but we had one natural advantage in that the fine wild grasses that form most of our hay have not the coarse, dry stalks of timothy and red clover, and consequently they pack much more closely. Since exclusion of air is the main requisite in making grass silage, this is fortunate.  At first we used diluted molasses as a keeping agent, but since the war we have used phosphoric acid.  The molasses mixture was applied to the grass in the silo from a homemade sprinkler and as we all tramped the grass down, Laurie's chief amusement lay in misjudging (?) the range of the sprinkler and so getting a liberal coating of the black sticky stuff over the bare legs of his sisters—nor was I always spared this indignity.

Since our early experiments with curing grass this way were successful, almost all the cut from the fields at the Point go into the pit for green feed and we then turn our attention to the field at Garron's.

When Morrill had succeeded in established grass on the fields near home, he decided to fence a piece of land for his sheep, and chose the old overgrown field known as Garron's, about half-way up the eastern side. He didn't attempt to clear this, but killed out the existing growth by a heavy dressing of sea-weed. Here we yard our sheep spring and fall, and in August we get from three to four tons of hay from the acre field. Here, too, we have a small camp (Do-Duck-Inn) where we keep sheep supplies and which serves as a half-way house for the gunners. It is a very unimposing structure, but we are proud of it as Morrill sawed every bit of the lumber from the rough and stunted trees of the Island and we all helped build it.

As Garron's field is so far from home, all the grass there is made into hay, which we bring to the home barn or store in the loft of the boathouse. We take our dinners and suppers along with us in the hayrack, and I cook them on the camp stove, although we eat outdoors in the shade of the trees. Almost always we have company at haying-time, often one of my brothers with his family, and some-times little chums of my children, so that our hay-making expeditions have the appearance and fun of picnics, although there is plenty of work accomplished each day. Occasionally we all find time for a swim, and the children run down to wade during every lull in the work. The beach at Garron's is flat, and of fine gravel and sand, in pleasant contrast to the large boulders that line the shore at the Point, and has no heavy surf to beware.

We spend all the long summer day at the hay-making and ride home on the loaded rack in time to do the chores and light the Light. In foggy weather Anne or I must stay at the lighthouse to tend the horn, even if the fog is not thick enough to interfere with drying hay; often the sun will be shining clear and bright at Garron's while the fog covers the Point and lies thick upon surrounding waters.

From Garron's on a fine summer's day, we look across a beautiful sheet of water. The sea is perfectly calm, "all starched and ironed" as we say. The mainland and Emerald Isle crowd close to Bon Portage in the still air and the faint musical note of a horn on a car hurrying through the sleepy mainland afternoon is clearly audible across the two miles of motionless water. The white wool tufts of the summer clouds are irregularly reflected and elongated in the flawed and wavering mirror of the sea. Tiny wavelets run gently in to murmur unimportant secrets through the tangled locks of sea-weed into the ears of the quiescent rocks, lying relaxed like shaggy monsters in this brief respite from the sea's buffeting.

Before we had our fields producing grass, Morrill used to eke out our hay supply by cutting and curing some of the wild grass on the savannah. This was very hard work, the footing was wet and uneven and broken bits of lobster-pots and driftwood made smooth mowing impossible. The hay was stacked on raised platforms, fastened against the wind by ropes and poles and left until the swamp froze enough to bear the ox, when it was hauled home for feed. It served the purpose for young cattle and the ox, but we never had a high opinion of its nutritive value.

You would be correct in assuming that all else is subordinated to grass and hay during the summer months: like so many things, a scarcity of it brings a full realization of its importance, and it has been a long hard struggle to bring into production fields to provide us with sufficient pasturage and hayland.

The third spring also saw us make our first attempt at raising sheep. We had not forgotten the books we had studied in Worcester, or the plans we had made, but our lack of capital made our start very insignificant. We purchased five ewes and a ram from my grandfather, who had always kept a flock. It had been composed originally of Southdowns and Leicesters but had deteriorated until the sheep we bought were merely good scrubs. They possessed one advantage—that of being perfectly at home in the climate and under the conditions that prevail on our Island range.

We hoped to add each successive year to the small nucleus with which we started, but the old man, seeing his flock dwindling from lack of care, refused to part with any more of them. Five were too few for even a start here, as our losses offset the gain in lambs, so although we had an occasional male lamb to eat and wool for socks and sweaters, we realized we would have to increase the number of our breeders if we were to see our flock grow. Four years after our start we were able to purchase twenty ewe lambs from a Digby farmer. These were mostly Shropshires, and have a close thick fleece suitable to weather conditions here. We breed to a Shropshire ram (obtained at half price from the Department of Agriculture) and expect to keep that strain predominate in our flock.

Our sheep do not lack for shelter, although we have no building for them. I have mentioned the thickets of tangled and interwoven spruce which slope to the very ground to break and withstand the sweep of the sea winds, and these form a more impervious wall than any building would provide. Then, too, the temperature never drops very low, so there is no intense cold to combat—once out of the wind the sheep are comfortable. The strong winds sweep much of the snowfall into the ocean, and most of the swamp and grassland is clear.

The sheep find their own feed all year; the swamp grasses and shrubs provide roots and succulent shoots, and the fir trees have tender spills and buds even during the cold months. The most plentiful and unfailing source of winter fodder for them is the dried kelp that lies all along the shores, and they consume vast quantities of it. Our sheep turn in disdain from hay while they eat dried kelp with relish. On this odd diet they thrive all winter and give us a good crop of lambs each spring.

The sheep's habit of kelp-eating carries with it a certain danger during severe winters. Once the cold becomes intense and the sea chilled we find some morning on awakening a narrow white line of ice at high water mark; the next incoming tide hits the iceline and splashes spray and water over and upon it and so builds up the ice. Then heavy seas pile drifting floes upon the ice already formed and the cold winds freeze the cakes solid in the wash and spray that the seas force among them. This is repeated until there is erected an ice-wall of several feet in height and thickness ringing the Island, and at places rising to miniature cliffs of fifteen or twenty feet facing the sea and gradually sloping to the land behind them. At low water the sheep go through breaks in the wall to find kelp on the beach below. If the flood tide should overtake the sheep at the face of a cliff, they would perish and be washed out to sea, so Morrill patrols the Island when the ice-walls are dangerous.

Another hazard lies in so much of the Island being low swamp. This freezes solid during cold spells and the sheep wander over it to feed, but in thaws there are many deep holes into which an animal might plunge. The most dangerous spot is the long narrow drain that cuts across the Island, the long swamp grasses protect it from the cold and hide it from view. Scarcely a winter passes but we lose one or more sheep in the drain.

The first few years we had wretched luck—all our lambs seemed to be rams! But gradually the flock has increased until we have over a hundred sheep, most of them breeders. And each year we have had several wethers to eat.

Many people do not know how excellent lamb and mutton can be. We think our Island-raised sheep are especially flavoursome, and all who have eaten ours agree. I have heard similar praise of those raised on Emerald Isle and Seal Island, perhaps the kelp they feed on gives them an appetizing flavour. Since we have no refrigeration I often sugar-cure (i.e. rub with a mixture of salt and sugar) the rounds of mutton, and these later boiled and sliced when cold make one of our most popular dishes.

Shearing day marks a big event in the spring routine. Until the war brought a shortage of labour Morrill hired three or four men from Shag Harbour for the day's work, and my chief concern lay in providing appetizing and filling meals for them all. When Morrill found he would be unable to secure help, he bought a shearing-machine and decided to try the job alone, with what help the children and I could give him.

The shearing-machine is run by a car engine, and this Morrill and Laurie carted to Garron's and set up outside the shearing-pen. It was in place and running smoothly before I took any part in the proceedings. I may as well confess now that engines leave me perfectly cold, though they are second only to ducks as an enthralling subject of conversation whenever Morrill and another man come within talking distance of each other, and Laurie and his father carry on long and apparently engrossing discussions concerning them. I seldom take any part at the installation of the various engines, beyond providing an intelligent (I hope) look of amazed appreciation at the wonder of the perfectly functioning machine, and the cleverness of my menfolk; and I delay my appearance in the role of congratulatory inspector until the "figgering" and hard work has all been done. And so it was with the shearing-machine.

The first step in harvesting our crop of wool is yarding the sheep, and this we did on the afternoon preceding shearing-day. We may not leave the lighthouse untended, so Anne decided to keep house, which included preparing supper against our ravenous return.

Laurie, Betty June and I set off up the western side to drive before us any sheep we found and so to round the northern end of the Island. The opening bars are on that end of the field and so we must approach it from that direction, and the only chance of collecting and driving all the sheep lies in keeping them between the beach and the woods or swamp. We started our first sheep from the woods at Red Bank, and as we went along they were joined by other flocks from the fields and thickets.

It was a beautiful spring day with a crisp wind blowing and a saucy sea slapping the rocks along the shore. We had chosen a time when the tide was high, so that it barred the sheep from attempting to turn back or run over the beach. Morrill joined us at Kelp Cove, and we all swung along, laughing and talking, stopping now and then for just an instant to enjoy the blue sea and sky, or the white lace of foam at our feet, sometimes to examine some unusual object that the sea had flung upon the beach.

At the farther end of Flag Pond we paused to rescue a ewe that had ventured out onto the black muck there and become stuck. We built a path of driftwood out to her and succeeded in getting her on it and safely on dry ground. She was a sorry sight, and when we sheared her two days later her fleece was still black and wet; but in the meantime she had presented us with a sturdy lamb.

Soon we turned the northern end of the Island with its wooded ponds and innumerable hiding places among the thick woods that come out to the shore in places. From then on, the greatest haste and diligence was necessary. Many of the ewes had lambs and had been walking a long way; now the lambs wanted to rest and nurse, so the mothers were perpetually trying to turn into invitingly wooded spots, and mothers and offspring kept up a continual chorus of "baa's": the lamb's plaintive and querulous, the mother's expressing exasperation with the whole business. Old wethers, wise from years of experience, took every opportunity to attempt a break across the beach. We quickened the pace of the drive to keep them from carrying out these movements. Laurie and Morrill watched the woods, I kept in the swamp, leaving the easiest position along the top of the beach to Betty June. Before the field was reached she and I, running back and forth over beach and swamp, were nearly as anxious as the lambs to call a halt. Sweaters and rubber-boots became hot and burdensome, and Betty June found it harder and harder to keep her watch over the sheep. She was barely ten, and the rough six-mile walk in itself would be tiring to a little girl without the running back and forth she was forced to do. When the field was finally reached and the sheep safely yarded, Betty June and I were glad to go to the beach and put our hot swollen feet in the cool salt water.

Morrill and Laurie caught two wethers on which to try the new shearing-machine and when we had things all lined up for tomorrow's work we went home to the evening chores and a belated supper.

We had poor weather that year for shearing, so the job dragged along for several days, but amongst us we handled nearly a hundred sheep. Morrill ran the machine, I helped him handle the fleeces, separated the poor and dirty portions from the good wool, Laurie tied the fleeces and bagged them and he and Betty June caught and brought the sheep to the shearing platform. Anne came up each morning to help us drive the sheep from the large yard to the shearing-pen and then returned to keep the Light.

It was hard smelly work; I started with a new suit of over-alls but before we had handled many sheep it would have taken a good nose to distinguish it from a fleece.   The little bottle-fed lamb we were raising at the lighthouse used to scent me from afar and come running to meet me with joyous bleats.   I am sure she thought me her long-lost mother.   My face and hands burned in the hot sun, and my back, like Morrill's, got stiff and sore from bending over. But I found it all most interesting, and the lambs were adorable, Betty June spent every spare minute in the lamb pen cuddling one or more of them.

When Morrill slaughters a sheep for food I often have him save the fleece for me.   This I wash and card for my quilts.   I find quilting a most enjoyable hobby; cutting and piecing the bright patchwork is light and interesting work for winter evenings and the warm wool-filled quilts are a comfort and joy on cold winter nights, as well as a source of pride when I have company and can make up several beds with gay new quilts both light and warm. Since the war I have put my quilting into crib-sized covers for the Red Cross to send to Britain.   The women of Shag Harbour save their flannelette cuttings for me, these with my own pieces make a top, I provide the wool and linings and quilt them; so far I have made twenty-two of these. It is impossible for me to join in the usual Red Cross activities so I am glad our sheep provide the means for me to help in this way.

From odd bits of inferior wool I quilt jackets for Morrill and the children to wear under their coats.   The men's I make from khaki drill, the girls' from dress prints, and I quilt the different sections separately before putting the garment together.   These garments take little wool and are warmer than sweaters—and far easier to make. I started making them before the present vogue for quilted jackets.   My inspiration was an inner down jacket I saw advertised for sportswear, and I imitated this for Morrill to wear gunning. He liked his so well that all the other members of the family demanded one, too.

At different times we have tried other ways to increase our income, but have not had any luck. We purchased three pairs of muskrats and turned them loose in the swamps where the water holes and ponds had a decade or so earlier been full of these rodents. One of them was seen for several years around the Lighthouse Pond, but we have reason to think the others were trapped and taken off the Island. We also tried nutria and had high hopes of them for a few years, but in spite of all we did (and we studied all we could learn about them and followed directions faithfully), they did not increase and thrive for us. So far our sheep have provided our only cash returns, although many of our other enterprises have saved on food costs and other outlays and a "penny saved is a penny earned."

## 11

## WRECKS

OUR FIRST WRECK came ashore during our third spring
here. One foggy morning in early May I was surprised
to see two strange men at the door. When I went to ask
them in they made themselves known as Captain Henry
Murphy and his son of Clark's Harbour; I had known
them slightly when I was a girl there. Captain Murphy
said, "We've been wrecked on the Island," but I thought
for a few seconds that he was joking and had merely
called to see Morrill on business. I soon realized that he
was in earnest and I sent for Morrill. We gave them a
cup of hot tea and something to eat; they were so utterly
exhausted from a two-day struggle against fog and a leaky
boat that they asked if they might lie down and sleep,

requesting that we call them in a few hours. On awakening they felt more rested and told us their story.

Captain Murphy, for years in command of steamboats, had been unable to secure a ship due to depression conditions, and after unemployed months ashore, he decided to invest in a small sailing vessel and enter the coastal trade. He bought an old vessel, the *Atlas;* the former owner bargained to make it shipshape and did put some repairs on it. Captain Murphy, with his son as crew, went to St. Mary's Bay and loaded with firewood which he planned to sell in Clark's Harbour. They were short handed but with good luck would have managed successfully on such a short run. However, the first day out the old boat began to leak, so that one man had to be always at the pump. Simultaneously the fog shut down upon them.

On the morning of the second day, after more than twenty-four hours continuous duty at wheel or pump, they were both too tired to use good judgment, Captain Murphy said, and he had lost his familiarity in reckoning his speed by sail after so many years in steam. When they passed Duck Island and entered the smoother water to the leeward of it, although he had failed to pick up the Groaner, he thought he must have passed the Point of Bon Portage (he was still two miles from it), and pulled his vessel into what he judged was the smoother waters of the Bay. Instead, he soon saw the surf breaking along the western shore of Bon Portage. He was then too close in to tack and clear the rocks, so drove his vessel aground to enable him and his son to reach safety, as they carried no small boat. The *Atlas* drove well up on the rocks, so that they were able to wade ashore with no mishaps. They left the sails set, as the wind was blowing directly on shore; they hoped the vessel would hold firmly aground and as the surf was not then heavy, they had a chance of saving their boat and its cargo. If they could get word to Clark's Harbour, friends with motor-boats would come and buy the firewood cargo and, thus lightened, the boat might be refloated at high water. Captain Murphy knew his family would be worried about him when he did not reach home that evening as planned, and was disappointed to learn we had no phone, and no way of sending information to the mainland, since the weather forbade an attempt to cross the Sound in Morrill's little boat.

All that day the wind held southerly and the fog blew past in heavy ragged folds. In the afternoon we left the children in Lem's care while Morrill and I went to look at the stranded vessel. The fog lay thick and heavy above the water and blew damply across the sodden shore and trees. It deposited a wet film of tiny globules on our face, hair and clothing, while an inadvertent brush against a tree or shrub brought a drenching shower upon us. We were within a few yards of the hapless craft before we could distinguish her outline through the driving mist. Her new white sails were gently cupped by the wind that pushed her directly on the shore and sent an angry short chop pounding under her stern. She looked beautiful but forlorn there alone in the driving spray and fog.

Captain Murphy and his son went aboard their ship later that afternoon and the Captain recovered some of his papers and instruments. They spent the night with us at the lighthouse, and when the next morning dawned clear and bright they borrowed Morrill's little boat; there was a fair north-west wind and the men set out under sail for Clark's Harbour. Morrill went to the vessel to see if he could get some of the instruments as the captain had requested him to do, but unfortunately the sea was now too rough for him to get aboard the vessel swept by the rising surf.

From the Lantern of the lighthouse we could see the masts and tops of the sails of the *Atlas* above the trees that

lay between us and her unhappy berth; and at noon
Morrill went upstairs to look at them. He came hurriedly
down exclaiming that he could see nothing, and the boat
must be breaking up. He and Lem left immediately,
hoping to salvage something for the owner. The children
and I followed more slowly, as they were small and the way
along the western shore rough and difficult. When we
reached the curve of shore that brought us within view of
the *Atlas* what a confused sight met our eyes! Cordwood,
sails, ropes, pieces of the wrecked vessel which was now
rapidly breaking up, and odds and ends from the tiny
galley and forecastle, were churned in one mad jumble
for a hundred yards along the shore, most of it surging back
and forth in the sea's wash, and becoming more snarled
and entangled with every wave that broke amongst it.
In the midst of this conglomeration, Morrill and Lem,
wet to their middles, were struggling with the mainsail
which lay with several cords of firewood awash amongst
its bellied folds. Captain Murphy had spoken of the sails
being new and expensive, so Morrill wished to save them
for him if possible. For a time the children and I gathered
pieces of the new sheathing that had lined the forecastle,
and piled it above the tide's reach; then I joined the men
in their efforts to save the sails, and by working strenuously
all afternoon they succeeded in salvaging the new sails and
spread them on the bank to dry.

The following morning boats came from Clark's
Harbour and gathered most of the cordwood that lay
scattered along the beach, so that the cargo, unlike the
vessel, was not a complete loss.

The shores from Cape Sable to Yarmouth are lined with
the memories and skeletons of wrecked ships, and Bon
Portage has its share of them, though few that finished
their voyagings on this Island have been attended by the
tragic loss of life that has marked the end of so many gallant

craft lost on other portions of this stretch of coast. "Uncle Gilbert," in his *Tales of the South Shore,* gives a list of the known boats that found their last berths about Bon Portage; as most of them were shipwrecked and forgotten before I knew the Island, I will mention only a few which hold the greatest interest for us.

The first of these was the *Anglo-Saxon,* wrecked on Duck Island rather than on Bon Portage proper, in 1841. She was a new clipper, and one of the finest packets ever launched in Boston, en route from her home port to Ireland. She carried a general cargo, much of it grain, as this was during the time of the Corn Famine in the old country. Another item in her cargo was tips of cattle horns to be manufactured into knife handles and similar products. Among the passengers were the members of a theatrical company. I have often tried to picture a theatrical company of that day against the backdrop of this bleak shore. Poor souls, they lost all their belongings, but they must have appreciated how fortunate they were to have escaped with their lives.

Uncle Gilbert has an earthenware plate from the *Anglo-Saxon* and also a few of the horn tips. The tips were given him by a friend who found them among the rockweed at Duck Island one very low tide, many years after all traces of the wrecked vessel had disappeared, I have heard of fishermen at Duck Island, who at exceptionally low tides would run down after a retreating sea, scoop up a busket of sand and run back before the incoming wave. In these buckets of sand they often found a gold coin or two, part of a considerable amount of gold which was lost with the *Anglo-Saxon.*

Another story tells how some sixty years ago two boys from Cape Sable Island accompanied their father to Duck Island, and while their father busied himself with his work the lads, like all boys faced with the combination of pebbles and a sheet of water, went to the tide line and began to skip stones. The older boy found several excellent pebbles at one part of the beach, small and flat and ideal for skipping across the little pools and shallow water left by an extraordinarily low tide. When his father called the boy even dropped a couple of the little stones into his pocket as he turned away from the shore. He claims he threw away every chance he'll ever have to pick up easy money, because, of course, the small flat pebbles he tossed back into the sea were tarnished coins from the wreck of the *Anglo-Saxon*.

The Salt Rock on the western side stands where a salt-laden schooner was wrecked, and thus derived its name. Most of this cargo was salvaged, carried through the woods on the men's shoulders to their boats on the eastern side and thence to the mainland.

One of the most tragic incidents in the maritime records of Shag Harbour was the loss of the *Belle* during the 1860's. I remember my grandmother telling me of her aunt Elizabeth, lost on a schooner that disappeared in a squall that struck while she was off Bon Portage, and in sight of home. Recently I wrote Uncle Gilbert to ask if he could tell me the name and a few facts concerning this schooner. In reply I received a most interesting letter, written in a firm, fine hand, and as clearly phrased as one could wish; Uncle Gilbert is now eighty-four years of age. He wrote me the story of the *Belle*.

Like nearly every other little hamlet along the shore of Nova Scotia, Shag Harbour built and manned her fleet of vessels and her ships and men sailed the seven seas. The *Belle*, however, was not built in Shag Harbour, but purchased "down Lunenburg way," and owned by men in Shag Harbour and Bear Point, a neighbouring settlement. She was engaged in freighting along the coast and made an occasional trip to Boston.

In the fall of 1869 she loaded with pickled fish, taking on most of her cargo at Bear Point and picking up the final part from a small boat that met her just outside Emerald Isle.   Uncle Gilbert, then a lad of nine, went in the small boat that carried the fish out to the *Belle*, so he remembers vessel and crew well, and is the last living person who saw the *Belle* as she sailed away from her home port on her final voyage.   The day was cold and Captain Nickerson of the *Belle* went below and brought up his seaman's coat which he tossed to one of the boys in the small boat to protect him from the chilling east wind.   Then the *Belle* squared away, and with a fair wind was soon lost to sight behind the southerly point of Bon Portage, while the small boat returned to the wharf at Shag Harbour, its occupants filled with a mixture of regret at parting, envy of those who sailed to more interesting ports, and hopes of high success for the voyage of their friends and relatives.   You may be sure many eyes watched the *Belle* out of sight.   No vessel sailed from the little harbours but left its anxious prayerful hearts behind, wives and mothers, sweethearts and friends, who knew only too well the long list of ships and their crews of loved ones that had returned no more.

All the anxieties and fears must have been replaced in every heart by joyous expectations of happy re-unions, when on October 17th, a schooner was sighted off Bon Portage and was taken by all from her position and appearance to be the *Belle*, now due to be making port.   The weather was almost perfect, its only fault to both the homecombers and those awaiting them, lay in there being scarcely a breath of wind, so the schooner made but slow way over a glassy sea, through air as sweet and warm as summer's.   Folks on shore began to think that their returning ones might not sit down to supper at home, as they had first hoped, but would certainly sleep under their own roofs that night.

Suddenly and with a sweep of fury no vessel could withstand, a gale with blinding snow struck from the north-west and hid the schooner from the anxious eyes on shore. Nothing more was ever seen or heard of the *Belle;* as Uncle Gilbert writes, "not so much as a splinter of wood to show what had happened to the schooner."

Theories were advanced to account for her complete disappearance. One is that the storm being so fierce, and the vessel so near home, the captain may have attempted to carry sail to reach the port that was so near. Another is that one of the passengers, a young lad, may have been at the wheel (since the weather was so fine and the vessel merely idling), while the others went below to have supper. His inexperienced eye may not have noticed the threatening clouds that formed so swiftly in what had been a clear sky, and the wind struck amain the ill-fated schooner before the hands were called to shorten sail.

Apart from the crew, most of whom were Shag Harbour men, there were also passengers, among them a boy and two women, who belonged in the village. In such a close-knit little community every family would lose at least one relative or dear friend, and the whole village be saddened by a great personal and communal loss.

After human fashion the bereaved ones began to hope that the sighted schooner had not been the *Belle*, and to watch for further word or sight of her. There was no lighthouse on Bon Portage then, and no one nearer than Shag Harbour had sighted the vessel, but as nothing further was ever heard of the *Belle* and she was known to have cleared from Boston, without reasonable doubt she and her human freight perished in the treacherous snow-squall, one of the worst ever experienced along this coast and without parallel at that season of the year.

In time, too, stories grew up to compensate for the lack of tangible evidence regarding her fate. I quote Uncle Gilbert's letter:

"Subsequent events that tended to show that the *Belle* was lost were, one afternoon my father and mother were standing out on their back-steps, when they saw a schooner outside of Bon Portage, apparently heading south. She was clear and well defined against the sky-line. They turned their gaze away for a minute or two and then turned to look again at the schooner, but she was not there. They looked to see if their eyes had deceived them, but there was no schooner there, and it was impossible for her to sail out of sight in so short a time, so they concluded it was a phantom vessel, to show the *Belle* would never enter her home port again. And again one evening as some elderly ladies were coming down the road, there suddenly appeared a bright beam of light, and rested on the roof of the store of William Crowell for a brief time, and then shot across to the roof of the store of Captain James Nickerson and was there for a few moments, and then shot off into the water, which the ladies took to mean that those two men were drowned in the loss of the *Belle* and would return no more."

In September, 1898, the steam ship *Express*, running from Halifax to Yarmouth with passengers and cargo, found herself in a very dense fog and with an unusually strong ebb tide running. The captain hoped to locate the Point of Bon Portage and then shape his course for the Tuskets. It was dead calm and there was no warning roar of the surf, so his first perception of how much in error his reckoning proved to be, was when his steamer trembled and lurched as she took ground and was held fast by the rocky ledge that makes the outer end of Bon Portage. The passengers were easily and safely put ashore and from the Island taken to the mainland; later most of her cargo was salvaged. A wrecking company from New York sent a boat, but it was found impossible to refloat the steamer; she soon broke in two and later was completely demolished by the surf.

My mother, then a young woman and living at Emerald Isle, made three sketches in oils of the *Express* as she lay held in the teeth of the rocky trap. The first, done September 18th, shows the steamer apparently undamaged, and the sea surrounding her is tranquil. The second, done November 18th, shows only the forward half of the ship, as the *Express* had meanwhile broken in two, and apparently the after part had been smashed into fragments and scattered, while the forward portion remained comparatively unharmed. In the third sketch, done at low tide, November 27th, angry seas are breaking over a bare hull and a lone mast, desolate under a leaden stormy sky. When that storm was over, nothing was to be seen where the *Express* had lain for many weeks. The rocks and seas had finished their sport.

But the *Express* was built on the Clydeside, and so built to last. Almost half a century later her two boilers still stand where they settled as the cruel rocks tore the bottom from their unhappy ship. They lie on the shore in front of the lighthouse, and the waves breaking over and around them is a familiar part of the view to seaward in that direction. The seas have battered them, washed over and through them, pounded them with stones torn from the rocky bottom and tons of crashing water, yet as the ocean recedes each ebbing tide, the boilers emerge, steadfast and undaunted. Of course they cannot many more years withstand the terrific punishment they receive almost unceasingly; they begin to show their scars and weariness. We shall miss them when they go, their long, gallant struggle against overwhelming odds ended at last.

All along the shore of the Point, caught between and beneath heavy rocks and exposed only at low water, are pieces of the metal railings and deck-plates of the *Express*. Morrill has made many linings for our kitchen stove from the still excellent metal of her deck-plates. Also, Morrill found on the shore a heavy brass lock, which must have been caught on the bottom for many years after the wreck of the steamer, and freed by a bad storm. He had a key made to fit it, and it is now in use.

The only other wreck of which any signs remain is the *Win the War*, built during the last war and lost soon after its close. She was salt-laden from Boston, and got off her course in the fog. Her crew (I think there were eight of them) made a safe landing and accepted the hospitality of the lightkeepers at that time, before leaving for the mainland. When we came here large pieces of the *Win the War* lay along the western side near the Salt Rock, where she stuck. The storms since have battered them and as she was of wooden construction, most of her timbers have been carried away by the sea at exceptionally high tides. A few large pieces of her sides still lie above the tide mark, and Morrill, as do other men in the neighbourhood, sometimes makes a fire at one end of a piece to obtain a few of the still excellent iron bolts which fall out as the fire burns the surrounding wood.

On the time-flattened top of the beach at Garron's, well above the reach of the highest tides, five or six broken ribs of some unknown vessel lie rotting. No sea but flying spray has touched them for many long years. They are sinking into the small rocks and gravel of the beach that has already covered the keel to which they are attached. Nettles and fragile beach flowers grow around and between the weather-beaten ribs, and small yellow lichens cover much of them. No one seems to know what boat left her bones thus stranded on this sheltered beach, nor what

USA 21
2001

ESSEX - ESSEX, MA 810
MIDDLESEX
DM
SEP 5
2001

Burlington Players Inc
POB 433
Burlington MA 01803
*Address Correction Requested*

# TO GILLIAN ON HER 37TH BIRTHDAY

*by* **Michael Brady**
*Directed by* **Rick Stewart**

*Featuring:*
Dana Bissett
David Bojarczuk
Lisa Burrell
Courtney Harmon
Matt Meier
Samantha Stein
Victoria Taylor

**BARBARA SPENCE**
**78 WILLOW STREET**
**WOBURN, MA  01801-**

Burlington Players

to **Gillian**
on her 37th birthday

September 14–29
Thu–Sat 8 pm/Sun 7 pm
Matinee Sep 16 at 2 pm
Park Playhouse – Burlington
**781-229-2649**

waters they furrowed before they were left to the long years of wind and weather that have thinned them to their present brittle decay.

Wrecks (apart from those caused by this war, and these I must not now mention) are far less common than they were a few years ago. Better lights and more powerful fog-horns, the replacement of sails by motors, and above all, radio, which gives a boat its location so promptly and exactly, have cut down shipping losses to a very small part of what they once were.

Let no one think, however, that the sea has been conquered and remains submissive. It merely bides its time, and is as cruel and ravenous as ever. Those who know it well shun over-confidence and do not trust it for a moment. We have had a small part in several occurrences in which the sea, fortunately, has been cheated.

The winter of 1934-1935 was the coldest we have experienced at Bon Portage, and the bitter weather continued well into March, although the salt-water ice, that had completely isolated us at times, disappeared during the first of the month. One March sundown as Morrill was lighting he was surprised to see a motor-boat near the western shore of the Island. We had seen no boats fishing all day, nor would we expect to, as most of the boats do not venture out during such weather. It was bitterly cold with a rising wind, and giving every promise of a wild, cold night, certainly not the time or weather for a small boat to be out, especially on such a dangerous shore, and the engine of this boat appeared to have stopped. What to do? Morrill's small boat would never live to turn the Point into the wind to reach the men, and yet he was reluctant to summon a boat from Shag Harbour if the boat we saw were not really in trouble. She flew no old coat or rag, nor did she show a hoisted oar, common makeshift signals of distress. The night was rapidly darkening, however, while the wind increased, so Morrill decided to signal for assistance.

He had previously arranged with some men in Shag Harbour that one fire on the Point meant "Assistance Wanted," while two meant "Doctor Needed." A year or two before he had put up near the lighthouse two large posts with metal brackets into which he could thrust a torch. So now he soaked a burlap bag in kerosene, and placing it in the post-bracket lit it and saw its lurid flare stream out into the deepening night. Leaving his brother, Leland, who was with us at the time, to replace the flare when it had burned out, Morrill then hurried to the boathouse to kindle a fire there to guide the hoped-for rescue boat into the landing place. After Morrill left I ascended at intervals to the Lantern, from where I could see the imperilled fishing-boat till darkness blotted her from view. Then I could only hope that she would be able to avoid being driven on the rough shore and smashed to bits before a boat could come to her rescue.

In Shag Harbour the signal flare was immediately seen, but no one could remember with certainty whether one flare was for help or a doctor. Taking no chances, a boat with four or five men started on at once while an attempt was being made to contact a doctor. The boat ran up the sheltered harbour, and then pointed out into the open sea towards Bon Portage. At once it began to ice up from the high wind and flying spray, and the men feared they would never make the crossing; they returned for a larger and abler craft and chose the best in the harbour. Again they started and this time reached the Island safely. Morrill met them on the shore and explained why he had summoned them on such a night.

In the midst of his explanation a motor-boat was heard coming around the Point from seaward. The Wood's Harbour men had discovered that one of their boats was not in harbour at dark, and a boat had gone to search for it. The flare on the Point at Bon Portage had told them approximately where to look for their missing comrade, so they had succeeded in locating the boat we had sighted and in taking it in tow. Once they rounded the Point they were in comparatively sheltered water and should reach harbour without difficulty. The Shag Harbour boat was thus relieved of further duties that night and returned to the village.

In the meantime, the only doctor who could be reached was at Pubnico, twenty-five miles away. He had already put in a full day's work tending a country practice over almost impassable roads—but he started at once for Shag Harbour. His car went into a ditch and he was forced to hire another; he reached Shag Harbour finally only to find that we had not signalled for a doctor at all. I believe he expressed his reaction to this in no uncertain terms, and if he did so he was not unjustified. However, we forwarded his bill for a call to the Department and I think he was finally paid for his trouble. Our Inspector said he would call Ottawa's attention to the fact that if the doctor were not paid under such circumstances, it might mean that medical care would not reach the Island in case of a real emergency requiring it. The misunderstanding was due to no fault or failure on our part, and what the Shag Harbour men did was done in a spirit of neighbourliness and a desire to help us, as none of them are under contract with the government to render assistance to the lightkeeper, and none of them imagined that a boat could be out on such a night. The fishermen all agreed that Morrill had done the proper thing in signalling for help. "If it'd been me," each said, "I'd a' wanted you to put up a signal fast as you could." As we always bemoan of such occasions, "If we only had a telephone."

Another incident occurred during one November, when a heavy sou'west fog breeze was blowing dankly in from sea. In the late afternoon Morrill and Walter, who had just arrived for some gunning, started out to get the shooting at the evening flight. Much sooner than we expected their return I heard voices and on going to the door found our gunners accompanied by two strangers. Morrill had met these men at Garron's and brought them home.

The strangers were two crew members of an American vessel that had been fishing about thirty miles off Cape Sable. These two, with their trawl-dory almost filled with fish and ready to return to the vessel, had found themselves cut off from it by fog and the rising wind. The older of the two men belonged near Yarmouth, and when they could not succeed in finding their vessel he decided their only chance lay in making land above Cape Sable. Fortunately they had a sail with them in the dory and the south-west wind brought them to the back of our Island just at dusk, but they had no idea what part of the coast it might be. They continued to follow up the western shore, as the breaking surf along that rough beach forbade an attempt to land, and finally they had sailed to the end of the Island, crossed the Northern Bar and reached the sheltered little cove to the south of it. Here they landed, and after anchoring the dory they started to explore. They seemed to have been walking for miles and miles over the rough beach they said, when Morrill found them. They had seen some of our sheep and knew they need not suffer from hunger, even if they could find no house or shelter. They had not eaten since three o'clock in the morning, just before they left the vessel to set their trawl, and it was now well into the evening, so I hustled about to get them a supper, and they did it ample justice.

They had scarcely reached the lighthouse, when the wind went in to the north-west with a heavy squall, and it began to blow hard. They praised their luck that they should have reached shore safely before the change of wind; this would surely otherwise have driven them back out to sea, and very likely have meant their doom, since a sudden change in the wind after the high seas raised by a strong southerly makes terribly wicked water off this shore, and in the cold and darkness even a trawl-dory could come to grief.

They stayed with us overnight and we enjoyed having them. Both were originally from Nova Scotia, but had sailed to many parts of the world and had the vivid word tricks of description that so many sailors possess.

When they left the following morning for Yarmouth, there to get in touch with their ship, they were concerned because they had no money on them with which to pay us! We assured them that we wouldn't have accepted a cent had they been weighed down with it, but wished them well and asked them to let us know how they fared. At Christmas each of the children received a gift from the younger man who signed himself "A Shipwrecked Sailor." The children's gifts are being kept for the time when they shall have children who will want to hear stories about life at a Light Station, and Anne's doll bears the name of "Elsie MacDougall" after Tom MacDougall, the man who sent it to her.

I mentioned this incident to a friend in the city and in answer got this comment, "In such a lonely spot I suppose even those fishermen would be interesting company." That is not the idea. Certainly I found them most interesting. They had had a variety of experiences and a knowledge of the world (not to be confused with worldly knowledge!) which I envied, but the reason I welcomed them and felt a pleasure in what I could do for them, was because they were men who had so lately escaped death; "Death had brushed them passing, but had turned aside." So, although I had done nothing to insure it, I shared to a limited extent their joy at their safety. My friend couldn't know that only the previous year, out of six men in similar circumstances four had been drowned at Seal Island. Three dories had become separated from the mother-vessel, and all had made Seal Island at dark; the men in two dories decided to land and were drowned in the attempt; the crew of the third dory waited until daylight and were rescued. A few years before a lone man in his dory, lost from his vessel, landed at Hawk Beach on Cape Sable Island. Men of the place found his body and the broken dory where the sea had scornfully flung them.

A few years after his short visit here, the name of the older man appeared among those lost from the rigging of their vessel one wild night in Boston Harbour. I wondered if the sea had claimed him at last. I am glad there were hearty men to feed and good yarns to listen to in Bon Portage Lighthouse that night; not an empty, broken dory or two sea-sodden bodies on the heartless shore.

One night towards the end of a hard, cold winter, while there were still considerable quantities of salt-water ice along the shores, Morrill and I watched a distant schooner burn and disappear. When we first noticed the red glow on the horizon and took the binoculars to look more carefully the vessel was already ablaze from stem to stern, clearly and awesomely outlined by fire. I stood watching in the lee of the lighthouse and Morrill went up to the Lantern to get a higher, wider view; but while he was still mounting the stairs and the boat was thus shut off from his sight, I saw the flames suddenly shoot up the two masts and make of them blazing crosses. They burned fiercely for a few minutes and then toppled to mingle their glow with that of the burning deck. After that the flames diminished and in a short time there was only an irregular blotch of flame colour along the horizon. The burning vessel was about eight miles from us, but ranged so that we thought it nearer the Cape Sable Light and should have been more clearly visible from there. The drift ice prevented Morrill from going to the mainland to send a report on the incident until amost two weeks had elapsed, and we never heard anything regarding the identity of the schooner. We hoped that some boat had been near to pick up the crew, or if they had been forced to leave the vessel in their dories, that the ice did not prevent them from making a safe landing on some close and friendly shore. Fortunately, the weather though cold was still and no high seas were breaking. Even from this distance the burning vessel was an awesome sight and in our eyes held all the possibilities for another tragedy of the sea. Again we thought of how we could have made certain of the crew's rescue—if we had a phone.

So many times we have found odd bits of wreckage along the shore and wondered what story lay behind them. We will never know, but we never cease to question and to manufacture possible explanations. You can conceive, perhaps, what scope for mental excursions a piece of mute and inexplicable wreckage offers three children with vivid imaginations and a rather extensive background of reading.

## 12

## WINDS AND SEAS

It was during the third winter here that we experienced our first storm accompanied by an exceptionally high tide and really heavy seas. The weather had been mild for February; no drift ice hampered travelling by boat, so Walter had come to spend a few days with us, sailing in a small skiff some eight or nine miles from his home on Cape Sable Island, a trip he makes quite casually even in winter. One morning Morrill and he had gone up the Island leaving me at the lighthouse with the children, and promising to be back for dinner at twelve. I don't remember the wind as being more than an ordinary gale during the night, I know we were not expecting anything more than the common run of seas, but a very severe storm must have been centred just off the coast.

By nine o'clock the mounting seas were pounding along the edge of the bank, tearing off pieces of the grassy turf and tossing them into the field. The tide was not due to full until noon, so I realized that something extraordinary was occurring. Throughout the morning the seas grew heavier and the tide continued to rise; mountainous seas broke high against the sea-wall back of the pond, and the wash and foam from them trickled in white streamlets across the beach into the quiet pool on its inner side. It was the first time I had seen this happen, as the sea-wall there is high and broad and forms a substantial barrier between the sea and the pond. The spray from the breaking waves at the Point with the wind behind it was driving against my bedroom window like a drenching rain. Soon the largest of the seas began to break over the bank near the Light and wash across the field to join the waters of the pond, which now, augmented by the sea-water pushing over and through the beach, came half way across the field, and was momentarily spreading, creeping up across the slight incline between it and the lighthouse.

By noon the water from the pond was almost lapping the edges of the barn, and was only five or six yards from the back door of the lighthouse, while the waves at the pond no longer broke when passing over the beach, but sped uninterrupted across the water now covering it, to flatten themselves against the further side, which now extended to our woodpile at its innermost boundary— over a hundred yards beyond its ordinary limits.

The lighthouse stands on a small knoll, so that the seas breaking over the bank only ten yards in front of it, were deflected from the building and washed down the slight slope to the pond, leaving pebbles and rocks, some as large as my head, strewn along its path over the field, and depositing dripping tangles of sea-weed on the few small trees in front of the lighthouse.

At no time did I fear the children and I were in danger; the wind blew with only moderate strength, and I thought the lighthouse could stand some little buffeting by the sea, since the main force of the waves would be spent on passing the large boulders that line the bank and the six-foot wall that the bank itself formed; but I did worry lest our cellar be flooded. My real concern was for the men, as I felt sure the lower parts of the Island must be awash.

The tide was full at noon, but for over an hour after it should have reached its peak I could detect no difference in the size and speed of the waves, nor in the depth of the water that covered the field; then gradually the waves diminished as the pull of the ebb reduced their height and lessened their onrush, and the sea began to recede, leaving the field strewn with broken bits of lobster-pots, buoys, stumps of trees, streamers of kelp and rockweed, the beautiful mauve shells of dead mussels as well as the dark clusters of those which at the roots of a stalk of kelp, had been broken from the rock to which they clung and tossed ashore with their attached kelp-stalk. With these were mingled all the odds and ends of debris that usually line the tide-mark of the beaches. By three o'clock the water had retired to its customary high tide boundaries, and was beginning to drop with great speed.

When the seas began to sweep in over the beaches along the shore, Walter and Morrill had both been at the northern end, but on opposite sides of the Island—Walter on the western side and Morrill on the eastern. Walter, finding himself on the low land back of Woody Pond as the sea began to pile in over the beach, and cut off from high land by the Salt Water Pond, now spreading as the swelling tide enlarged it, was forced to climb a tree and remain there until the water went down enough to allow him to wade through it towards the lighthouse.

Morrill was safe on the high land at the extreme northern end of the Island, but anxious to return to us at the lighthouse as he didn't know what danger might threaten us; so he left the high land and started homeward down the eastern side. He walked along the beach top as it afforded the highest and firmest footing. When he came to the low portions of the beach, he would brace himself to withstand the force of the breaking surf; then run through the shallow water along the crest of the beach in the lulls between the wave as it rolled across the rocks and into the flooded field or swamp beyond, and the tremendous suction of its backwash. Had he lost his footing both sides of the beach would have been equally dangerous, as the waters over the land were as deep and strong as those outside the sea-wall. At the narrow low swamp back of Kelp Cove the seas were sweeping across from both sides of the Island and meeting with considerable force in the middle of the savannah. Huge pieces of wreckage, weighing hundreds of pounds, were washed in from the western shore and still lie where the sea dropped them in the centre of the swamp.

Morrill finally succeeded in reaching the boathouse safely, but found he could not follow the path home as it was too deeply inundated; so he made the remainder of his way through the thick woods along a higher ridge some distance inland from the path. I was thankful to see him safe at home, but shuddered to think of the risks he had run to reach us. Neither of us knew what might have become of Walter.

Morrill had been forced to be on duty all the previous night, keeping the outside of the Lantern windows cleared of a wet, clinging snow, which if allowed to remain and build up on the glass would have shut off the beam of the Light. His struggle home on top of a sleepless night left him weary; so after eating he went to bed, requesting me to waken him at three o'clock if Walter had not returned, and he would then go back up the Island in an attempt to find him. At three Morrill was still sleeping the sleep of exhaustion, and as the tide had not yet ebbed to any extent I decided to allow him another half-hour's sleep, and hoped Walter would turn up in the meantime. Just before the half-hour had elapsed I saw Walter wending his cautious way along the beach top, and soon he and Morrill were making comparisons and exchanging accounts of their experiences.

The tides continued higher than normal for the two following days, but each successive tide ceased below the boundaries set by its immediate predecessor, and by the third day they no longer flowed above the usual lines of high waters.

That was our worst experience with a high tide, none since have ever quite reached the record boundaries set by that one, although several have swollen until they flowed without break over the beach and a wave kept its shape until it surged into the woods and swamp a hundred yards or more beyond the normal margin of the pond. It is these excessively high tides that wash over the path and make keeping the road in repair an unending task; and the rocks and trash they left scattered over the field at the Point was a factor that influenced our decision to turn that field to pasture rather than use it as hayland and to make a hayfield on the hill, beyond and above the reach of the abnormally high tides.

The wind that reached us with that record high tide was not as strong as many we have had. The lighthouse lies north and south (roughly) and presents its narrowest surfaces to the winds from these directions, but we get the full sweep of an east or west wind, and these are our most trying. A strong east wind seems the worst of all that blow. The whole lighthouse trembles and vibrates to its force as it pipes mournfully around all the corners of the ells and porches and whistles shrilly past the tower. The iron trap-door that leads to the Lantern is lifted and dropped upon its metal frame with a continuous rattle, punctuated by an irregular bang, as a particularly heavy gust strikes the lighthouse and sucks the air through the Lantern ventilator with immense force. Windows rattle and the whole house is filled with the pressure and hum of the wind. The noises caused by the wind added to those of the pounding surf which accompanies a high wind make it difficult at such times for us to hear each other speak.

After a night of such winds, Mike used to have exciting stories to tell Betty June of how his single bed in the room directly beneath the Lantern had been blown from side to side, and only by the most strenuous efforts had he succeeded—just in the nick of time—in warding the bed away from the walls, or prevented it from capsizing, like a storm-tossed boat in a crowded harbour. Betty June thought this most adventurous, and her enthralled questions would bring forth in answer more and more lurid details from Mike. Finally he would demand, "Do you mean to say *your* bed never moved none in all that wind, and the lighthouse pitching and tossing like it was?"

"No, not that I can remember," Betty June would reply in a puzzled and reluctant voice, "Unless," she would add brightening, "I was asleep and didn't know. Perhaps it *did*, like yours."

Our bed is like Betty June's and never goes careening about in the unseemly fashion described by Mike, but there have been nights when I have been unable to sleep for the vibration and noise—I, who so love the sound of the sea and the wind, and most of all, my sleep!

The greatest wind that ever struck us was in November of 1938. One very mild afternoon the wind sprang up suddenly from the south-west, and inside an hour was blowing a screaming gale. I think if it had blown with equal force directly against the lighthouse, the chances are it would have blown away parts of the tower, or might even have flattened the structure completely; but striking cornerwise as it were, its full strength was not brought to bear on the wide surfaces of the building, and it succeeded only in blowing away two braces from under the Lantern and the storm door off the western porch. The Lantern atop the tower rocked and swayed to the sweep of the gale.

The wind picked the top off a completely flattened sea and sent the spindrift across the field so thickly and continuously that nothing could be seen but the driving white spume for a height of fifty feet; it resembled a dense snow-squall during a blizzard.

Morrill waited to be sure that the lighthouse would withstand the wind, and then grabbed his gun for what he believed would be the best afternoon ever for ducks. Before leaving he said to George, newly arrived from Ontario and somewhat puzzled by our Maritime weather, "There's one thing you might do while I'm gone, George, empty that pan of wood-ashes for Evelyn."

"Sure thing," replied George obligingly. "Where'll I put it?"

Then he saw the joke as he realized what would happen to him and a pan of ashes if he stepped out into that wind.

Morrill's high hopes of especially good gunning were not fulfilled. Ducks in large flocks flew past him; but the wind blew so strongly he could not hold himself or his gun steady enough to shoot; and then he realized that if he hit a duck he would never retrieve it, as the wind would carry it so far neither he nor the dog would ever find it. It was that afternoon that he watched a duck, unable to move against the wind, the only time he ever saw one that could not "stiver to windward"; for several moments it beat its wings with all the strength it could summon, but was held immobile by the force of the wind sweeping down and across the bar. Then it swung about with the wind, set its wings and was out of sight in an instant.

When Morrill left home the ground was soft and wet, the air sweet and warm, and he was dressed for the mild Indian summer day. About three o'clock the wind hauled to the north-west, and long before sunset the ground was frozen solid, and the windows thickly frosted. Morrill was stiff with cold and exhausted by the buffeting of the wind when he returned.

"*Our* geography book said," George remarked, "that Nova Scotia does not have extremes in temperature."

Luckily no small craft from this vicinity were out when the gale struck so suddenly, and a few barn roofs blown off was the extent of local damage.

The hurricane that swept the Atlantic States in 1938 did not reach us. We heard of it over our radio, and listened continuously as the U.S.A. weather bureaus tried to plot its future course; for a time they expected it to turn in this direction, and Morrill made some preparations against this contingency, as we would be forced to leave the lighthouse and move back into the woods on some of the highest ground that the Island affords. None of our trees are exceptionally tall, but we hoped some of the largest and toughest would weather such a blow, and even survive being flooded some distance up their trunks. Morrill collected strong ropes, lantern, clothing and a little food, as we should leave the lighthouse and be past the open fields and low swamps before the storm reached here, or it would be useless to start, as our greatest danger would lie in the tidal wave that accompanied the wind. At about half-past ten in the evening we heard that the storm—fortunately for us—had turned northward and inland rather than out to sea, so we went thankfully to bed.

The following morning was most beautiful, no breath of wind stirred and the sea lay smooth and motionless. But soon big waves began to form in that quiet water, and huge sleek mounds of water rose as if by magic, swelled to a height of twenty feet, moved slowly forward until their green translucent crest became top-heavy, then the very tips curled over in a delicate ruching of white; and the rest of the wave, still as smooth as glass and as transparent, soon fell like a cascade from its greatest height in a crashing smother of foam that spread in lacy patterns over the silken waters beneath it. The contrasting greens and white were unspeakably lovely.

"See," said Anne Gordon, "like Christopher Robin says, 'the green curls over and the white falls under.'"

Those were the most beautiful waves we have seen, because of their stately dignity in forming and breaking, and because of the beauty of the placid water in the midst of which they formed and dissolved; but they were by no means the largest we've watched.

Often when heavy seas have formed before a southerly wind, the wind will change its direction and blow from the north, now opposing its strength to the impetus it had formerly given to the seas. This blows the breaking tops back from the crests in glorious arches of white foam. The picture of horses tossing their manes comes at once to mind, and I find myself mentally quoting Matthew Arnold's

> Now the wild white horses play,
> Champ and chafe and toss in the spray.

If these conditions prevail during a sunny afternoon we behold an extraordinary beauty as the waves rush in along our eastern shore; every crest forms a rainbow as it is blown back and falls in prismatic loveliness into the white foam behind the wave from which it was torn. Then the waves are like graceful dancers with scarves of surpassingly fragile texture and delicate blendings of colours, and they move in the most stately and perfect rhythm.

It seems that the heaviest seas roll in at night, and their speed and roar are like those of an express train as they tear past up the Sound, and their inner fringes are caught among the rocks and break along our shore. The water surrounding the Island is shallow, and the seas break out some distance from the shore; during the worst storms they break all the way across the Sound, well over a mile. To see their white-crested tops streaming past in the darkness with such speed and at such a height is awesome in the extreme, but so fascinating that Morrill and I spend hours watching them, even on cold winter nights when we crouch in the shelter of the lighthouse and call each other's attention to the more stupendous combers as they take their place in the endless rushing procession; and glimmering indistinctly in the weird light that seems to emanate from their foaming crests, smash and smother the black rocks and shallow water before they disappear into the deep night, filled with the thunder and roar of their passage.

Always now these nights of wild splendour are tinged with a feeling of sadness for me. It was on just such a night that I learned of my father's death. In fact, I had been listening to the radio to hear more details of what was expected of the bad storm then in progress when I heard the news of his passing announced. It came as a sad shock to me; he had been ill but my last word from home had been that he was recovering. I wanted with all my heart to be with Mother and the others of the family at that time, but I had little hopes of being able to join them, for such a sea as was then running would make it impossible for me to get off the shore.

Later in the evening Morrill came to me and asked me to join him in watching the tremendous seas smothering all the shores. I knew he hoped to divert my mind with the beauty we had shared so many times, so I went with him. The roaring seas seemed unreal and dreamlike then, though I can see them plainly in my mind's eye as I now write. There was no sympathy in their wild power, but their stupendous beauty filled my eyes and mind, if it did not ease my heart.

Through the night the weather relented; when I awoke next morning the wind had changed and had already beaten down the waves, so that I was able to start on my sad homeward journey with little inconvenience.

The only time that the seas seem to assume a malignant aspect towards us is when there is illness in the family and they prevent Morrill getting off to a doctor; and even then we are more likely to express our resentment towards a government that leaves an employee and his family in such an isolated spot with no means of getting in touch with medical assistance—in this day and age of radio and wireless!—than we are to blame the seas and weather.

So many times a telephone or similar convenience would have saved us heart-wringing anxiety, and in Morrill's case, hours of pain and illness brought on by having to go by boat to Shag Harbour when he should have been under the doctor's care. Since it would be possible to land the doctor from a big boat nine out of ten times when Morrill cannot launch his small craft we feel our hazards in that respect are rather needlessly increased.

We found this true when Betty June was coming to join the family and no woman would risk coming on to care for me, because of the isolation and lack of communication. No one could take me and my two children in to care for me either. Many days that winter Morrill and I went off in the little open boat to try to make arrangements for a place at which I might stay and returned from a fruitless trip tired, cold and discouraged.

It was then that Clayton and Sade proved friends in need. Sade offered to take me into her home and care for me and the children and this in spite of the fact that she herself had a large family, many of them still small. If there is a silver lining to every dark cloud, in this case it proved to be their kindness and thoughtfulness to me and the children, and we have always counted their friendship as clear gain from that trying time.

But a baby is something about which plans can be made far ahead. This is not true of other illnesses or accidents and the only means of summoning help or a doctor is to hoist the flag on the Lantern rail. This leaves much to be desired—in heavy winds it means a tremendous struggle for me to get it in place, there on the wind-swept deck. In foggy weather it cannot be seen, and has gone unnoticed all day when there was no wind and an overcast sky.

The only time I have been seriously ill was during a rough spell when Morrill could not travel, and I was better before the doctor could get here. It would have meant much to my peace of mind to have been able to talk to the doctor over the phone during the three or four days when I lay hoping for the best and wondering how my children would make out if I were not to come through the illness and they were forced to adjust themselves to the world outside Bon Portage after a sudden and tragic break. At such times I wonder if I have done right in keeping them here where they are dependent on me, not only for mothering, but for much of their companionship, and for their education. This dependence on me is to a somewhat lesser extent true of Morrill, too, but he or I would be equally lost in any world that did not contain the other.

We are fortunate in having a doctor that never shirks the rough disagreeable journey whenever the weather per-

mits the boats to bring him.   He has always brought relief
with him so we have come to feel that the worst is over
when we see the boat bringing Dr. Wilson.   At such times
when the seas prevent his coming we have been fortunate
in managing somehow to "make out."

The sea is not always in a boisterous or angry mood,
its mountainous waves seem never to have been when it
lies placid and quiescent under the summer sun or a clear
winter sky.   The angry roar and turmoil as it lashes the
shore in a fury of destruction softens to gentle whispers
and good-natured chuckles among the rounded rocks, and
nothing could be more charmingly innocuous than the
beautifully calm aspect it presents.

Between these two extremes lay many variations of
appearance and behaviour, the "feather-white" of a northerly blowing down the Sound, the surly grey of a short-
chopped easterly, the merry blue nor'westers of the fine
summer days, and the soft warm wavelets of a dry easterly
—there is an infinite variety, probably never in a person's
lifetime would the ocean present an exact repetition of a
former appearance.

Then there is the sea under the moon's light.   Never
can I be too thankful that our southern bedroom window
looks upon the full moon rising above the tide at its fullest
flood, so that the restless waves among the rocks outside
the window are in the full glory of its magic silver light.
It is in the moonlight, when the eye is not enchanted by
the contrasting colours that the sun brings out, that the
beauty in the movement of the tossing sea becomes
apparent.   Its molten silver weaves and undulates, curves
and circles about the rocks in its wash, rises and falls,
advances and recedes with such grace and beauty of motion
that often I tear myself away from its wonder with the feeling that such unearthly loveliness is not to be drunk in too
long draughts.

And once between me and an orange moon in a silver gauze of mist, a ship came sailing. Standing close in after rounding the Point, so near it seemed I might run my hand along her moonlit bulwarks, her masts and spars were silhouetted blackly, but the softly bellying sails were indistinct with mist and golden moonlight. The water talked under her bow and gurgled along her side, but I heard no sound of human voices above the creak of her gears and the whisper of the gentle breeze in her sails and rigging. She might have been a "Phantom Vessel"; I thought of the *Belle* making harbour at last, and I wondered for a moment if the anxious ones that had watched in vain for her coming, now asleep in the churchyard atop the hill all these many years, perhaps had stepped out upon the road for a clearer view and were shading their eyes in the moonlight to catch a glimpse of the silent sails, so long and vainly awaited, now stealing towards the harbour and home after all the hopeless years; and if perhaps a ghostly crew would be greeted with spectral tears and smiles by the shadowy watchers. The ship passed through the blaze of the moon path and stole silently into the darkness of the shadows from the shore, and I knew she was merely a fishing schooner seeking a safe night's anchorage.

## 13

# BOATS AND LANDINGS

IN SHAPE Bon Portage is almost straight and so its shores offer no really sheltered coves. We often wish we could take it by both ends and bend it into a horseshoe shape, as a giant might a piece of stout iron—then we would have a wonderful anchorage and the dangers and difficulties that beset us when launching and landing a boat would all be ended. Since that wish doesn't seem likely to be fulfilled, we must make the best of what we have, and Morrill has accomplished wonders in overcoming many of the unfavourable conditions that prevailed when he came.

The first few years we were here he could do little more than try to keep the landing which was already in use clear of the rocks that the sea continually heaved into it, and to widen it somewhat.   Our first boat was not much larger than a big dory, so the landing sufficed for the time being. This boat was fitted with oars, a mast for the small sail we made from sugar-bags, and an outboard motor.   The outboard was not very satisfactory in such rough water as we travel since it became wet and so rendered useless much of the time.   However a larger boat with an engine was out of the question, because we could not bring it ashore with the facilities we had at the time, and could not always leave it moored off on account of the frequent heavy seas.   So for the first four years we managed with the little boat, although after two years Walter succeeded in finding us a small, light marine engine, and this proved much more serviceable than the outboard motor.   Still it was a long slow journey across to Shag Harbour in the little boat, and if there was even a slight breeze, it meant a wet trip.   Morrill went many days when I wished him safe ashore, but in moderately windy or rough weather that would mean nothing to a larger craft, our little boat stayed on the bank.

Morrill has done much "figgering" since we arrived at Bon Portage, most of it to good effect, so he soon started "figgering" on the landing situation.   When he asked local opinion, he was told that nothing had been found that would serve his purpose here, a slip or ways would not stand the pounding of the seas, particularly when there were ice-cakes about.   These jam under a structure, and then as the tide rises, exert a terrific pressure upward,  or they smash down from the crest of a sea upon anything beneath them.   No one held out much hope of his being able to construct a landing place that would hold against sea and ice.

Morrill, however, was determined to try to improve conditions as they then existed, and after watching the action of the sea on the breakwater and landing, and considering it from every angle, he began to construct a slip as soon as the third spring brought warm weather for working. He first deepened and widened the original old landing place, and extended it several yards to seaward. The preceding winter when he cut his firewood he had selected suitable poles and timber for what he planned to do, and had hauled and piled it in the boathouse field, near where he was to work.

With Lem to help, he dug trenches and sank cross-timbers with attached upright posts, between two to six feet below the surface of the landing, according to the contour of the adjacent beach. These uprights provided the posts to which he nailed stringers of heavy poles down both sides of the landing, with a width of fifteen feet between them. Across the stringers he nailed pole skids at three-foot intervals.

The men followed the tide out as it receded and retreated before it as it turned and flowed over their work. Morrill sank his cross-timbers to a good depth because he believed the sea did not tear up the skids until it had gullied all the sand and soil from around and beneath them, and this he determined to prevent if at all possible. He graduated the heights of the tops of his posts, from surface level at the bottom of his landing to an elevation that would allow the top of his slip to be at the same level as the crest of the beach. This made an incline of fifteen to twenty degrees. Nothing except the small exposed portion of the sunken posts was made to withstand the force of the sea; his idea was to offer as little resistance as possible, and allow the sea to wash under, through and around, but not against his work.

This was our first slip and it worked fairly well with our little boat, the heavy seas and ice seemed not to bother it, but washed through it without loosening the poles; but the sea piled the lower part, which was level with the sea-bed, full of rocks, and this meant that every two weeks or so a day must be spent pitching out rocks and clearing the landing. The winch at the top of the beach aided in hauling up the boat, and launching over the skids became much easier than it had been over rocks and through gravel. One thing had to be watched. During bad storms kelp and rockweed would tangle and twist round and round the cross-pieces and build up such an accumulated weight that it sometimes broke one of the skids. Moreover, if such tangles froze it was impossible to launch the boat through them, so Morrill sometimes had to take an axe to cut a passage through the ice and kelp in order to get his boat in the water. If possible Morrill always goes to his slip after a storm and cuts away this kelp before sufficient quantities collect to do a great deal of damage.

I spent a nerve-racking hour or two watching him at this work one winter afternoon. As a large sea receded, Morrill would race down over the wet and slippery skids with a hunting knife in his hand, and in the few seconds before a fresh wave started in, he would hack and cut at the kelp which had twined and twisted around the poles, then turn and rush back up the slip, arms outspread for balance, only a few inches ahead of the oncoming crest; and with churning water and rocks under the open skids beneath his flying feet. The incoming wave would wash clear for him the kelp he had cut and loosened. He claimed it saved time, but watching took years off my span of life, I am sure. When *I* am forced to land on the skids, and Morrill is not there to steady my steps, I get down on all fours and climb it as I would a ladder.

The spring after Morrill constructed the slip we got a larger boat. It was really a small motor-boat, much like those the fishermen use but on a smaller scale; we had it built at Cape Sable Island, and it was powered by a Starr car engine. She was a sweet little craft, and we always meant to name her, but never got around to it. Anne and Laurie always called her *Green Flasher* from the way her dark green keel flashed above the surface and contrasted with the spray and the white of her hull, when she was going fast or through rough water.

Then we had hard luck. The following spring the breakwater was demolished by the sea, and all the boulders and rocks that had been used in its construction, as well as those that had piled up behind it during the many years it had stood in the path of the sea, were tossed and thrown across Morrill's new slip, covering the poles and filling the landing to the level of the adjacent shore; and at the same time changing the level and contour of all that section of the beach. So again Morrill was back to trying to pull up and launch his boat over rocks and gravel, and to removing the boulders from the landing as the sea tossed them in. The sea never seemed to tire of this—but Morrill did.

Now came a time when we kept our boat on a joan-pole about a hundred yards off-shore from the landing place. We bought canvas and made a covering to shed rain and spray, but when we expected a bad storm Morrill brought the boat ashore and hauled her up over the rubble in the landing, rather than risk her sinking at the joan, or breaking free and being blown ashore and smashed, or out to sea and lost. This was by no means a complete or convenient solution to our trouble. It was awkward, and none too safe, to row in a small skiff out to the boat, and wait until Morrill had unfastened the grommets of the covering and rolled it back until there was room to step aboard, while both boats pitched and tossed in the seas. I, for one, never enjoyed the time we spent rolling at the mooring as Morrill got the engine in running order, and Betty June often became seasick before we began to move. It was equally inconvenient on the return trip; and our boat on the joan was a constant source of worry to us—Morrill never woke at night to hear a rising wind or the roar of seas breaking on the Point, but his mind flew at once to his little boat more or less at the mercy of wind and weather.

We made a bargain with one of the young fishermen of Shag Harbour: he had the use of our boat for lobstering (the boat taking the customary seventh share of the earnings) and he "tended" us. That is he brought us our weekly supplies and mail and left them at the boathouse and also undertook to respond to our distress signals if we should need help. This proved a great help to me when Morrill became ill from getting out of bed while suffering from a heavy cold and working all one afternoon to help save a fisherman's boat. I had managed to get the flag hoisted when I found Morrill too sick to move, but although boats were anchored under the lee of the Point no notice was taken of the signal until they went into harbour that evening, when they informed Elroy, who had our boat. He came on at once, but as Morrill was no worse he didn't bring the doctor until the following morning. The arrangement we had made with Elroy proved a great help to me during the weeks Morrill lay ill, and he proved kind and helpful beyond the terms of the contract. He carried the doctor back and forth, brought supplies, and best of all, made me feel I was not entirely on my own although the children were too small to help in any way.

He asked, "Have you got a fairly large piece of red cloth?"

I replied that I had an old red tablecloth.

"Just the thing. If you need help, or anything goes wrong, fasten your red cloth to the far end of the clothesline. I'll keep watch for it as I go out to tend my pots, and as I come in by. If I see it I'll come right ashore."

Though I never had to fly my old red tablecloth in distress, it was comforting to know that if I did someone would see it and respond.  So we managed again, but felt most keenly the lack of a telephone which would have saved Morrill the long weeks of pain and illness since a phone call to the large boats would have brought one of them to the aid of their hapless comrade and would have saved Morrill having to struggle in the cold and wet when he should have been in bed.

Morrill was convinced that his method of constructing a slipway was correct, so the following spring he again went to work, but this time he made his slip wider and higher, and found it more satisfactory.  This slip is still in use.  Neither it nor the previous one extended to the extreme low-water mark, so there are always a few hours each day while the tide is out, when it is impossible to land or launch our boat.

When making his first slip Morrill used dynamite to blow some dozen large rocks from the entrance of the old landing.  These had always caused trouble when the tide was low and I was glad to see the last of them with their possibilities of disaster.  One was directly in the middle of the narrow entrance and more than once the boat had caught on it and threatened to capsize as he attempted a difficult landing.  Once with me and two small children in the boat he had broken an oar on an obstructing rock as we landed in a rough sea.  Although the government steamer lands lighthouse supplies at our slip, and uses the landing, we were unable to obtain any assistance from them in the cost or work involved in the improvements made.

We now have our third boat.  Each one we have bought has been a little larger and abler than its predecessor, and this is slightly over twenty feet in length, with a beam of five and a half feet.  It was built in Shag Harbour and is of the same type as the boats of the district though smaller.

Our colour scheme does not vary: all our boats have been white, with a green keel and under-water line, while the inside is a light brown. We all take a great pride in our boat, it replaces for us in some respects the family car of people in different circumstances, and often the annual cleaning and painting becomes a family undertaking.

Since in landing safely much depends on the speed with which the boat can be removed from the reach of the following seas, Morrill had a hauler-head installed in the bow of his boat and had it geared to his engine. The hauler-head is a wooden cylinder, about six inches in diameter, which revolves when in use. In the lobster-boats the pot-line is passed around it, and as it turns it winds the lobster-pot to the surface, saving the men the back-breaking labour of pulling up their traps. Morrill used it similarly with his hawser; in rough weather the hired man (and now Laurie) waited at the water's edge with a heavy rope which was attached to strong timbers at the head of the landing; Morrill drove the boat at full speed upon the slip, seized the rope, passed it around the revolving hauler-head, and stood back to keep free the line coming off the cylinder. The boat "walked right up the skids," as he says. But when Laurie grew big enough to use the boat occasionally, Morrill considered this arrangement rather dangerous, as moving rope can be very treacherous, especially when attached to an engine. Then, too, the weight of the hauler-head detracted from the boat's seaworthiness, making her heavy by the bow. So he made another change, and now has a car engine at the top of the slip; it is connected to his winch and the pulling of the boat is done with that, after the hawser has been carried down the skids and fastened to the bow of his boat. As can readily be understood, both these arrangements need someone on the bank to bring the heavy rope within reach of the man in the boat; and a trip to Shag Harbour means a half-day job for both Morrill and Laurie, as Lo must be on the bank to give a hand with the launching and again to bring the rope to Morrill on his return, and this task interrupts his school work most frequently of any of the chores.

Our boats were each made with quite a deep keel and this presented a difficulty when Morrill first attempted to haul them up the skids, as once they left the supporting water they tended to fall over on one side or the other. To overcome this Morrill had the boat-builder bolt pieces of two-and-a-quarter-inch hardwood stock, six inches wide and tapering at the ends, on each side of the keel for about two-thirds of its length. They increased the width of the flat surface of the keel from nine to twenty-one inches and overcame the boat's tendency to topple. These pieces do lessen somewhat the boat's speed, but since safety and ease in launching and landing are of paramount importance here, we feel this diminution of speed is negligible.

Morrill also rigged a turntable at the head of the landing, so that he can easily turn his boat bow first, ready for launching. This turntable, he says, required the greatest amount of "figgering" of any of his undertakings, and all the fishermen or mechanically-minded friends who view it are impressed and interested in the details of its performance, but I fear I cannot do it justice (to be perfectly honest I don't understand the thing!), so I'll make no attempt to describe it. The boat is always left turned and everything as nearly ready for launching as possible, in case of an emergency. The actual launching is done mostly by pushing on the stern of the boat after the poles of the slip and the keel of the boat have been brushed with old machine oil kept for that purpose; the incline of the slip and the pull of gravity do the rest; a rope from the winch is left attached to the boat's stern, and a check on the boat's way down the greased poles is afforded by pressing a stick against the revolving drum of the winch, thus stopping the rope from unwinding and so also stopping the descent of the boat down the skids.

The engine is started before the boat is launched, so that once she is in the water the propeller blades grab and she is headed out through any waves that may be breaking into the landing.  If the seas are too large or continuous, with no lulls or "breaks" between them, we just can't put the boat in the water.

The girls and I and any passengers there may be get in the bow of the boat before she starts her run down the skids, she slides along and plunges her bow into the water at the bottom of the landing, rolls a little to one side or the other, takes her bearings and we are away.  Then we all move back to the stern except the steersman who sits amidships on the engine box.  We are so accustomed to this method of leaving the shore that we sometimes forget to warn others of the splash and roll as we take the water, and to assure them of its lack of danger, and only remember too late as we hear their startled gasps and see their frightened clutch at the sides of the boat.

All this planning and work with boats and landings that we may have contact with the mainland once a week or fortnight—if the weather permits!

I learned to run our second boat, with the idea of making an occasional trip to Shag Harbour, but went off alone only once.  That was the year the slip was under rocks from the breakwater and we left the boat off-shore on the mooring.  Morrill felt he should not leave me to manage mooring and covering the boat, so that meant he must be at the landing to set me off and to meet me, which took a great deal of his time.  Then, if there is any possibility of the fog shutting in (and there almost always is) we cannot simultaneously be away from the Light.  It didn't seem the trip was worth the trouble involved, so I gave up the idea.   Now Laurie can run the boat and I can leave with him, it only remains for me to find the time to get away.

I'm afraid "a woman running around in a boat" would not meet with local approval.   One of the men on the wharf remarked to me on the single fine weather trip I made, "I don't believe Morrill thinks as much of you as he lets on.   If he did he'd never allow you off here alone in a boat."

In enumerating our boats I mustn't forget to mention the skiff Morrill bought the year we were forced to keep the boat on the joan and row in and out to it in a small skiff which could be easily pulled over the rocks.   Clayton had taken Ashford and the Richardson family to Clark's Harbour to spend the day.   While there Morrill saw a skiff that he liked and bought it.   He pulled it aboard the big boat and we brought it home with us, Clayton coming in to our landing to drop us off first.   Lem was supposed to watch for our coming and meet us at the mooring in the small boat, but no Lem appeared, although we waited and waited.   Finally Morrill decided to row ashore in his new skiff and get the small boat for us.   He knew the skiff, which had been lying on the bank in the hot sun and wind for weeks, would leak like a sieve, but he gambled on reaching the shore before she filled and sank.   So he rolled his good trousers well above his knees and—of all things for the job at hand!—got his pipe drawing well, while Clayton slipped the skiff over the side.   Then emitting clouds of smoke and rowing for dear life, Morrill started for shore.   The skiff sank lower and lower as Morrill rowed more and more furiously, and we stood in the big boat and cheered him on.   He made it; but it was close.   As he rose from the thwart, still dry, the water lapped across it.   Clayton, his blue eyes twinkling, slapped his knee and shook his head.

This little skiff, which proved too light for much service offshore, we afterward placed in the pond near the lighthouse, and in it all the children learned to row. It was ideal for that purpose, being small and light and having oars which they could easily handle. I was as sorry as the children were when it finally went to pieces and our plans to replace it were postponed from year to year. As I write I can hear Laurie's hammer from the shed where he is constructing its belated successor. I am not supposed to see it until it is completed, but from the description Laurie has given her as to how it is turning out, Betty June suggested he name it *The Ugly Duckling*.

Besides our own craft, the Department maintains a dory here for the use of the Keeper; the one now here is about sixteen feet long, and is known as a "double-ender"; it has both ends pointed like a skiff, but has a flat bottom instead of the keel that marks a skiff. It is very convenient for purposes which do not warrant launching the boat, but we almost never use it to travel to Shag Harbour.

Although Morrill is very cautious (too much so, the rest of us sometimes grumble) about taking the children and me in the boat when the weather is stormy or unpredictable, a few times we have been caught in dangerous circumstances.

When Morrill was taking the children and me off to Shag Harbour there to await Betty June's birth, we were nearly swamped in getting beyond the line of breakers. My trunk was in the bow, and the boat low in the water from the weight of us all; before we were far from shore we saw a big comber forming directly in front of us; and as it moved upon us it appeared that the bow of the little boat was not going to rise to it, but that the crest of the wave would pour down over us and "level us off" leaving us helpless against the following seas. Then slowly, so slowly it seemed, the bow rose and we slid over the top of the sea and down its smooth back, and were out beyond danger when the next wave formed.

One fine winter day we all piled into our boat (it was in the days of the first and smallest one) and set off to visit Ashford and Jean. They had been to Bedford and we were anxious to hear all the news from home. We planned to stay at Emerald Isle until the ebb, as that tide usually cuts down any wash of the sea on the shore, but on our arrival we found Ashford and Jean were still away, so there was nothing to do but return home.

When we reached our landing we could see that there was a heavy sea running, but Morrill watched for a lull and went in. We hit the skids fair and square, and in a twinkling Morrill was out of the boat, had grabbed first Anne and then Lo from their places in the bow and tossed them into a windrow of seaweed that lined the beach above the reach of the waves, then he raced for the winch with the painter to haul up the boat. As we struck the skids I started for the bow from my place aft, and was out of the boat before the following sea hit her and washed in over the stern. Then I did a very foolish thing. I meant to help Morrill by holding the boat straight on the narrow slip against the wash of the sea while he pulled it up by the winch. But instead of pulling against the boat, I went to the opposite side and tried to pit my weight and strength against the sea by pushing. What I should have foreseen happened. The next sea hit across the boat, filled her and washed boat and me off the slip and down among the rocks and water beside it. Fortunately I fell clear of the boat and was not injured, but "more by good luck than good management."

Then came, to quote Morrill, "the devil's own job" to get the boat back on the skids and out of the wash of the sea; as fast as Morrill could get her partly emptied and pointed towards the skids, while he ran up the slip to his winch a wave would break across slip and boat and wash her again among the rocks below the level of the skids. At last, during a lull in the size and speed of the breakers, he succeeded in getting the boat started up the slip to safety, and my small assistance no longer needed, I crawled over the poles of the slip to the children. They still sat in the kelp and seaweed where Daddy had tossed them; quietly watching what was going on.

Our children early learned to do as they were told, quickly and without fuss. I have been amazed sometimes as I've watched small children argue and coax when told to do something and seen them obey only after long and patient persuasion. Ours were often naughty, no angels at all, but I never remember having to punish them for not obeying promptly, and I certainly would have done so, knowing that their very lives might in many conceivable circumstances depend on quick obedience. Of course we always tried to explain an order the reason for which seemed obscure to them, if circumstances allowed us to do so, but often there was no time for explanations and coaxings. They never cried in the boat, even Betty June, who was subject to sea-sickness, made no outcry. If they were frightened, they sensed that they could best help by not distracting Morrill's attention from the job at hand. Nor did they make any fuss when the weather or sea upset our happy plans for a picnic or a boat trip. Perhaps because even a child can sense the futility of fussing at the ocean!

As for myself, I have learned the meaning of fear since coming to Bon Portage. I had been startled, nervous perhaps, before but not afraid as I know it now. As a young girl I had a canoe on Bedford Basin and I took a delight in paddling it out on windy days for the joy in pitting my skill and strength against the wind and water. Always at the back of my mind at such times was the thought of what

I could do if the canoe capsized. It never entered my head that such an occurrence might end things for me. The same was true when I was around boats at Emerald Isle. If I thought anything might go wrong I considered the possibilities for saving myself, my chances always looked good to me. The fact that I was a strong swimmer and at home in the water no doubt added to my sense of confidence. All that ended when I came here. Coming into the landing in rough weather with two or three little ones beside me in the boat, and looking at the cruel water, the unyielding rocks, I knew I would stand small chance of saving myself if things went wrong, and what of my children? I could see no way that I could possibly save more than one of them, and that only I realized, by the grace of God. I have known fear and a sense of helplessness that I never could have imagined before coming to the life here. Yet I think it is good for us mortals to come, now and then, against the realization of our own insufficiency. Strong fear, like other powerful emotions, can leave us cleansed of pettiness and humble, with a fuller conception of how much lies beyond and above our own puny powers.

## 14

## DUCKS AND GUNNERS

IF THE weather, and the resultant state of the ocean by which we are surrounded, is the greatest single influence in our life here, then it seems to me the next greatest is black ducks! In fact, during the fall gunning season the weather is considered subordinate to the ducks and is viewed merely as good or poor "gunning weather" and a strong cold northerly is deemed the sweetest breeze that blows.

The season for duck-shooting here now opens October 16th, and for weeks before that date Morrill talks and thinks of little else. One bright afternoon last fall I suggested we go up the savannah to pick a few cranberries and Laurie, Morrill and I set out. Unfortunately for my plans the swamp where I had expected to pick cranberries lies next to Flag Pond, with its vivid reminders of ducks and shooting, and the season opened the following week. I spent all afternoon carrying swamp hay and driftwood for Laurie and Morrill to construct duck-blinds along the inner shore of Flag Pond! You'd think cranberry sauce, instead of being a favourite dish, never existed.

For weeks before the opening day of the season, the letters between my brothers and Morrill consist of questions and answers regarding the number of ducks "tending" our ponds, the way any new dogs are "shaping up," the state and probabilities of the weather, and plans for the arrival of those who are coming for the first day's shooting. Perhaps in the corner of the letter I'll find the garrulous message, "All well" as a concession to family gossip.

My brothers Douglas and Edgar seldom miss being here for the opening day, Ashford sends his regrets that he cannot be "up the Island on the warm side of a cold rock," and the others get here only occasionally. For my part I look forward to Opening Day as a sort of family reunion; indeed some years my only contact with any of the family was with the brothers who came gunning. Quite often friends from near by also join us for the sport, arriving at the lighthouse the preceding evening, so as to be on the spot for the shooting at daybreak.

The gunners arrive with hunting clothes, guns, rubber-boots, shell belts, boxes of shells, dogs and cartons of dog-food, heavy coats, overnight things, parcels and a big box of books from Dad and a box of preserves from Mother. These are deposited in the kitchen while we all laugh and talk and try to tell one another all the news about every-thing. The little lighthouse sort of groans, gives at the sides, bulges in odd spots from the pressure within, and then settles itself rather contentedly to hold firm for a few days.

On the evening before the Big Day the men remind me of children on Christmas Eve. Their faith in a favourable wind and lots of ducks remains unshaken by experience. The values of the various blinds and berths are discussed; a place is apportioned to each gunner; a different course of action laid out for each exigency of weather or variation in the behaviour of the ducks; the number of shells to be taken, with the size shot and brand of each are long and earnestly debated. If one of my brothers' wives is along, she and I sit silent and neglected in a corner, overwhelmed by the scope and magnitude of the operations under discussion.

Late at night we get to bed, various cots and makeshifts having been arranged, at least two alarm clocks set, and things settle down for a few hours. "Settle down" comparatively speaking, of course, as Morrill tosses and turns and mutters, afraid he might oversleep and thus betray the faith reposed in him as official waker-upper. Since gunners from Shag Harbour arrive here early in the morning, it would never do for our party to be late. At five o'clock the alarm goes off and Morrill springs up. He makes the fires and starts breakfast, then rouses the others. This he does by going to the stairdoor and squawking loudly on the small horn-like instrument made to entice ducks within range, and called a "Quanker." I wonder it wakes them, since they are doubtless all dreaming of ducks quacking and it should blend right in with their dreams.

Morrill prepares breakfast that first morning, I smell the bacon and coffee but doze until the noises of departure cease, when I arise to extinguish the Light and clear away the cluttered kitchen, preparatory to getting breakfast for the non-gunning members of the family.

The men do not return to the lighthouse during the day, but eat a lunch up the Island, of late years at "Do-

Duck-Inn," the camp which Morrill built at Garron's to hold the fencing and equipment for shearing, but also strategically placed for gunners since it can be reached by crossing a few hundred yards of swamp, so saving the long walk to the lighthouse in the middle of the day. My brothers all consider it the most important building on the Island.

Once breakfast is over I start immediately to prepare lunch for the gunners and this must be sufficient for two meals, a hearty one at noon and a "mug-up" before the evening shooting. I gauge gunners' appetites by allowing just twice what I think they can possibly eat; nothing ever comes back but they assure me they have plenty. Laurie helps me pack the lunch into cartons and then harnesses the ox to carry it to the camp. A big pot of thick chicken soup (to be rewarmed at the camp) is the standard hot dish; then there are meat sandwiches, crackers, homemade bread and butter, pies, jam and cookies, bottles of cream and milk, tea, sugar and coffee. Dishes and a cream can of drinking water make up the rest of the cartload, and Lo sets out to have his lunch at the camp with the menfolks. I get a meal for us at home and tidy the house. The latter is accomplished by skirting the outer edges of things but never attempting to move or straighten out the knapsacks, shell-boxes, guncases, etc. I see the house is clean before the gunners arrive and I clean up after they go, but after all, there are more important things than house work on the first day of the season! And by now it is time to start one of those more important items—a big dinner of roast black duck for when the men arrive home around eight o'clock. They always do justice to what I have prepared and loosen their belts as they sit back for their after-dinner smokes.

I have been known to receive help with the dishes from my masculine company the evening before, but never the evening after, that first day's tramping over beach rocks and through swamps. Then, too, there are usually a day's bag of ducks for each to be picked and cleaned. Sometimes there are more than fifty ducks to be handled and it is after midnight before they are finished. I leave the kitchen while the cleaning is being done—a dirty, smelly job that would dampen my ardour considerably, were I a gunner. My rule is, "them as shoots, picks" and Morrill calls this fair enough, but most of the women hereabouts clean all the ducks as a matter of course.

After the plentiful game on the first day there are fewer ducks around until we begin to get colder or stormier weather and our gunners soon leave for home, although some of them return later for additional shooting. Not all our gunners are relatives, nor do they have to travel so far to reach the Island. Friends from Shag Harbour and near-by districts often come to spend a day or two at the lighthouse and go gunning with Morrill. The first friends we made in Shag Harbour were two men who came for a few days' shooting, and through them we came to know their wives and families. Clayton, whom I have mentioned, was one of them and he and his family have proved friends in need.

Clayton was one of the best shots around and had killed many ducks yet always he would return from a day's sport shaking his head and vowing, "Some day I'll get my revenge on those black-ducks!" Like all earnest gunners he believed the ducks are elusive and wary solely and vindictively for the purpose of thwarting gunners and making them wait around miserable in the wet and cold. Morrill shares this belief and becomes so exasperated at the maddening performances of the ducks. "The sons-a-guns!" he'll say, as if their perversity passed all comprehension.

Part of the fun of gunning, as of fishing, I am convinced lies in the yarns that good gunners love to spin. Every

little detail of wind and weather is remembered and enumerated.  I have heard hundreds of these tales as the men
sit around cleaning their guns after a day's shooting and I
dodge and weave back and forth, under, over and among
gun barrels and ramrods with greasy rags attached (as well
as innumerable rubber-booted and outstretched legs) as
I try to prepare a meal or wash my dishes.  After listening
to the stories and noticing the similarity of detail for
some time, I thought, "Why, I can tell a gunning yarn!
I believe I'll make up a good one and tell it to Morrill and
the others some time."

So I did.  Alas!  Like Queen Victoria they were not
amused.  Since that brash effort I have treated all phases
of gunning—including the yarns—with due respect.

When the duck season used to open on the first of
October the mosquitoes were still out in full strength over
the ponds and swamps.  A gunner arrived home one
night with a new alibi: he hadn't been able to shoot straight
because the mosquitoes had been driving their "stingers"
clean through his ear-lobes and clinching them on the
other side.

But the following evening when he again returned
empty handed, he was greeted with such jibes as, "Well
you can't blame it on the mosquitoes tonight," and
"No mosquitoes tonight with this north wind, boy."

"That's right," he replied, "no mosquitoes out tonight."
Then in a slow drawl with frequent pauses, "But the
wind—whistling through them holes—the mosquitoes bored
last night—well, you know—I wasn't used to it.  It
sounded right down queer—and put me off my aim a
mite."

Walter is the local visitor who comes gunning most
frequently; few winters have passed without one or more
visits from Walter.  Sometimes he gives Morrill a hand
with whatever work is in progress, often he and Morrill

spend a few days duck-hunting. Walter is easily discouraged, time without number he has arrived back duckless to drop dispiritedly into a chair and declare, "This ends it. I'm all through gunning. Getting too old. Going to hang up my gun for good." I offer consolation and encouragement, knowing that by the next morning he will be as keen as ever.

Walter doesn't know just what to think of some of Morrill's "rigs and contraptions" as he calls the various devices Morrill has made to overcome some of the difficulties of the place, partly because Morrill seldom tells him the truth about what purpose they are to serve. One spring Morrill made up a wooden tank for dipping his sheep; it was eighteen inches wide by about five feet long, its sides and one end straight, but the other end out of which the sheep walk onto a platform was slanted, not unlike the stern of a trawl-dory, only more so. It was a queer-looking rig, I suppose, to a fisherman whose mind naturally turns to boats, and Morrill found Walter examining it with a puzzled air.

"What might you call that?" Walter demanded.

"Well now, I'll tell you," said Morrill, "I made it for gunning in the Salt Water Pond. You see it's flat bottomed and will be fine in the shallow water there; it's deep enough so I can get in and crouch down out of sight," suiting the action to the word, "then this end . . ."

"My God, man," Walter interrupted in the voice of one who at last sees proof of suspected insanity, "Not in a contraption like that! You'll drown yourself."

I know Morrill would be pleased to have me share the shooting with him, but somehow I cannot bear the thoughts of killing. This is not very consistent of me, I realize, as I eat all game with relish. I do enjoy accompanying Morrill when he goes gunning and I go as often as I can leave the house, which is all too seldom. As I go for the sake of the walk with Morrill and to enjoy the outdoors, it really matters little to me whether or not we see and shoot many ducks, though naturally I do not stress this heretical attitude on my part.

Even when we went for a Sunday walk the first winters we were here, Morrill would insist on taking me to all the places where there might be ducks. Just in the midst of crossing the savannah, as I was poised on a tiny islet of raised moss and wondering if it would not sink beneath my feet before I could jump to another hummock, Morrill would be sure to hiss urgently, "Down. Get down," and point upward where I would see a duck or two flying towards us. Have you ever tried to flatten out on a wet hummock that you had doubted would be big enough to step on? Up to that time I hadn't either.

Or, Morrill would come close to whisper, "There should be ducks right over the beach here. Wait a minute and then crawl after me."

Then he would creep along, almost prone, with his dog, also flattened out in the moss and grass, inching along behind him, while I followed awkwardly on all fours—not even the promised sight of a duck could induce me to crawl through that wet, cold moss. My cap was always the wrong colour and I was supposed to tuck it into my pocket, lest I frighten the ducks! But in one respect Morrill showed remarkable foresight in picking a wife—my hair is a neutral brown and blends well with both swamp grass and rock-weed. Thank goodness.

Some evenings when Morrill planned to shoot as the ducks flew into the water holes in the savannah, he would place me in one small point of woods while he went to the one north of it. At such times I was supposed to either watch, and if any ducks came over me, step out and wave my arms in hopes of frightening them within gunshot of Morrill, *or* under other circumstances keep out of sight entirely, so as not to startle them. I well remember Morrill's parting words one evening as he left me to take up his position: "Now you stay here. Don't frighten the ducks. Whatever you do *don't let them see your face.*" He assures me now that he meant my face would be most easily seen by the ducks, but I wonder. A face to frighten ducks.

At times Morrill regrets taking me along. One evening we took our place behind a large boulder below tide mark and prepared to wait until some unsuspecting ducks feeding in with flood tide, should come within range. We waited and the tide crept gradually higher until it was lapping the base of our rock and half way up my rubber boots. The water was not quite freezing, but I decided my feet were, and I timidly suggested that I go home and thaw out, while Morrill waited for the ducks.

"Oh, you're not cold, dear, surely," said Morrill. "Don't go home yet. Look, right back of us here is that kelp bank. Go put your feet and legs in that, get right down in it. It's warm as toast, honestly. I've often got warm that way."

Perhaps he had, with his moisture-repelling oilskins over his high rubber boots. I was wearing woollen breeches, a fur jacket and knee-length boots, and my imagination, though partially benumbed by cold, was still functioning sufficiently to present a picture of the interior of a wet, decaying bank of kelp. Fortunately the situation, and my feet, were saved by two unwary ducks swimming into gunshot, and after Morrill got them he decided we'd go home.

The gunning expeditions I enjoyed most were when we built ourselves a blind on the savannah and waited for ducks to fly in over us. We took a hatchet along, cut some branches from a spruce and choosing a small group of spreading, stunted trees in the savannah, built them up with our branches until we and the dog were hidden as we crouched there. When the ducks flew in it was so dark that I saw nothing before Morrill swung his gun up, there was a crimson flash and roar, then he whirled in the opposite direction and fired again. The dog was out and away, but soon back with first one duck and then the other.

When we returned home Morrill gave me the gun, ducks and hatchet while he stopped to put up his dog. Tiny Anne and Lo met me at the door with the usual inquiry, "How many ducks, Mummy?"

I replied, "Daddy didn't have any luck, but see, Mummy got two with her hatchet."

The next time I returned empty handed. No hatchet, no ducks. The children were disappointed, "Mummy, you *should* have taken your hatchet."

The dogs are not so pleased when I accompany Morrill gunning. They feel definitely that woman's place is in the home and not tagging along when a dog and its master want to go for a little sport. Peggy was very jealous, and although she had been trained to keep behind, she would watch her chance and edge between me and Morrill, half tripping me, until I learned to walk well apart from him; and she would immediately thrust her head between us if she saw any signs of my closing the gap that separated us. I usually humoured her because I knew how she loved Morrill and considered me the wrong corner of the triangle, but if the going was rough or slippery and Morrill wished me to take his arm, he would have to speak very sharply to Peggy or slap her nose to make her stay behind us. If we were waiting in a thicket for the tide to rise sufficiently for shooting, Peggy would be told to lie behind us, as we sat chatting side by side. In no time at all Peggy would have wriggled over and little by little would succeed in pushing me aside and squeezing herself close to Morrill. Then she would relax with an air of triumph and contentment, after a supercilious glance or two in my direction.

Although Rags, our first dog, and Ted, the present duck dog, are both Chesapeakes with brown coats, Peggy was a cross between a Chesapeake and a Labrador retriever and had a black coat, though she kept the chest and build of the Chesapeakes.

Morrill claims that a dog will not be much good in the cold rough water here, no matter how carefully trained, unless they love the sport and are really keen on getting the ducks. Peggy certainly lived for her gunning jaunts with Morrill and nothing deterred her once she saw where a duck had fallen. She learned to dive after wounded ducks, and often caught one that had dived before it could return to the surface. When the surf was breaking too heavily for a dog to swim through, Morrill could often watch for a lull and send Peggy out through the momentarily lessened seas. Then, when she turned to come in, he watched the line of surf and would toss a stone or two beyond the breakers to keep her paddling there, until he whistled, and Peggy would come riding in on a wave that would deposit her at Morrill's feet. Sometimes she was too eager to wait for Morrill's directions, but started out alone. If the seas were deep, as off the Point, she dove through them before they broke, but in shallow water this was not possible. Once at the Kelp Cove I saw a wave pick her up, carry her several yards inshore in a tumbling smother of breaking water, and smash her down upon the close-packed sand; I thought every bone in her body must have been broken, but she scrambled to her feet, shook the sand and foam from her coat and turned to the sea again. On this attempt she timed the breaking seas better, was soon past them and had retrieved her duck.

Sometimes Morrill and I pick lovely clear days or evenings for our gunning trips together, at other times we

go when the leaden sea and sky are dour and foreboding.
Each aspect of the weather has its own fascination. We
have walked back together when the sky was still faintly
tinged by the sunset, and the brighter stars were reflected
across the serene ocean to the tiny pools among the rocks
at our feet, while the starlight on the snow-covered beach
and fields made walking as easy as in daylight. Again,
after lying hidden behind a rock and camouflaged with sea-
weed, the sullen grey sea before us and over us angry clouds
that whipped their ragged edges almost in our faces, while
sea and sky looked equally malignant, and the beach and
crowding trees only slightly less hostile, we have picked our
way home by flashlight over driftwood and through puddles
in the face of a rain sweeping in from the sea.

Although the duck-shooting has provided us with much
pleasure and brought us new friendships, it has also been
the cause of our greatest discouragement in the life here
and of (as far as we know) the only ill-feeling between us
and our neighbours in Shag Harbour.

For thirty years or more before we bought Bon Portage,
no owner had lived on the Island to enforce his rights, and
the lightkeepers had control over the government property
only. Consequently a certain element in the district had
been accustomed to having their own way about coming and
going over the Island, making use of wood for pot-bows,
gathering the berries and shooting the ducks, without so
much as by-your-leave; and they were reluctant to admit
our rights as owners.

First we found we had to put a stop to shooting before
the season, as some gunners, mostly boys scarcely old
enough to have a gun, were shooting the ducks in the
Ponds as early as August. Then we found there was some
jealousy, because the Shag Harbour gunners thought our
guests were getting too large a share of the ducks. We
decided in order to save any further hard feelings, and also

to help the black-ducks which were becoming scarce along the Atlantic seaboard, to have the Island made into a Sanctuary. Apparently local political pressure was brought to bear against this and we were forced to abandon our idea of Bon Portage as a Wild Bird Sanctuary, though I never see the ducks so happy and safe in our ponds in the summers but I regret that our plans could not have been carried through.

When Morrill's strict enforcement of "no shooting before the season" began to bear results in the increased number of ducks to be had each opening day, many Shag Harbour gunners, not satisfied with having free access to all the shooting at other times, began to come on that day as well and it finally ended in words between our guests and the Shag Harbourers and in general hard feelings.

Morrill had tried to explain his attitude and to talk things over with the Shag Harbour gunners, after all they are our neighbours, many of them had been friendly, any to whom we had appealed had been kind in helping us out with their boats, and we would be dependent on them in times of trouble. But among them were some who talked grandiloquently of old deeds and grants and "Fishermen's Rights" (which is supposed to give them a right to a few rods inland from the beach) and to claim that Morrill did not really own the Island and couldn't enforce his control.

We were sure our deed would hold, we had had legal advice that no such "Fishermen's Rights" existed and it looked as if we should have to prove our ownership of the Island by declaring it private property and arresting the first trespasser. Once we had proved our title we felt sure we could come to an understanding with the better element in the place. In no case did we plan to refuse the Island's gunning to those men who had been friendly and willingly co-operated in observing the game laws here.

I think we overlooked the country store debating clubs. No doubt the matter was talked over and discussed *ad nauseum* without Morrill's side of the question ever being presented or considered, until they convinced themselves and each other that Morrill, an outsider, was being greedy and selfish and infringing on their rights. They were affronted by our having more "outsiders" (my brothers and friends) coming to shoot, although we would never have dreamt of objecting to anyone they had cared to bring to the Island as their guest. I deeply resented their assumption that our choice of visitors should be limited by their opinion. In all their discussions no one seems to have remembered the many other islands in the vicinity that were open to everyone, nor to realize that the only reason for good shooting on Bon Portage was the trouble Morrill had taken to enforce the observance of the opening date.

Our chief difficulty in the whole matter lay in the fact that we do not own the foreshore, that strip of beach lying between high and low water marks. It is Crown Land, so the men of Shag Harbour (and we, and the world in general) have certain rights along the shore of the Island, including, no doubt, the right to shoot there. On the other hand, we own everything above high tide mark and the greater part of the shooting is done on and over our land.

The Shag Harbour gunners declared (with but one exception) that if Morrill attempted to keep them off the Island the opening day of the season, "Every man with a gun in Shag Harbour" would be along the foreshore that dawn and if they got no ducks themselves they would see that our friends got none either. Furthermore, they would henceforth refuse the use of their boats to us and to our company.

We felt we must assert our ownership of the Island but we hated to think of Morrill facing hostility every time he went to the Mainland. We decided we would have to make near-by Wood's Harbour our port of call although it meant a longer run for the little boat. We felt heartsick and discouraged at the turn things had taken, we had hoped we were beginning to be accepted as belonging to the place.

Finally one of the Shag Harbour men proposed a compromise, and after some discussion an agreement was reached. The Shag Harbour men gave up all rights to the foreshore on the opening day of the season and promised to treat us as kindly as before in regards to their boats. In return Morrill allowed them all the shooting in the Salt Water Pond, the little Northeast Pond and one side of Woody Point, while they kept strictly above Flag Pond and Kelp Cove. Except when we have company the Shag Harbour men are welcome to shoot anywhere on the Island, and any time but the first day our friends go where they please. Since then we have had no trouble, though I hear all is not sweetness and light amongst the Shag Harbourers that shoot on the Northern End. We have heard no more of our not owning the Island and I think many of the men now feel that Morrill was merely trying to protect himself, not being greedy or infringing on anyone's prerogatives.

I was glad when the trouble was settled amicably; I had never dreamed of "quarrels with our neighbours"—way off here in the ocean, but so it was!

Most of the ducks shot here are black-ducks, some of which breed on the Island but most of them come from the inland lakes and ponds as they freeze over and cease to provide feed. Other birds here are Teal, Shell-ducks, Whistlers, Coots, Old Squaws, Sea-ducks, a few Geese and an occasional duck we are not able to identify.

Usually sea-ducks are not plentiful along our shores, but önce in a great while huge flocks make a brief sojourn here. I shall always remember one such flock. There had been a heavy wind and high seas, then overnight the wind changed, so that the water in the lee of the Point was the most sheltered for some miles around. When we woke in the morning we were amazed to see what appeared to be a blanket of ducks spread over the surface of the sea, stretching for half a mile up the shore and extending outward for a depth of a hundred and fifty yards. The seas were not breaking but rising in lazy swells, and each wave passed beneath them, ducks rose and fell, so closely packed together that no water was visible between the individual birds. I have never seen anything remotely resembling that sight; there must have been thousands of sea-ducks on that strip of sheltered and unbreaking water, many of them the beautifully marked drakes, or pieds as we call them, whose glossy black and dazzling white seemed to predominate over the more sober browns of the females. Walter, who was here at the time, said he had heard seamen tell of similar "rafts" of ducks off Newfoundland and Labrador, but neither he nor we had ever seen the like along this coast.

From all the ducks that are picked at the lighthouse, the feathers come to me. I make pillows for our own beds and present a pair to each of our friends and relatives who get married. I have a pair of pillows made from duck feathers my mother had when she started housekeeping almost fifty years ago, and I cannot tell that they have lost any of their resilience. One thing must be guarded against, pillows containing the wild duck feathers must not be left in the sun or near a fire, as the heat draws the oil and ruins both feathers and ticking.

So apart from the many appetizing meals which they provide, the wild ducks also serve other purposes, the most important being the sport and insurance against boredom or loneliness that Morrill finds in his gunning and the friends it brings to the lighthouse. Laurie is a chip off the old block. He shot his first duck last winter and already, at fourteen, considers himself an experienced gunner.

## 15

## SCHOOL DAYS

WE HAD scarcely got Betty June safely into "the family circle," as Anne loved to phrase it, and were settling into the changed routine that a baby makes necessary, when a new problem arose. By late summer of that year Anne was five-and-a-half and mentally ready to start school. Morrill's brother was with us as help, making a family of six, one of them a baby and none able to lend a hand at the multitude of tasks that confronted me each day. At that time we had practically none of the time and labour-saving improvements that we acquired slowly but surely throughout the years, no engine for washing, no convenient supply of soft hot water, and I still lacked the speed and skill that constant repetition has brought to many household tasks. I felt that I must start Anne's lessons but couldn't see how I was going to find the necessary time, since I think no phase of a child's education needs the constant help and supervision that the first year's work requires.

However, I have found in many of the tasks we have faced that the difficulties, when actually confronted, do not prove as insurmountable as they had appeared. I knew Anne was quick mentally and possessed of an amazing grasp of and appreciation for the children's books I read to her, and that she had an unusual memory for words and stories.

I felt sure an hour's supervised study each day would give her the most of what she would acquire in the first year at a public school. The thing was to find the hour! Often during that winter I could not find a minute, not to mention an hour, until the evening after the baby was in bed and the chores finished. This was a poor time for Anne to put her mind to lessons, and I worried at the handicaps that seemed to face her, yet at the end of the school year I found that she had learned the essentials of the primary work and would rank high in the list of scholars in any school.

The next term was easier. We had no hired man, the baby needed less care, and Laurie was old enough to do lessons with Anne, instead of distracting her attention and arousing her envy as he played in freedom while she was forced to study. I was able to allot some time to teaching them during both morning and afternoon and each learned more quickly with a fellow student. Since they were so near an age they studied many subjects together. I had a child's table, made for me on my seventh birthday by my father, and this became the "school-table" (it is still so known, although the children have all outgrown it for several years). Each had a kindergarten chair which was the right size for the table. I bought a piece of blackboard cloth, which tacked to the outside of the cupboard door and fitted with an eraser dangling on a cord beside it became their blackboard. They had white and coloured chalk and did much of their work on the blackboard as well as drawing and printing for fun after school hours.

About this time we had several exceptionally cold winters, and throughout the months of severest cold the school equipment had to be moved into the living-room as the kitchen proved too cold and draughty for the children to remain in it for any length of time. (Each winter sees a few days on which we have to do our school work in the warmer living-room.) The blackboard was tacked up on the wall and became a source of great delight in the evenings when the children found their Daddy would draw for them Walapuses and Galumpises. Since I never could draw these "frabjous" creatures, and they varied from evening to evening, becoming more ridiculous and complicated as time went on, I won't attempt to describe them. I never heard of any curriculum containing a study of them except that of the Bon Portage school.

Anne and Lo had letter and numeral cards, a few map jig-saws, and any helps I knew of and could afford, to make their lessons interesting. Lo early showed his ability in numbers and his total lack of it in spelling—this still hampers him in written work. Anne's spelling and reading came to her with little effort, but she found numerical work more trying. One thing in which my lack of time for teaching showed disastrously was in their writing: both are poor penmen, I think because I could not always over-see their writing and they formed bad habits that I could not spare the time to make them overcome.

Until Anne was in Grade 5 and Laurie in Grade 4, I taught them myself from text-books that I had kept from my teaching days, and those supplied by the Shag Harbour

School District. Then I read a newspaper article on
the Correspondence Course provided for children isolated
as ours were, and after some correspondence with the
Department of Education for the province, Anne and
Laurie were enrolled under the Correspondence Study
Division which is centred in Halifax at the Nova Scotia
Technical College.

The parcel of lessons that arrived shortly afterward
looked most intriguing; and the new books, many of them
different from the ones we had been using, were hailed with
joy. Though we had nearly finished the work of the
grades they were studying, and the Superintendent of the
Course had written that they could take up the lessons
where new work began, the children were so pleased with
their new assignments that they decided to do them all,
and they finished twenty of the prescribed thirty lessons
before they stopped work for the summer. They started
in March, so I felt that they must have had a good understanding of the grade's work under my tutelage and felt
relieved that this was so. The last ten lessons of the
grade were finished before the children began the next
year's work.

My children found the lessons interesting and instruc-
tive, and personally I think this Correspondence Course
excellently fills the need for which it was designed. The
Correspondence Study Division sends out a year's work,
divided into a number of weekly assignments—in the lower
grades the number is usually thirty or thirty-five lessons
to cover the work of a grade. My children ordinarily
completed the year's work before the end of May. When
a pupil completes a week's assignment it is sent to the
Nova Scotia Technical College for marking and grading.
An unsatisfactory lesson must be repeated, making use
of the explanations and help that comes back with the
corrected paper.

For the common school grades the Department of Education provides materials and paper on which to work and stamped envelopes for mailing the completed lessons. When pupils reach the High School grades they provide for themselves everything but the Course of Instruction which includes the lesson assignments. They use the same texts prescribed for regular High School work.

In the lower grades the children are sent the usual text-books for the province and also a few excellent additional books, partly to replace the oral lessons that would be given by a teacher, and partly to compensate somewhat for the extra books on certain subjects that would be available in school libraries.

I think it would be possible, and not unduly difficult, for a child of average intelligence to obtain an education with no other help than what the Correspondence Course provides. Of course, a member of the family who could help when difficulties arise would make his studies easier, but the teacher who marks his papers will answer questions and explain any part of the work which the pupil does not understand from his texts and the additional information that accompanies each lesson assignment. I try to discuss the lessons and to help my children with any troublesome points, since to wait for explanations from their teacher might mean delays of weeks, here where the mail is so infrequent during the stormy months of winter. I like, too, for them to read their literature aloud to me, since I should be sorry for them to miss the music of poetry and the cadences and smoothness of good prose. I do not agree with the modern tendency to stress the length of time in which a child can read a selection; speed will come with reading, and the garbled and half-baked ideas I have heard quoted from articles, which on reading prove to be completely innocent of such content, would make me very loath to drop the old stress on the *meaning* of a selection.

Laurie prides himself on the speed with which he reads, but he sometimes misses a finer point, while both girls, who never think of speed, read as quickly and grasp what they read more completely.

When Anne and Laurie started languages, Latin and French, I tried to help them with the sounds and pronunciation, although I think a class is more suitable for this work than a single pupil and teacher, unless that teacher speak the language fluently and well. As I acquired my knowledge of languages more by eye than by ear, I am not such a teacher, and I am afraid instructors who give their pupils a speaking acquaintance with foreign languages are still all too few, practically non-existent in the smaller schools. Laurie did not care for French and dropped it in Grade 9. His pronunciation would have to be heard to be believed and he had no patience with their idioms. "Well, why don't they say what they mean?" he would demand in exasperation. He can see more "sense" in Latin, but it is not his favourite subject. Anne, on the other hand, likes languages and does better work in them than in mathematical or scientific subjects.

The children have a regular time-table and we strive to follow it. School time extends from 9 to 11:45 in the mornings, with a recess from 10:30 to 10:45; and from 1:30 to 3 or 3:30 in the afternoons, with at least an hour's study in the evenings when they have reached High School, or when behind in their lesson schedule. When we had a hired man we kept rather strictly to our time-table, except in case of sickness on my part or on the part of one of the pupils; but since the war, Laurie's lesson hours are often interrupted or postponed from sheer necessity, because there are so many things about the Light and even more about landing and launching the boat, that one person cannot handle alone and which must be done.

Betty June started her school career with the Correspondence Division and has made good progress. I think Anne and Laurie got a more solid foundation in Arithmetic from the older texts and methods that I taught them than the prescribed texts have given Betty June. Another lack that can scarcely be avoided in a Correspondence Course is in drawing lessons, although the first few grades have picture appreciation lessons and some drawing instructions. I had given Anne and Laurie lessons in drawing such as I had used when I was teaching, but when Betty June started her education I had three pupils in three grades and could not find opportunity to work any extra subjects into our crowded day. I did make an effort to oversee Betty June's writing lessons, and at present she bids fair to become a good writer.

The teacher who marks the papers for the lower grades is most friendly and takes a personal interest in her pupils. She and Betty June carry on an intermittent correspondence, and Betty June includes her among her "penpals." We are still hoping she will come some day to pay us the visit she has promised. The teacher who marked the work for Grades 7 and 8 turned out to be a friend of my father's, who startled and disconcerted Lo (who had no idea of his teacher's identity) by threatening to tell his grandfather if he did not improve his careless writing! In the High School grades the papers on the various subjects are marked by different instructors, so there is not the same opportunity for a personal feeling to establish itself.

Both Anne and Betty June write "poetry"; Anne is shy about letting me see hers, but I share Betty June's enjoyment of what she has written. Betty June wrote her first verse as a lesson assignment when she was eight. She did it so effortlessly and quickly that I encouraged her to keep trying. It was no masterpiece but as a poem on "First Snow" I felt it was as good as I would expect from a Grade 4 scholar:

> The forest is silver
> The ground is white.
> The earth is blanketed
> Softly with snow,
> Children are laughing
> Wherever you go.

Then she wrote about the dancing waves, "a frill on the dress of the sea," which I considered showed imagination.

The only bit of Anne's verse I know I came across by accident on the back of an old calendar. It dealt with a dashing but heartless (apparently) buccaneer who sang this refrain:

> "Oh, I can love little or I can love long,
> I can find a new sweetheart when the old one is gone,
> I can tell them I love them to give their hearts ease,
> But when their back's to me I love whom I please."

Both girls when smaller wrote stories and "novels" but Anne did much more of this than did Betty June. I have never seen these works, but I know from her compositions that Anne expresses herself well.

When Anne was in Grade 9 she received a brochure sent by the Correspondence Division of Manitoba's Department of Education to pupils of the similar division in other Provinces. With it was a letter asking the recipient to write Manitoba's pupils about life in his or her Province and to send the letters in care of the Correspondence Division. Anne was surprised and impressed by the variety of Manitoba's beauty spots and wrote a letter as requested. I am sorry that I didn't read it as she got in reply a very nice letter from Miss Pearman, who was in charge of Grade 9 English in Manitoba's Correspondence

Division, saying that she liked Anne's letter so much she was mimeographing it and distributing it to her Grade 9 pupils throughout the province and asking them to write Anne personally. Well, naturally we were all very puffed up about this! Anne received about forty letters from Manitoba boys and girls, most of them nicely written and very interesting, and she answered them by a group letter which Miss Pearman again distributed. Anne sent all the letters she had received to her grandfather to read, and he was very pleased to think she had made such a good impression with her writing.

Letters play a large part in our lives and the girls carry on rather a voluminous correspondence with "pen-pals," cousins and friends. Laurie refuses to put pen to paper except under the most drastic coercion.

To get back to our schoolroom—while the children soon learned to work along at their lessons without a great deal of help, it can be understood that during lesson hours I was tied pretty closely to the schoolroom—otherwise known as the kitchen. A little help to each of three soon runs into time, then there were reading lessons and dictated spellings that needed my attention, so that lessons and preparations of meals and the ordinary chores that are done in the kitchen filled in most of my day. As all three were normal healthy children, considerable coaxing and prodding was often necessary to get them through their day's assignments, and extra fine days or unusually interesting events more than once played havoc with our time-table. My being tied to the kitchen during school hours made it very difficult to keep the work in the rest of the house under control. Much of it had to be postponed until Friday after school and Saturday, with the baking often pushed over into Sunday, so that my week-ends were too busy. Washdays also were hard, as much from the strain of trying to keep the youngsters at their lessons while I was forced to be absent from the kitchen, as from the actual labour involved. Laurie, as might be expected, welcomed these opportunities for a little diversion as Heaven sent, and he usually improved them by teasing Betty June so that she accomplished little more than he did.

The little kitchen was cramped and crowded with three pupils, but when Anne reached Grade 9 and Laurie Grade 8 they were promoted to new quarters, that is, they were allowed to work by themselves at the big table in the living-room, though this necessitated a great deal of running back and forth (up and down the three steps between kitchen and living-room) on my part. Though Anne was by this time a conscientious and hard-working student, Lo still tends to skylark if left too long to his own devices.

Anne and Betty June are good scholars, they do their work well because they enjoy their lessons and wish to send in creditable assignments. Laurie can do as well as they, but he does it only because I give him no peace otherwise. I often think it is a shame that I should have to add the supervision of his lessons to all the many things the mother of a teen-age boy has to oversee, such as clean hands and ears, combed hair, to say nothing of table manners and the proper treatment of a younger sister. However, though he nearly drives me to drink with his slow-motion studying and I must be a source of constant harassment to him, he seems to forget and forgive once school hours are over. He feels that this love for studying must be a feminine failing, since Anne and Betty June share my attitude for it, and as such he endeavours to show a proper masculine tolerance towards the question, although he is often sorely tried. Morrill is every bit as anxious as I for Laurie to get an education, but since he leaves the school-work in my hands, and his remonstrances usually take the form of a mild, "Now, son, you want to get your lessons done as Mother says," he does not appear as rabidly irrational to Laurie as I must with my perpetual "school work first."

Laurie's education does not stop with what he learns from his books. At fifteen he knows and understands the engines and mechanical devices about the place, can run the boat, drive the ox, run the mower, make hay, care for the Light, identify the planes for our A.D.C. work and turn his hand to innumerable jobs. Best of all, he is completely dependable at all these tasks. Taking everything into consideration, I think he is getting a great deal from the life here; he is learning to be self-reliant, and that work can be interesting and a source of contentment as well as a means of livelihood. He loses, however, the fun a boy gets from group games, and the joy of being one of a gang.

We have been especially fortunate in the many books and magazines that come to our home, and the children have a knowledge of current literature as well as of the old classics. Much of this was due to my father's kindness in sharing with us his excellent library, including his "Book-of-the-Month" selections, and in forwarding us his magazines. These, with periodicals to which we subscribe and a yearly gift of *The Reader's Digest*, give us quite a variety of reading. Among ourselves we often give books for birthdays and Christmases, the modern cheap reprints of classics are certainly god-sends to folks situated as we are away from public libraries and with insatiable thirsts for reading. Several of our books have been read and re-read by the children until they barely hang together. Laurie loves particularly books of exploration and most of all those dealing with the far North; he must almost know by heart Peter Freuchen's *Arctic Adventure*. Among more recent books his favourite is *Storm*, by George Stewart: the weather plays a big part in our life here, and he found this book extremely fascinating. Betty June's favourite books are now the "Anne" books and similar tales by L. M. Montgomery; but she reads everything that comes to the house. Anne Gordon would probably choose Dickens as her favourite author.

Dad also kept me more or less posted on educational developments. Though he retired from active teaching some years before his death, he did not lose his interest in schools and teaching, and always kept us in mind so that he was often able to send us interesting and helpful material.

I feel that the children do not get sufficient religious instruction as it is impossible for them to get to church and Sunday School except on rare occasions. When they were small I always spent some time with them each Sunday afternoon, reading and explaining stories from Sunday School papers which friends sent us. They still receive and read these papers, and now Betty June and I play and sing a few hymns at the piano each Sunday morning; the children were taught the childhood prayers and we opened school each morning with the Lord's Prayer, Betty June as youngest learned to say grace at table, but this is not regularly observed and I realize that all we do is very casual and leaves much to be desired. Although I am not a member of any church and no great believer in doctrines and forms, I do think every child (and aren't we all children in this?) needs the spiritual atmosphere that the church and its established ritual gives, and the sense of being one in a community of spirits seeking the Divine. So many children now do not have this influence in their lives and I am sorry mine are amongst them.

When I was a child my father gave me that excellent book for children, *Hurlburt's Story of the Bible*, and Anne early began to read this. It is now read to shreds and tatters and on Betty June's tenth birthday I gave her a new copy. I suppose mine are as familiar as most children with the story content of the Bible and they will read more from the Bible itself as they grow older. I hope, too, that when they have the opportunity they will attend church and find there spiritual strength and realization of the brotherhood of man that Jesus taught and that has been so persistently and tragically forgotten. I do not think attending church is an end in itself, but I think it can be a help to an end, the developing of that inner essential self we call our soul.

Another lack we have not been able to circumvent is instruction in music and this I deeply regret as both Anne and Betty June show signs of having musical ability.

I never had the advantage of a musical education—the salary of a schoolteacher with a large family didn't run to any frills. Often on Sunday afternoons when I was small Mother would play on the organ and sing for us some hymns and old songs; but the organ was left behind when we moved to Bedford and it was not until I was teaching and able to purchase a piano that there was again a musical instrument in our home. I had hoped to learn to play the piano and thus fulfil one of my dearest dreams, but teaching took most of my time and it was not always possible to find an occasion to practise in a small home full of lively brothers and friends of all the various members of the family. Before I had learned more than the notes and one or two simple tunes, I changed my school and never again before my marriage had an opportunity to study music. I always felt this lack of musical education was a great disadvantage to me, both socially and in my teaching, apart from the fact that I loved good music and would have enjoyed above everything being able to play some instrument, quite for its own sake.

When I married, my piano was left at home and the first few years at Bon Portage we could not afford to have it moved and it would have been useless for me to hope to find time to play it.

Morrill had been more fortunate than I and had had
some instruction on the violin. Anne Gordon early
showed a love for music and a desire to learn to play her
Daddy's violin, so the Christmas after she started school
lessons Santa Claus brought her a half-size violin. She
was overjoyed. Morrill took time each evening during the
fall and winter to teach her. He started with fifteen-minute
periods, and I taught her the notes and counted time for her
to practise during the day.

Many a time I looked at my floor, sadly in need of
sweeping, looked at Anne's eager little face and her tenderly
grasped violin, and said, "Sure, Mummy will help you a
little while." Then I would turn my back and shut my
mind to the work that waited and count the time for Anne's
violin exercises. I hope she remembers that I did what I
could to help her and forgets that my housework was often
neglected.

Before many years Morrill felt that Anne had learned
all he could teach her and she was able to get a great deal
of pleasure from her music; she still does, although she
has had no further instruction.

Anne was still small when she played her violin for a
Captain Kenney (retired) who came to spend a day at the
lighthouse. He was pleased with her playing and said,
"Do you know, I have a violin in my clothes-closet at
home. I bought it in Boston one time, I thought I'd learn
to play it but I never could pick out more than a hymn or
two. They tell me it's quite a good fiddle. Next time
you're off to Shag Harbour I'll give it to you."

And so he did; one day as Morrill was passing he
brought the violin to him and insisted that he take it to
Anne. We shall always feel grateful to Captain Kenney
and think Anne was very lucky to have a good violin given
her so unexpectedly. I am sure if the Captain knew the

pleasure it has given her and the pride she takes in her violin, he would feel repaid for his kindness.

Laurie also started to play on the violin. He did very well, too, but he found it "too much like lessons" and dropped it. As for poor little Betty June, we've been so busy of late years that Morrill has never had time to help her with the violin.

We had Morrill's phonograph when we came here and a fairly good, though not large, collection of records of classical music. Then, when we had been here five or six years, we bought a radio and that has been a marvellous link with the outside world; but as the children's lessons occupy most of the evenings and we cannot sit up late enough to get the best musical programmes, we do not get as much enjoyment from the wonderful music it brings over the air as we would like. The reception here is wonderful and we have enjoyed some of the programmes to the full, when we have felt that the next day's duties did not demand that we get our rest. One winter I was able to listen to almost all of the Metropolitan's Saturday afternoon broadcasts by re-arranging my work schedule, cleaning the living-room and scrubbing and waxing the floor during the hours the operas were on the air. After we had had the radio a year or two we lent our phonograph to Clayton when he was ill, and later to another invalid, so it is still in Shag Harbour, although I doubt if it is still in operation.

Then at long last, after we had waited for eight years, came the dawn and we could see our way clear to pay for having our piano shipped to us and hire a boat to bring it on. Morrill had long before decided that if we could find money for the moving expenses, that he could "figger out" a way to get it on the Island. We were all in a state of great excitement when we learned that the piano, shipped from Bedford, had arrived in Shag Harbour.

No one in the village seemed very hopeful of our chances of getting it to the lighthouse safe and sound, but finally Morrill persuaded one of the men to use his boat and lend his assistance for the purpose. Several young men offered to come along to help.

It goes without saying that the trip was left until a suitable day presented itself, one that was "slick calm," and with no seas breaking at the Point, since it was necessary to land the piano near the lighthouse. We had no cart that could carry it from the boathouse landing, and no means of lifting it into one, if we had. Finally a perfectly smooth day arrived and Morrill went to Shag Harbour to help and oversee operations.

It was comparatively simple on the Shag Harbour end, as the wharf there has a derrick-wheel by which it could be lowered and many men to lend a hand. It was not put into a big boat, but on a platform of boards across two trawl-dories that had been lashed together, and this double dory with its raised load was towed behind the motor-boat. The trip across the Sound was made at high water, so that the tide was beginning to ebb when they reached this side. The trawl-dories were rowed in to a comparatively level stretch of shore and when grounded were left until the tide had receded from around them; then heavy planks were laid as skids from the dory sides and over the rocks. Then our man-power (five men strong) went to work. The piano was pushed and pulled along the planks until it reached the bank. The bank at this spot is eight feet high and Morrill had planned to make with his planks an inclined plane up over it and utilize his ox to help pull the heavy load. The men were impatient of this delay and so somehow, by main pushing and pulling, they got the load up over the bank. The rest was easy sailing. The ox was harnessed to the load and he dragged it along the path to the front doorsteps where the men again took over.

When the piano was unpacked from its crate it went easily through the door, up the three steps to the living-room and into the corner where the stairway forms a large alcove. That was a great moment, I can tell you, when we at last saw it in its place! Morrill informed me it was here to stay, he would never tackle the job of moving it off the Island, and the other men nodded their approval of this statement. Getting it here was quite a job, but when Morrill started to pay the men they wished to take only the price of the gas used. The owner of the boat said he considered it only neighbourly to give a hand at such an undertaking. Well, we thought it was fine of them, but we insisted on paying them something, though little enough, for all their trouble.

The children were so pleased and happy with the addition to our home! During the first week I had to partition the time into fifteen-minute periods, so they could all have an equal opportunity to "play." The piano had been played very little since I bought it eleven years before and the keys were still stiff, so I encouraged them to use it all they liked after explaining to them how to be careful.

It is surprising how much enjoyment we have had from the piano, considering the fact that none of us could play a note when it arrived, as I had forgotten the little I once knew. First it affords us a great deal of pleasure when our friends and relatives visit here and play for us. Morrill often gets out his violin and plays, too, although his fingers are so terribly stiff from the hard work he does that he can play only the simpler of the lovely pieces he formerly knew. We have grand sing-songs in the evenings (when someone will play for us) and the children are allowed to sit up until it is over and I serve hot cocoa and sandwiches or toast and jam. No musicale was ever so gala an event nor half as much fun as these evenings are for us all.

I have learned to play simple songs and hymns and although I don't flatter myself that my playing would be tolerable to anyone else, nevertheless it is a source of real enjoyment to me. I know I can never hope to play well, even if I had the time and the instruction, as my hands are small and stiff from the hard work I have done and do. Then I seldom have time to spare for practise—from the time the spring work starts until the long autumn evenings come again, I never touch the piano except on Sunday mornings to play a few hymns for Betty June. Throughout the late fall and winter I take an hour or so for the piano each evening after supper unless other duties prevent, but my improvement year by year is very slight indeed. Only a person who has felt the same sense of frustration and hopeless longing that has filled me when I have sat dumb and bound before a piano could understand the joy I get from playing a simple tune. This is quite different from the pleasure I receive from listening to good music.

Anne, with the knowledge she had gained from learning to play her violin, soon could play the piano for her enjoyment and ours. Laurie is completely indifferent to the piano as he was to the violin. Betty June is learning to play with the help of instruction books, and loves it. I wish with all my heart that we could give the girls a musical education but at least they have learned to love music and can, if they really desire it, take up its study when they are more advantageously situated for it and earning the money for such a training.

Being on the Island holds complications even for owning a piano: it has never been tuned since its arrival here, and so far I have not been able to contact a tuner who might make the trip to the lighthouse to do it for us.

Besides the "book-learning" that the children receive, a life such as we lead here opens many avenues to knowledge about the world in which we exist. Birds and flowers lead us into learning a great deal as we find and identify new specimens in the books we have on those subjects. Nature herself is very near and real, not only the pleasant, calm-faced Nature that most children meet on country hikes and summer vacations spent on a farm, but also Nature in her tantrums, sulky and obstinate, and in her violent rages that leave one awed and helpless. These off-spring of ours should not grow up with an overweening sense of their importance in the scheme of things as a whole.

From the time Anne, and then the others, started asking questions about the world surrounding them I have endeavoured to answer those questions relating to sex neither more nor less fully than others. Mating and birth among the wild animals and our domestic stock are accepted as naturally as they occur in the phenomena of the various seasons. I think a reticence about adult love is natural between parents and children, but I hope I have never shown any embarrassment in discussing or explaining any questions that have been brought to me. When Betty June was coming, Anne and Lo, although they were very small, shared our plans and happy anticipations.

No doubt the children have heard less of the evil vocabulary of school-age youngsters than they might have heard attending school, but I am under no delusion that they have not encountered plenty of it. There seems to be no way in which parents can protect their children from that unpleasant phase of childhood, but at least we can see that they have accurate knowledge to counterbalance the nasty whisperings. None of my children will ever suffer the disillusioning shock I felt when I was informed in the trenchant language of a girl companion all the facts (albeit somewhat twisted) leading up to and including the birth of my adored baby brother.

Since money, or the lack of it, plays so great a part in the life of us all, Morrill and I decided when Anne and

Laurie were very small to acquaint them with money and its use. There is little opportunity here for them to run to the store for candy and ice-cream, but for that reason they would be less familiar with the value of what was bought for them. So before they reached school age they were started on their "allowances." Saturday was "pay-day" and each week they were given as many cents as there were years in their age. This was theirs to spend when they went to Shag Harbour, to save for special things like an extra ball or a jack-knife or towards Christmas gifts, or to put in their little banks and later into a savings account at the bank at Barrington. When war broke out they all had money enough to buy at least one Certificate, and now of course their savings go to the purchase of War Stamps.

Laurie earns extra money by salvaging abandoned buoys and other lobster gear that the storms bring ashore and selling them to the fishermen. He really earns this money, driving the ox up and back over the wind-swept beaches, and working in the cold wet kelp to collect the gear. The green glass balls, the size of large grapefruit, that are used as floats and called "bobbers," are among the things he saves to sell; we all keep our eyes open for bobbers as we walk along the beaches, since one of them means ten cents for Laurie. He has bought himself a .22 rifle and several things dear to boyish hearts that we could not afford to buy him, and has a sizable amount in War Certificates. He knows what every dollar means in cold hard work, and while we hope he will make his living in an easier fashion, he has learnt that money doesn't grow on bushes.

The girls have both of necessity learned housework and the cooking of simple meals, since when I have been ill it has been a case of "Root, hog, or die." When Anne was too small to manage alone Morrill lent a hand at the cooking and although she was glad of his help she did not always approve of his methods. She was only twelve when she wrote her Grandma:

"Mummy is sick and Daddy made cookies. The kitchen was a cloud of flour and Daddy was rushing back and forth, saying, 'Where's this?' and 'Where's that?' Daddy is a very energetic cook. Sometimes I think he uses too much energy and not enough discretion."

As for the ability of our children to mix with the outside world only time will tell us that. They have never been unduly shy, the number of guests who visit us here have helped in preventing that. Anne Gordon is this year staying in Bedford and studying Grade 10 there. Her letters sound happy and interested in her work, she seems to have made some friends and her marks place her among the better scholars in her class.

When the children were all younger and too small to go to Shag Harbour to see their friends, they made out splendidly with The Gang. I never belonged and know very little about this group and indeed they are nearly forgotten now; I think they were mostly cowboys, as they were products of Anne's imagination and at that time all her interest lay in the Wild West. Betty June was usually the victim of Indians or robbers and as such spent much of her time waiting contentedly to be rescued by The Gang; she was too small to play a more noble part or to go "galloping" about the fields and through the woods. Each portion of the Island had a name and imaginary inhabitants—we still speak of one open bushy stretch as "The Rudds' Country" from the name it bore in the days of The Gang, though I don't know where the name Rudd came from.

They all played well together, but Betty June is almost four years younger than Laurie, while little more than a year separates him from Anne; consequently the two older ones treated Betty June with no little condescension. Their most telling remark, if she ventured to join in their reminiscences (!) was, "You weren't here then: you were only a little angel up in Heaven."

This angelic state was their own idea of an existence before the present one; Betty June is not one, however, to be relegated indefinitely to the background (even a heavenly one).

One day I was listening as the two older ones were describing the fun they used to have, when every Sunday morning they were allowed to come into Mummy's and Daddy's big bed for a frolic and tussle with Daddy.

"*Every Sunday morning* we'd do that," concluded Laurie.

"I used to . . ." began Betty June.

"You weren't here. You were only . . ." started Laurie in the old overbearing way.

But Betty June had heard that one too often. "Well, *I* don't care. I used to get in bed with God *every* morning."

This left Laurie completely nonplussed.

The children have never lacked for pets. Although the dogs cease to be pets when they outgrow puppyhood, there are always cats and kittens to be loved and Anne's favourite "Pinknose" has been with us for twelve years. Other friends have been "Gulliver the Gull," who arrived out of the fog one day and stayed for two weeks to be pampered with every delicacy that the children thought might appeal to a gullish appetite, only to leave as suddenly and unexpectedly as he arrived; and Jack the Canada gander, who spent a summer in and around the Pond, but left when the wild geese flew over one lowering fall evening. Most appealing of all were three tiny wild rabbits that had been deserted by their mother. Anne, by feeding them warm milk from a medicine dropper, kept them alive for a week or so, and was tragically sorry when they died.

Each new calf is claimed as the special pet of one or the other of the children. Tiny orphan lambs are much loved and we have raised many on bottles, even bringing up a sturdy pair of twins in this fashion. (Morrill, who really knows better, but cannot overcome the temptation to create a stir over nothing, caused quite a sensation at the time by asking at the Shag Harbour store for two nursing nipples as there was "a pair of twins at the light-house"!)

As can be imagined the theatre and moving pictures play a very small part in our life. None of the children have ever seen a play or more than half a dozen pictures. When "Snow White" was presented as a matinee in Barrington we made an effort and took the children to see it. Of course they loved it and so did Morrill and I. But it was a run of eight miles each way in our little boat and while we were in the theatre the fog shut in, so that we had the long run back in the late foggy afternoon through waters with which we were not familiar, having been to Barrington by boat only once before. We would not make the trip except for some special occasion, and now we cannot leave the Light and are homebound.

Children are born actors, I think, for Anne and Laurie began acting out the stories I told them when "The Three Little Pigs" was still their favourite; I suppose Laurie was two and a half that winter. Laurie acted the parts of all the little pigs—I can see him yet, his head well inside the cardboard carton that was the house of the pigs, but his fat little bottom bulging above and behind it, though apparently invisible to the wolf, who, only slightly less rotund, but wearing an old fur neckpiece to prevent any possible mistake in identity, rapped loudly at the top of the carton and demanded to be let in.

Anne had a very vivid imagination and she never curbed it. I think it was too much for Laurie at times.

In the midst of a series of commands from Anne, "Now, Lo, you're . . ." and "Lo, you be . . ." I often saw him stop, stand up and say to himself distinctly and positively, "I Laurie Morrill Richar'son," as if he feared he might lose his real identity altogether in the make-believe world that Anne was so rapidly building about them both.

"Hansel and Gretel" was another great favourite when the children all became a little older; it was written as a play in one of their Readers. Morrill and I used to be impressed for the roles of father and mother in the first act, after the living-room furniture had been completely disarranged and all sorts of old garments dragged in to supply costumes. Morrill was a great trial to the rest of the cast, he would *not* learn his lines, and insisted upon substituting the names of the most exotic foods for those of the plain fare he was supposed to produce from his bundle. Then he would be dragged off-stage and instructed anew, and finally disregarded in despair, and the show would go on to the climax, when Anne as the witch was thrust into the oven (her head put into the old phonograph cabinet) and Hansel and Gretel went on their way rejoicing.

Betty June particularly would glory in taking part in a school play. She recites and reads clearly and with expression and has a love of posing and posturing that would serve her well.

Anne is now away at school and in a year or two at most Laurie must leave home for further education. That is one of the greatest disadvantages here. I would so much prefer to keep them with me during their High School years and to share and enjoy their experiences through these last years of adolescence; I remember the fun and interest life held for me at that age and I have always enjoyed teen-agers. But since we feel it is better for them to get their education, regardless of how greatly we miss them, and since we cannot well change our work to a place where there is a good High School, I suppose we must resign ourselves to parting with them sooner than we otherwise might. We faced that possibility when we decided to come here: but then the years before they should be grown stretched so far into the future it seemed we would almost never reach the time when such a break must come. Now as we look back, how short those years have been and how swiftly they have flown!

## 16

# THE SEASONS COME AND GO—
# SPRING AND SUMMER

THE WISH to put into words and perhaps share with others a little about our life here and what it means to us has been in my mind for several years. There has never before been an opportunity to do this, since by the time Betty June ceased to be a baby demanding all my attention, the two older children already needed every minute I could spare for help with their lessons; and my evenings, which I might otherwise have utilized for writing, I spent in keeping abreast of new texts and in assisting with studies.

The break in the established routine of our life here, caused by Anne's absence, and the lessening of my duties as teacher that this brought about, seemed to increase the urgency of my desire to write, since the first change so often brings others in its immediate wake, and I wished to tell something of our first years here before events altered our mode of living too greatly.

Our life here has gradually assumed a quiet rhythm, following the changes of the seasons, with many small diversions and interesting variations, but essentially no more affected by them than the regular rise and fall of the tide is affected by the changing weather.

We have been, I think, an exceptionally close-knit family; the phrase Anne Gordon loved to use, "The Family Circle," meaning all of us as an entity, the parts of which joined as completely and indistinguishably as those of a circle, has seemed very apt. If the life here has brought to the children more duties and fewer opportunities for fun than we might have wished, we early learned to make the most of every small break in the routine, and were often able to disguise a necessary task as a chance for a picnic or a boat ride. We all, I believe, are able to drain the last drop of fun and joy from every pleasant occasion.

Each season has brought its own delights, its new interests, and each contains a day or two that we make special ones. I took great pains to establish a ritual of procedure for each during the first few years and then the children tended to carry on and elaborate as they grew older and could take a bigger part in any preparations. Birthdays, Easter, Valentine's Day, Hallowe'en and, of course, Christmas, each provided interest and work for busy little fingers for many days preceding it and made bright breaks in what might have become a monotonous succession of days that varied little one from another. Each special day has its own dish without which it would not be complete, and the children soon learned to take a part in its preparation and embellishment.

Spring here begins, not on the official date of March 21st, but on that day when one of the children comes in to announce triumphantly, "The boats are out!" Our Island lies in that arm of the Atlantic known as Lobster Bay, and for at least half a century lobsters have been the chief product all along this section of Nova Scotia's coast. Its proximity to the Boston market early gave this district an advantage in such a perishable commodity, and the business increased rapidly until it soon became the mainstay of the Southshore fishermen. The handling and selling of lobsters has passed through various phases and developments, and has its ups and downs, but lobstering has remained the money-making industry for the fishermen along many miles of this shore.

The boats used for lobstering have changed with the times, and engines now do all the heavy, back-breaking work, but to counterbalance this somewhat, more gear must be handled "to make a dollar" and fishing must be done further offshore. No longer can one gather a dinner of lobsters by going down among the rocks at low tide and pushing aside the rock-weed, as old folks can remember doing; the boats now run out as far as twenty miles to haul some of their gear. The dories and pinks first used for lobstering would present a startling contrast to the sleek forty-foot craft now used by most of the fishermen. Even the first motor-boats showed little resemblance to the type now in use. I remember the first of these that appeared along the shore, squat, tubby little affairs, open to wind and water and known as "gasoliners." Perhaps the nickname borne by the first one owned at Clark's Harbour gives as vivid a picture as any words I can use. From her wide ungraceful appearance and perhaps, too, from the sounds her engine made, she was known throughout the district as "The Old Hen."

The Cape Sable Island boats are now known in the harbours of Nova Scotia and along the New England coast; it is claimed they can outlive anything their size in a storm, and I have never seen more strikingly graceful lines.  This is the type of boat used by the fishermen of Shag Harbour and all the surrounding districts, and are now built in many places along the shore: Shag Harbour's own boatshop turns out many beautiful craft in the course of a year.  Each owner feels a pride and affection for his boat that is scarcely surpassed by his feeling for his children —good, loving fathers though most of them are.  Powered as the boats are with big car-engines and with their high bows flinging aside the flying spray, they make little of very dirty weather and present a picture of nonchalance and ease as they cover a stretch of rough water that would have punished the smaller boats of a few years ago.

When the winter ice is gone from the harbours and shore-line, and the worst storms seem to be over, the lobstermen begin spring fishing and the boats that have been lying snug in harbour throughout the winter start to appear in the outside waters.  Boats from the mainland dot the Harbour and Sound as well as the waters around Emerald Isle and Bon Portage.  Boats from Cape Sable Island hurry by the Point with high-piled loads of traps and gear for Seal Island and Mud Island to the westward.  On these Islands the fishermen will live in their "shanties" and "cook-houses" and fish the surrounding waters all week, returning to their homes only for week-ends.  It takes heavy weather indeed to prevent the boats from going home Saturday afternoon and returning to the Islands twenty-four hours later.

The boats that fish from Mud Island, and have to be hauled up over skids there, must sacrifice the comfort of the "cud" (as the cosy, built-in forward part of the boat is called), for lightness in weight.  They are fitted instead with a water-proofed sprayhood which is arched across the bow of the boat and sheds the spray and breaking seas.  Usually the boats from the islands travel in groups for safety and convenience when making the week-end trips, and I never tire of watching them as they pass the Point, particularly in stormy weather. Often they go out of sight behind the seas, and rise again on the crest of the following wave, as light and buoyant as a feather in a breeze. But they present the most fascinating spectacle when driving into the teeth of a strong wind and heavy seas. They seldom lessen their speed (many of the men claim it is safer and drier to push right along), but go over and through the waves, sending water and spray arching high above their sides to fall several feet astern. The high sheer bows now in common use keep most of this water from falling into the boat and the new boats are made with scuppers to carry off the water from the tight decks; but a few years ago when the bows were lower and floorboards loose, many a trip was made with one man at the wheel and the other at the pump. The boat leaps from the crest of one wave to another, often the keel cleaves only air from the bow to where the grip of the propeller blades hold the stern to the water, and the boat rises to an unbelievable angle before smashing down into the next sea. The boat seems to revel in this, it shakes itself from the surging water and leaps forward again. I know as I watch that the boats are large and seaworthy, but they look like shapely chips in the immensity of the surrounding ocean.

The boats do not go out to haul their traps in as heavy weather as that in which they make the run to the Islands. There is a limit to the wind and sea in which they can manœuvre their boats so as to "run down" the small buoys that mark where their pots lie, but the days on which they do go out would present impossible conditions to any but a fisherman.

There are few accidents, miraculously few considering the number of men engaged in the hazardous business. The men are cool and steady; they know their boats and the ocean as I know my kitchen stove and the floor it stands on; most of them are descendants of men, who for almost two hundred years have fished these waters; and they start to learn their trade in boyhood. They make no claim to courage. "A man's a fool or a liar," said one of them, "if he says he's never been scared in a boat. I've been scared often enough. I've thought more'n once I'd never see shore again. Any man'd be a little mite afraid. He don't hafta set down and cry about it. He should do what he can to help himself. But a man that's made his living on the water many years, he's been scared."

In the spring the storms are not apt to be as wicked as they are during the winter lobster season, and as the weather grows warmer and finer there are many days when the fishermen's work lies in beautiful and easy waters. I envy them as they glide past the Point, their bright boats reflected on the motionless mirror beneath them and their engines purring contentedly.

As soon as the men get some number of pots in the water and begin to fish further from shore, they spend all day away from the home wharf and many of the Shag Harbour boats lie off the Point of Bon Portage "between tides," that is, while they wait for the slack water which comes when the tide has ceased to flow and not yet started to ebb, and the similar pause between the alternate tides. As long as the tide races in or out, the buoys which mark the traps lying many fathoms below are pulled under the water and cannot be detected from the boat. Since the time of the tide varies slightly from one fishing ground to another the lobstermen are able to pull a great many pots before all the buoys are pulled under by the power of the rise and fall of the ocean's breathing. It looks neighbourly to see the boats at anchor in the lee of the Point although they are not near enough for any communication with us on shore. They visit back and forth among themselves, "tying on" to an early arrival that has anchored, so that there are often five or six boats tied together in a group and the men go aboard one of the craft to relax on the sun-warmed floor-boards for a chat and a cigarette. Soon we see cosy smoke curling from the cud chimneys and we know the men are cooking a few lobsters for dinner and boiling a pot of tea.

Once the boats are out we begin to make up our mouths for a mess of lobsters, since sooner or later (and we hope sooner) Morrill, on his way to Shag Harbour will meet a boat and be given a few lobsters. That first meal of lobsters is a treat that ranks with the first roast black-ducks of the fall. In these days of rationing, I feel almost guilty when I mention the way we prefer our lobsters prepared; but from the days when my grandmother cooked them thus for her visiting grandchildren, lobsters to me have meant "Creamed Lobster." Let's pretend, as Betty June says, that the war is over and we can use butter and cream with a clear conscience.

First I melt plenty of butter in a heavy frying-pan. When this is hot, but not brown, I add my lobster meat and brown it in the butter. It doesn't brown really, but reddens, and the butter in the pan becomes red from the colouring of the lobsters. I add salt and pepper generously and then milk to come well up about the fish, then set it back to simmer half an hour or so, adding more milk if it evaporates too much. Just before serving, I remove the pan from the heat and add from one-half to one cup of rich cream, depending on the quantity of lobster, and lastly a tablespoon of lemon juice or vinegar. Mother always served with this her home-made brown bread, and the two complemented each other exquisitely; I often serve it so, but usually we have mashed potatoes and a red and green vegetable; in the good old days I served home-made mustard pickles also.

Though this is our favourite lobster dish, they are not to be despised in any form and are delicious eaten from

the shell.   The fishermen who have them nearly every day
of the season for a hot meal in their boats say they tire of
them but, of course, we do not have them often enough
for them to pall upon our appetites.

Early in the spring Morrill saws his firewood.   He used
to hire help for this but recently he has been forced to
manage with what assistance Laurie and I can give him.
I throw blocks to relieve Laurie for short spells or give a
hand at the lighter end of a piece too heavy for Morrill
and Lo to handle alone.   When Morrill was small his father
had several lumber mills and the smell of sawdust and the
sound of the saw buzzing through wood take for him the
place that the smell of hay and the sound of the sea on
the shore have in my memory.   It is too bad that our
Island wood does not offer opportunity for him to do
more with it, as he enjoys putting lumber through his saw
for rough boards and similar pieces.   The buzz of Morrill's
saw and the sound of his engine is very like that of the near-
by boats, so that I am never sure which I hear as I work
about the house, especially when the breakers dull the
sound of both.

Of the birthdays, Anne's comes first in the year, on
March 3.   We have always tried to make very special days
of birthdays, and have had gifts, even if small and inexpen-
sive, to mark them.   Often a kind aunt or grandparent
would send a remembrance.   The gifts are wrapped and
put on the breakfast table at the place of the honoured
member of the family.   Of course, he or she is greeted by
"Happy Birthday to You" and likely a "birthday spanking"
by Daddy and the other little ones.   Birthdays call for a
freezer of ice-cream and a cake with candles and decorations.   When Anne was small we bought fortune-telling
favours to put in the cakes (tiny thimbles, boats, etc.) and
these are washed after each cake and re-used year after
year, their interest never seems to pall for the children.

Coins of a value corresponding to the number of years in the recipient's age are also placed beside the breakfast plate, and after each birthday the weekly allowance naturally increases by an additional cent. We have never yet been able to have a party: the girls' birthdays come too early in the spring for safe travelling for children, and Laurie's comes in the midst of haying; but each birthday is celebrated as a family festival.

At my childhood home Easter was considered simply a religious season, although we had the traditional dishes of ham and eggs, and wore our new hat and coat (if we were lucky enough to be having one that year) to church or Sunday School. Perhaps because I was over-anxious that my children should not miss any of the joys of childhood in spite of their isolation, I soon inaugurated the coming of the Easter Bunny, and Easter became an exciting occasion; often aunts and grandparents sent boxes that augmented the small trinkets and coloured eggs which I prepared, and the caps that the children set out the preceding night were filled to overflowing. As soon as they were big enough to do so, the youngsters painted and decorated hard-boiled eggs for the family and also for some neighbouring children who were not apt to have many eggs even at Easter.

Sometimes I think it is a mistake to make every occasion one of gifts and feasting, and perhaps if I had it to do again I should consecrate Easter as an entirely religious holiday, here where the commercialized aspects of the day would not be brought to the children's attention. However, they have had much innocent pleasure from the coming of the Easter Rabbit, and I do not forget to bring to their notice the deeper significance of the day. Each Good Friday I read to them the story of the Cross on Calvary, and on Easter Sunday that of the Resurrection as told for them in their *Story of the Bible* and we sing some

Easter hymns, while in our ears and before our eyes the
sea and land and skies shout aloud Spring's ever-recurring
miracle of resurrection.

The dainty little white violets are our first flower har-
bingers of spring; they appear along the edges of fields and
stone walls a few days before the earliest of the vivid
dandelions toss out their golden manes.    I miss so much the
pussy-willows and delicately-perfumed arbutus that ushered
in spring to my childhood, neither of these grow on the
Island.    But soon the mossy carpet of the woods is covered
with many exquisite and fragile blooms, the shrubs burst
forth in hardy and flamboyant colours, and every available
vase and container in the house has its fragrant bouquet.

As on every piece of land where any planting or farming
is done spring brings its ploughing, harrowing and seeding.
It brings, too, the new calves and lambs, the little pink
pigs and tiny puffs of chickens.    It brings shearing and
whitewashing and a thousand and one jobs that all of a
sudden pop up from nowhere and demand instant attention.    It brings fog and rain and bitterly chill damp winds
from off the cold ocean, but it also brings an ineffable blue
of sea and sky, new warmth from the sun, and sweet winds
that have blown across the blossoming land and hasten to
us with the perfumes they have gathered.    It brings the
birds, the robins and the song-sparrows and many a little
feathered passer-by that stop here for a rest of a day or
two on their way, and pay for their suppers with songs,
unfamiliar and thrillingly sweet.    Some day I hope to
have time to study and identify the strange songbirds and
water-fowl that pause here on their long flights—to and
from where I have no way of knowing.

On the first of May each year the swallows arrive.    I
welcome the brave song-sparrows and their first rapturous
lyrics to spring, undaunted by belated snow and sleet, and
we have many other sweet-voiced though shyer feathered

neighbours, but the swallows are my favourites. They are so busy and bustling, so friendly and unafraid, and often so impudent. In close formation they wheel and swoop upon the cats in power dives that force the disgruntled felines to lie cowering in the grass. Though the male has one short song that is sweeter than I would expect from their perpetual twitters and chirps, they loose most of their ecstasy in flight.

These swallows build their mud nests under the eaves of the various sheds and barns and stay with us until the young are grown and expert with their wings. I say they build along the sheds and many of them do, but really that is an understatement. They build anywhere and everywhere, they nearly drive us frantic at times with their persistence in setting up their mud houses wherever the fancy suits them.

I had my first skirmish with them before I had been here a week. Our back porch had been made of rough lumber, and across the ceiling had been nailed one or two flat boards a few inches wide. As I opened my kitchen door one morning and stepped out into the porch I saw a swallow flying about the porch ceiling, and after a leisurely circle or two he flew through the porch door and was gone. But not for long. Soon I heard great twitterings and twirpings, and I stepped out again. He had gone to fetch his little bride and now was showing her the perfectly marvellous apartment he had located. He pointed out to her in boastful accents his excellent judgment in such things and the many advantages this afforded over anything they had heretofore inspected. She made one or two doubtful but wifely little twitters, it was really not very airy and perhaps would be cramped when the children began to fly, but he silenced her objections with a brilliant burst of salesmanship. She chirped that he really was the most wonderful husband and out they went. In no time at all they were back with building materials. Well, really, I couldn't have them building their nest and raising their family in my back porch; I worried enough about its lack of sanitation as a place for handling milk and cream without the extra hazards that a family of swallows would present. So I took my broom and shoo-ed them out, closed the door and informed them that the apartment they had been inspecting was definitely not to let. They couldn't credit such selfishness on my part and hung about hopefully, so for over a week, whenever I opened the back door to step out, two flashes of steel blue and brownish white swooped past my head and with joyful chirps deposited some mud and straw on the board they had chosen as the site for their home. I felt most heartless, but I persevered in my cruel course and in time they must have found some other nest-spot, although no doubt their early housekeeping was tinged with regret for the perfect home I had denied them. Before another spring the back porch was sheathed and painted and lacked appeal for house-hunting swallows.

When Morrill removed the pipe that led from our outside water puncheons to our kitchen tank he closed the hole only on the inside until he had completed some alteration he had in mind. Before we realized what was happening, a pair of swallows had found the small opening and built a nest between the two walls. After the babies hatched there was considerable commotion, and our guests paused in amazement on hearing a family of swallows separated from the kitchen by only a beaverboard wall. By this time I was accustomed to their racket and wondered for a moment what was causing the puzzlement on our visitors' faces.

They build in Morrill's feed shed, and he must remember to fasten the door just so, every time he goes in or out, leaving enough room for the comings and goings of the swallows but not enough for the cattle to get at the feed. If he forgets and closes the door he is given a terrific scolding. He knows he did all in his power to dissuade them from building there, but he says they make him feel guilty in spite of himself. All one spring we waged a perpetual battle to keep them from building above our water-puncheons, and each spring a pair is determined to build in the empty silo. Since this must be closed off before the little ones can fly, Morrill has to keep watch and destroy the nests repeatedly before the eggs are laid.

When the young swallows crouch on the roof of the oil-shed for their first flying lessons, I watch fascinated and hate to leave the vicinity. First the father and mother fly the few feet between the shed and the broad top of the garden fence. They assure the youngsters that it is not really hard, and when one or two of the bolder ones succeed in making their first wobbly flight, what praises and applause they bring forth from their proud parents! This rouses the envy of the little ones watching and they determine to attempt the flight also. Soon all have flown but one, who crouches disconsolate but rebellious, close to the safety of the warm shingles at the roof's edge. The mother returns from the fence and talks encouragingly, but with no results.

"I'm scared," he whimpers.

"Scared! Nonsense," says his mother. "Do you want us all to be ashamed of you, the only one in the family that can't fly?"

"I don't care. I don't want to fly. That's too far," and he hugs closer to the shingles.

"Far!" The mother loses her patience at last, and with a swoop and a push of her wings, descends on the exasperating youngster. He finds himself to his complete amazement fluttering his awkward wings, actually *flying* to where his brothers and sisters sit in a state of unstable equilibrium on the garden fence.   Then they all have a great time, flying back and forth, twittering and chirping and incessantly calling each other names.

With some of the cold, wet fog-breezes that blow in from the sea during the changeable weather of spring come other feathered folk, though the imagination rejects them as messengers of spring.   I mean the stormy petrels, those queer black birds, known also as Mother Carey's chickens, that walk the watery waste.   They come only at night and in the most dismal weather.   They fill the fog and damp sea-wind with their weird cries and bump into the Lantern and lighthouse as if they were eagles in size.   We sometimes find one temporarily stunned and a few kill themselves in flying against the thick windows of the Lantern. They are attracted and bewildered by the light beams, and continue their harsh cries and wild flights till daylight.

Each spring Morrill finds a nest or two of young black-ducks tucked in the grass under the overhanging boughs of a low spruce.   Last year Edgar and Laurie found a covey of tiny blue-winged teal, and these they declared the cutest ever, so quick and diminutive.

During our first few years on the Island we noticed no gulls nesting here, but now the swamps are full of them and the air above all the centre of the Island is filled with their whirring wings and raucous cries much of the year. The children find their nests of large speckled eggs and see the young learning to swim in the shallow ponds each spring.   Later we see many of the spring broods in their drab grey swimming near shore or in awkward flight.

Looking across the wooded part of the Island from the Lantern, we see one old tree that towers several feet above its fellows.   This is the tallest tree on the Island by several feet and is much admired as a tree to be climbed.   The children have named it the "Hawk's Tree"; as you might guess it is the home of a pair of fish-hawks and here they raise a family each year. We see other varieties of hawks as well, but I think they have their nests on adjacent islands.

Altogether the Island has many birds that mate and raise families here each spring, and the only ones to whom we really begrudge its hospitality are the crows, though they are probably the most numerous of all. They steal our seeds in the spring, destroy young black-ducks (and even came into our duckyard to carry off most of a brood of tame ducklings one spring), spoil innumerable shots for the duck-hunters in the fall, and are generally a nuisance and a detestation. They fairly blacken the sky as they rise from the kelp banks where they have been feeding, and startle my breath away when they ascend in huge flocks from the trees that line the path to the boathouse when I happen to pass at night the place where they are roosting. We can do practically nothing to curb them, although Morrill destroys eggs and young each spring wherever possible, and kills off a few in the fields with a .22.

For me, as for most housewives, the spring brings house-cleaning and sewing. As spring is late along the coast and winter clothes and winter heat stoves are useful until May and often later, I make no effort to start my spring cleaning until fairly late in the season. During March, any spare time I can squeeze from the day's demands I put to quilt or mat-making. Each spring I like to work the rags that have accumulated throughout the preceding months into mats: the woollen and silk pieces I hook into rugs, while the cotton ones I braid and sew into mats. We use an extraordinary number of these mats, especially in the back porch. The very weather, wet and foggy, against which most housewives close their doors, demands that we leave our porch doors open to the wet, driving winds, lest we fail to hear (and so to answer) any boat-horns that blow. Consequently the porches are often wet and with the men tramping back and forth between house and garden, they would be in even a worse state than they are, if I did not keep the floors well covered with ab-absorbent mats.

It is useless for me to think of leaving my pupils while I work at housecleaning, so it must be postponed until most of the year's school work has been finished and I can give my attention to my own tasks. I must admit I find this one of the most trying disadvantages of their getting their education at home. It is hard to possess my soul in patience and see the lovely spring days go by without being able to start my work, and to know that before I can finish housecleaning Morrill will be needing my help at silage (we begin to make it in the latter part of June) and at outdoor tasks that follow close on the heels of one another, planting, weeding, whitewashing and hay-making. It usually develops that I race to finish my housecleaning before the grass reaches the stage for cutting, and thus the housework becomes more of a task than it otherwise might be. Last year I lost the race, and some of my interior painting just didn't get done at all.

While the children still need supervision and assistance at their lessons I do the spring sewing, hem sheets and pillow-cases, let out hems and seams for the growing children, make new dresses, shorts and shirts, and perhaps make over a coat that has been passed on to us; generally licking into shape our not extensive wardrobes. Sewing further clutters our small rooms already full of school books and appurtenances of family life, and means one more job to be crowded into a full day; but it is surprising how much can be accomplished once the long spring days arrive, and the delight of the children in new garments for themselves or me, more than repays the effort that goes into them.

Finally I do get my cleaning done and there is something very satisfying in seeing the rooms all scrubbed and shining, freshly painted and papered, curtains and bedspreads as crisp and white as the near-by foam, clean new mats on the floors and everything as ship-shape as is possible in an old building that has seen better days.

Early in May the government steamer usually arrives with supplies for the Light and brings the Inspector on his annual visit. Many people think that we are supplied by the government with a great many of the necessities for living here, but such is not the case. The steamer lands kerosene oil for the dwelling as well as the Light, but this means of illumination is practically the only thing supplied us by the Department that would not be provided for any rented dwelling, and the rate of rent which is figured as part of our salary is extremely high for this section of the country. We may also purchase coal through the Department at cost price, but we do not need to take advantage of this opportunity. The box of cleansers and supplies for the Light and any lumber for repairs or new buildings are usually landed at this spring call, and we unpack them and stow them away for future use. The Inspector looks over the lighthouse and outside buildings, notes our requirements for the coming year and discusses with Morrill any questions that may have arisen since his last visit. For many years Mr. Morrisey came on these yearly inspections and we looked upon his visits as upon those of a friend. We felt a sense of personal loss when we learned of his sudden death a few years ago, and we remember his thoughtfulness and many kindnesses to us gratefully. We have met nothing but friendliness from all the men of the Department with whom we have come in contact, and we are made to feel that as long as the Light is well cared for and the other prescribed duties performed satisfactorily, we are very much our own bosses.

One of the first things I attempted to make the surroundings of the lighthouse more homelike was to have a small flower garden. Many of the more delicate plants will not withstand the cold fogs and strong winds, but some of the hardier flowers grow profusely. I made several attempts to have various flower-beds around the lighthouse with no great success. Then one spring I dug up and planted a small plot in the shelter of the one big rock that the government field contains; it is near the west side of the lighthouse and the building and rock together broke most of the wind from my flowers. Morrill put up a picket fence, we whitewashed it and I had one of the most successful gardens one could imagine. I planted nothing fancy except some dahlia bulbs that Dad had sent me, and even these did remarkably well. Every bloom was larger than any of its kind I had seen on the mainland, and I was so proud!

But the conditions of soil and climate that caused my flowers to grow so luxuriantly had the same effect on weeds and grasses; and with only limited time to put at caring for my little plot (the vegetable garden must always be weeded first) I waged a losing battle for two or three years. The small size of the piece of ground made it impossible for Morrill to reinforce my efforts by ploughing, so I reluctantly abandoned my little flower garden. Nothing can be planted without being securely fenced because the cows feed in the lighthouse field, so my flower garden of late years has perforce been limited to a row or two along the top of the vegetable garden to give us cut flowers for the house. Once I had started teaching the children I had less time than ever for gardening, as land and scholars need their most attention simultaneously: the children are finishing their year's studies when I should be putting in seeds. But some day we plan to put a picket fence around the lighthouse and I shall have hardy blooms of brave and joyous colours and some of delicate perfume to greet me when I step outdoors, to add delight to the fine days and to replace the sunshine when the fog hangs low.

By the middle of May the children can usually run barefooted on the warm grass, at first for an hour or so at noon.   To the country child nothing is so deliciously patent of spring as the feel of the warm earth and the soft sun on feet that have been shut up for the long winter in heavy boots and woollen socks.   On that first fetterless day my children race like mad up and down the grassy path, their pale feet like wings in their new-found freedom and weightlessness, so that they hardly seem to touch the grass, but to skim along above it.   Soon they coax to go wading, and as the water itself would dampen (not to say chill) any undue ardour on their parts we give our permission. Morrill and I seldom have the courage to go swimming before the end of June, but the children get in a few times before that.

When they were small we used to take the youngsters down on the sun-warmed rocks of the Point and they waded in the shallow pools left by the receding tide.   Sometimes we would sit on the rocks and let the waves break over and around us.   But the water was too cold to make this altogether enjoyable, and too rough to allow us much peace of mind where the children were concerned; Laurie was swept off his feet once and only Morrill's quick grab saved him from being battered against the rocks.

When Anne was about seven we discovered the Pool and its possibilities.   Just beyond the end of Morrill's cleared fields, lies a piece of level shore known as Saddleback.   I have never heard why it was given this name, certainly not because of any physical characteristic of the place.   At Saddleback the shore extends seaward with a very slight incline for several hundred yards, and along one part of it the sea has hollowed out an oval pool, some twenty yards long and eight yards wide, and has built on its seaward side a miniature ledge of rocks for its protection. At half tide the water in the little pool lies only three feet deep in its centre, but as the tide flows the hollow fills with water pushing through the rocks that line it, and this incoming water, warmed by its passage over the sun-soaked seaweed and rocks, mingled with the water that has lain in the pool under the sun, is of a pleasant temperature for swimming. The trick is to catch the tide at that stage when the water in the pool has been deepened enough for swimming, but not yet augmented by sufficient outside water to be chilled unbearably. Some fine warm summers we have had many wonderful times in the pool, almost every day swimming and splashing there together; but just as often a cold, foggy summer limits our swims to very few. Of course, the pool leaves much to be desired in many respects. The shore is rough and rocky, the pool itself is small, it offers no opportunity for the children to learn to dive, and often after a storm it is dirty with broken kelp and rock-weed; but we have had some most enjoyable frolics there, and we always emerge refreshed and exhilarated.

When we go swimming in the pool our dressing rooms are little open glades in the spruce thickets. Mine is carpeted with tiny exquisitely-perfumed twin-flowers, and a small spruce with stiffly-extended boughs makes an excellent clothes hanger.

By the first of June the lobster season is over and the fishermen turn their attention to other harvests of the sea. Most of them go out daily to near-by "banks" or shoals for cod and haddock, some go further and stay out for a few days; these latter fish for halibut; while some try the water off the Point and similar spots for pollack. Most of these fish are shipped fresh to Boston and other markets, but the pollack are salted and dried for home consumption. We of the South shore consider good dried pollack much superior to cod, so we dry cod for those who don't know any better and keep the pollack for our own winter's use.

As the boats come in from fishing on a fine summer evening, each escorted by a cloud of flashing white gulls, and all unerringly duplicated on the smoothly shimmering water, they add a vivid touch of life and colour to the perfect background of sea, sky and distant dark shores. I see them again in memory when I think of swimming in the pool, so often they skirt the shore as we leave the water and start homeward to prepare supper. Many of these boats have nets set off the Point to catch herring or mackerel which they use for bait. Occasionally we beg a mess of herring from them. If you have never eaten little herring, fresh from the sea, rolled in cornmeal and fried in pork fat, you have missed one of the sweetest dishes the ocean provides.

Not all the boats stay at home and fish the neighbouring waters. From each little hamlet a few of the bigger and newer boats go each year for the sword-fishing off Cape Breton. We see them passing in groups of four or five, one following close in the wake of another, unmistakable with their slender look-out masts and long platforms jutting forward from the bows. They leave in June and return in September, usually with a profitable summer's work behind them.

Many lightkeepers eke out their none-too-munificent salary by fishing on the side. Morrill never has. He found, from a tentative attempt he made one spring, that even lobstering, which pays the highest returns of any branch of the fishing, demands too much time and effort in launching and hauling his boat to be a profitable side-line. However, during the last two summers he has carried a fishing line with him in the boat when the fish are in the Sound and often stops for a few minutes to catch a haddock or two on his way back from Shag Harbour. We eat what we need fresh, can some and dry the others towards our winter's supply. Those who have never eaten haddock

until it has been iced and handled several times and are
of the opinion that they do not care for fish have been
amazed when here at the quantities of fish chowder or
boiled haddock with cream and butter sauce that they consume.   Fishermen assure me that fish cooked immediately
after being caught, as they do in their boats, surpass what
I cook in flavour.   "From hook to pot" seems to be the
best rule when cooking fish.

I have never caught a salt water fish.   Of late years
Morrill and I cannot leave the Island together, and to tell
the truth fishing holds no great fascination for me.   Years
ago Morrill took Laurie and me out to try our luck one oily
morning when the feeding gulls showed that there were
pollack close to the Point.   Mildred was here and she
undertook to keep house for me to go and in return I was to
mind her little daughter for her to try her hand at it the
following morning.   Unfortunately, Morrill needed my
help at changing the chain on the joan-pole before we went
fishing, and we lay a few yards off-shore rolling broadside
on to the greasy swells for half an hour.   I assured myself,
"I'll feel better once the boat is going again," and so I did
as long as the boat kept moving and the wind was in my
face.   But we had no sooner stopped the engine to fish and
began to roll in the lazy ground-swell, than I was forced to
abandon my line and crawl into the bow to lie flat on my
back.   In a few minutes poor little Lo joined me there;
our distress was too much for Morrill and shortly after he
disgustedly reeled in his line and took us home.   He refused
to consider taking Mildred next morning and she didn't
get fishing until last summer, seven years later than her
promised trip, when she went a few times with Morrill and
caught some good-sized fish.

By the first of July our wild strawberries are ripe and
although they are not as plentiful as we could wish, they
do provide us with fruit for many suppers.   When I can

possibly spare the time I love to go picking strawberries; another result, I suppose, of my childhood at Emerald Isle when each of us youngsters were sent forth daily throughout the strawberry season with a large earthenware mug which was supposed to be filled before we returned. The strawberries do not grow here in such generous quantities as they did at Emerald Isle, perhaps because we do not have as much grassy pasture land, but their flavour is as exquisite and as satisfying.

Last summer (as if we didn't have enough to do already!) we tried our hands at gathering Irish moss for which there is now a demand since the war has cut off the former European sources of supply.

This Irish moss is a sea-plant growing along the rocks and ledges that lie where the sea covers them, or leaves them exposed for a few hours at most during the lowest tides. The plant itself is graceful, made up of thin fronds that sub-divide into tiny delicate fingers of slippery, glittering opaqueness. Under water it grows in rounded tufts and a small rock covered with it reminds me of a large and yellowish head of cauliflower without its encircling green leaves, and like the cauliflower each tuft is made up of numerous smaller flowerets. When the tide has ebbed from about the tufts they lie flat and droop from their roots which attach themselves strongly to the rocks that are covered with a thin layer of silt. Where the rocks are washed clean by the changing tides no Irish moss is found, and as far as we have been able to observe, it ceases to grow where the water is deeper than two or three fathoms. It is brownish before being picked, varying from a yellowish brown where it is most exposed to the light (even though it comes through the water) to a deep purplish brown where it grows on the dark undersides of rocks.

After it has been gathered, cleaned and bleached, it is used commercially in bases for ice-cream, candies, cheeses,

some medicines, and other things.  I use it in the preparation of dishes wherever I would otherwise use a plain
gelatin, and "Irish Moss Spanish Cream" is a favourite
dish in spite of its mongrel nomenclature.

Along almost all the shores of Bon Portage the rocks and
reefs lying at low tide line are covered with Irish moss;
and for two or three summers before we made any attempt
to get it we had seen dories from Shag Harbour gathering
it at low water on the full course tides.   The men in these
dories were equipped with long-handled rakes by which
they tore the plants from the rocks and threw them into
the dories.  This moss was then bleached and dried in
Shag Harbour and sold to the agent for a firm that handled
it in large quantities.  The bleaching process was what
prevented our trying to gather it before.  This is done by
alternate drying the moss and dampening it in salt water
until it loses its brownness and becomes a light straw colour;
we have no wharf or similar place where this could be done.
When last year, the agent announced that he would buy
it unbleached we decided to see if we could earn a little
extra cash at this work.

The waters along our shore are more often than not too
rough to allow working from a dory, and since this method
also presented difficulties to us that did not affect the men
who could bring their moss to a wharf, we decided to pick
it from the rocks at low water and pack it into large burlap
bags.   Then we found cutting it much quicker than picking,
and finally Morrill and Lo discovered that they could use
rakes to gather moss in a few feet of water while the girls
and I cut what the fallen tide left lying limp and flat along
the sides and tops of inner rocks and ledges.   Practice at
the work brought speed and introduced short-cuts; in a
short time we had worked out a system that went something like this:

First we found it paid us to put our time to mossing only during a week at the time of the full moon and another week at the dark of the moon when the tides have their greatest variations, or what interested us, their lowest ebbs, and thus left exposed the most moss-bearing rocks and for the longest time.    Each low tide suitable for the work offers us about three hours during which we can gather the moss.    We begin to work when the first moss-covered rocks are exposed, following the tide down, gathering our greatest quantities while the slack water lasts and retreating before the incoming flood.

We dress warmly in heavy sweaters, woollen breeches and warm socks in rubber boots (all the oldest and most worn that we possess); we usually end by getting wet to our middles by the heavier seas brought in by the flooding tide, but we try to postpone this as long as possible and in cold, foggy weather the girls and I take extra care to keep out of the reach of the seas.    Morrill and Laurie, working strenuously with long sweeps of their rakes, find their activity keeps them warm, but we, cutting among the inner rocks, move less and tend to become cramped and chilled.    Only on the warm afternoons do we discard our sweaters and we never find the heavy nether garments too warm, though once we are wet it matters little what we have on.

We take our utensils: sharpened knives, and buckets with holes bored in the bottoms to allow the water to drain out, for the girls and me; rakes and large wire lobster-baskets for Morrill and Lo; numerous feed-bags and ropes for tying them when filled; and off we set for low water line and the Irish moss.

The girls and I cut the moss from the rocks and when our buckets are full we empty them into a bag, left above low water line on a high shelf of rock above the reach of the sea.    Morrill and Lo pull up their hip-rubbers and work at the plants still under water, stripping the rocks with their rakes and knocking the plants off the teeth of the rakes into the metal baskets. When their large baskets are full they bring them in and empty them into the waiting bags.

It is tiring work, especially on the back, but it is not as monotonous as one might expect. The Island at low tide line might be in a different world from the fields and beaches we know so well. The growth among the rocks and the tiny inhabitants of the clear pools have an interest and fascination of their own, and new aspects of the under-water roots of the Island open to us as the tide recedes, or as we work further and further away from our starting place. We usually begin by stripping the rocks near the Point, but as the season progresses we daily move further up the Western Side as each new strip of shoreline is cleaned of its growth of moss, until we are working almost to the Kelp Cove and a long way from home.

In foggy weather it is cold, damp work and the sur-roundings are weirdly depressing as the black fog, hanging low along the dull water, shuts out everything but the rocks and reefs that loom up threateningly whichever way we turn, their heavy manes of lank sea-weed drooping forlornly about them. The sea sucks and slobbers among the crevices of the moss-covered ledges, and at one spot the round, slimy sides of the battered boilers from the *S. S. Express* tower above us like squat and obese monsters rising from the ocean bed. The cold water soon numbs our hands as we try to pluck the tempting clusters of moss just beneath the surface, and our feet become chilled from standing in the cold water of the pools as we clean the rocks that form their outer edges.

On fine days it is a pleasant job, with the warm sun colouring the lovely marine plants and dainty shell-fish in the shallow pools, and shimmering across the shining surface of the sea. If there is a slight surf running it adds interest and contrast to the placid outer waters as it purls in creamy suds among the rocks where we work. Once the tide turns and starts back in over the rocks our time for mossing is limited and we are no longer careful not to get wet. Since the incoming tide increases the surf (and it is seldom there is not some wash along the shore) our boots are soon full and we are wet above our knees. The sea drives us back, back, until the moss is all once more under water and we must wait until another low tide to gather more.

Then Morrill and Laurie finish filling and tying the heavy wet sacks and carry them up over the slippery, sea-weeded rocks to the top of the beach, while the girls and I make a trip or two over the rough shore to carry the buckets, knives, rakes and baskets with any empty sacks there may be, to where the men have piled the bags of picked moss. Laurie goes to harness the ox for carting our moss to the lighthouse, as sometimes we work half a mile from home up the western shore and a good tide's gleaning will yield us fifteen to twenty sacks of the heavy wet moss.

This gathering moss can be dangerous work after a bad storm. Though the girls and I, working among the inner rocks, are seldom within reach of the seas, Laurie was once swept off the ledge on which he was raking and into the deep water beside it. Fortunately he was not carried out by the backwash and he regained his feet in shallower water before the following breaker swirled about him. This frightened us all and made us resolve that after bad storms we would not work at the mossing. A large sea coming in with the flood will sometimes break twenty feet inside the one that preceded it, and is apt to be followed by two or three of equal size. We would have no means of rescuing one of our party if he or she were swept into the undertow and tide whirls that lie close to the shore off the Point, even if the smashing seas should spare their prey. So, as long as the surf that follows a storm thunders in along the shore, we stay out of its way.

Once the bags of moss are safely home at the lighthouse field, and we have stepped out of our sodden clothes and boots and into dry garments, we are ready for the next step, for our work is by no means over. Now the moss must be dried, and this we do by spreading it thinly over all our flat roofs, and when we have a large quantity in various stages of drying, on the strip of beach where we dry our hay and which has been cleared of its larger rocks for this purpose. We all work at spreading it in the fine mornings—on the roofs of the barn, manure pit, silo, hen-house, pig-house and back porch; and at evening we all go to re-gather it. We sweep it into piles on the various roofs and then stuff it into bags. Here in our damp winds it seldom dries sufficiently in one day, and must be re-spread for a final crisping. Fog or rain spoils it for sale, so if fog shuts in or a shower comes up, we must hasten to bag it before it is damaged. When it has been properly dried and bagged, Morrill takes it in his boat to Shag Harbour and sells it.

July and August fly by, crowded with company, silage and hay-making, mossing, swims, berry-picking, caring for the garden, housework, cooking and canning. Though summer is our busiest season it is the one I enjoy most; I like working out of doors, and above all I am free from the strain of keeping the children up to date in their lessons and I can plan my own work without having to give first consideration to the school time-table. If we are able to take a short vacation, it comes near the end of August, and makes a break before starting the fall work, although I begrudge the time spent away from my beloved Island home in its loveliest season.

## 17

## FALL AND WINTER

By September it is time to start a new year's lessons, and as in other schools we begin the term with high hopes and great enthusiasm. Alas! as in many other schools, this praiseworthy spirit is not always sustained, and soon Laurie begins to grow restive and uninterested and we all lose that first fine ardour.

Our falls are lovely, fine and clear with no early frosts. The sea is warmer than it has been all summer so some of our grandest swims are enjoyed after lessons are over for the day. Morrill and I miss the vivid fall colours of the hardwood trees that made the fall season so gorgeous among the hills that surround Bedford, but even in autumn the Island has a charm of its own. The sea is never more affable than on a crisp fall day, and even the little ponds reflect "October's bright blue weather." The higher swamps blaze forth in scarlet shrubs, and our few hardwood, mostly birches, show a golden gleam among the dark green fir and spruce. The savannah grass and reeds ripple in the breezes like a field of yellow grain and the soft white clouds in the deep blue sky send shadows down to dance amongst it.

Morrill and Laurie begin to discuss plans for the coming duck season; there is much whittling, painting and refurbishing of decoys, and I am called upon to exclaim over the realistic turn of a new duck head or a change in the shape of a tail. I begin to prepare the warm clothes we will need for winter and to put more time at knitting the necessary socks, mittens and sweaters.

Some fine fall day we all go cranberrying and gather enough for the winter. Roast black-duck and cranberry sauce are as inseparable in our minds as ham and eggs; we also use the berries as a fruit dish for suppers and for luscious pies. Cranberrying day is declared a holiday, a lunch put up, rubber-boots donned and off we all go to spend a glorious day in the open once more after several weeks of being cooped up at lessons. Betty June first went for cranberries when she was two and a half; she had her little cup and picked berries, too. We gathered the gleaming ruby red and speckled brown "spice" berries from their mossy beds until we had a flour bag nearly full. Our berries are smaller than those usually marketed, but they are sweeter and lack entirely the bitter tang that the larger berries have. We stopped at noon, made a fire, ate a hearty lunch and after resting a bit resumed our picking; by four o'clock we had enough berries and made our weary, contented way homeward through the lovely autumn evening. Until the last few years our swamps provided us with an ample crop for our own use and plenty for many other pickers who came from the mainland to gather them, but for some unknown reason our swamps have yielded no berries for three or four years and we have gone to Emerald Isle for them. After the berries are picked they are stored in a cool, dry place and keep their flavour and succulence until spring.

At the end of September we get our root crops dug and safely stored in the cellar: smooth red carrots, wine-red beets, pale turnips with their mauve tops, pallid, uninteresting-looking parsnips, blue and red potatoes. These are followed a little later by round, green cabbages and in lucky years a box of plumed celery with its roots in mud, to last us till Christmas. Before this we have canned our excess perishable vegetables, although there are still a few belated beans on the scarlet runner poles. Morrill closes the cellar windows against the chiller breezes of fall.

Then comes pig-killing day or days, with its boilers of water to be heated for scalding; and then the sugar-curing of hams, shoulders and bacons, the making and canning of head-cheese, the packing of the fat pork in coarse salt for beans and frying, and the trying out of the snow-white lard for shortening.

It is good to go down cellar and see our rows upon rows of bottled fruits and berries, canned and jammed and jellied, with other rows of canned beans, peas, small carrots, beets and greens, meat and fish, and in pre-war days a shelf full of home-made pickles and relishes. Then there are large crocks of fat pork, one of sauerkraut, bins of potatoes and other vegetables, cabbage hanging from the ceiling and the box of celery in its corner. The cellar presents a very different aspect indeed from the bare and empty one of our first winter here.

Sometime during October Morrill brings on our winter supplies, food staples for us and bags of feed for the stock. The former are placed in the pantry store-room and the latter in the feed shed. We also look over our medicines and see that we have a supply of the simple remedies for colds and minor injuries on hand. Though our falls are generally fine and late, winter has been known to shut in by the end of October, so we take no chances and prepare as fully as we can for any unusual behaviour on the part of the seasons. We always have on hand some extra bags of flour and we keep more vegetables than would suffice for the needs of the family alone, in case the sea should bring and isolate here unexpected guests. Our sheep and cattle would provide meat in an emergency.

In October the screen doors come off and the storm doors go on, the banking of sawdust is put around the dwelling, and the woodshed is filled to the last inch of space. The heat stove is installed in the living-room and sheds its cosy warmth about us as we gather in the long fall evenings to read and study and sew. We leave the storm-windows off until the last possible day, usually until just before Christmas, because once they are on the wind blows salt and dust in around them in spite of all we can do, and after a few storms they become very dingy and darken our rooms on dull fall days.

The lobstermen start their winter fishing on the first of December; ordinarily by the end of the month the water is too cold for the lobsters to crawl and most of the boats are pulled up for the winter, although a few hardier souls continue to haul traps until, or unless, salt water ice prevents them from leaving the harbours. It is during this fall or winter season (it is known by both names) that the greatest losses in gear occur, since that is the time of the heaviest storms. Two years ago the fishermen in this district suffered the worst losses they have sustained since our coming here.

The opening days of the season were clear and fine and all the boats scurried back and forth piled high with loads of traps to be dumped along the nearer shores; and soon the Sound and the waters about our Island were dotted with the white buoys that mark where the pots lie. All the boats first put their traps "inside," that is near the shores of the Islands and points, until they soak up some water and become heavier and less likely to shift position on the bed of the sea, then they are lifted and carried out to deeper water further from land. Most of the big boats fish the more distant grounds, leaving the inner places for "skiffers" and men in other small craft. So, while the traps were still new and buoyant and still in the shallow water near the shore, a storm broke. Immediately the seas began to lift and roll the light pots and soon we saw them being washed ashore. At first most of these traps were not badly damaged and Morrill spent all one day pulling those that were in good condition out of the reach of the seas, so that their owners might salvage them when the storm abated.

He has found, however, that all too often the men who own the gear never get it, some one else is ashore first and takes all he can find and take off in his skiff. Each man knows his buoys from the painted marks upon them and his traps from his handiwork in making them, but after each storm there is more or less hard feeling and accusations of gear-stealing among the men. Since Morrill doesn't know who owns which, all he can do is rescue what he can and wait until the storm is over for the men to claim their own. He is never thanked for this, and is often afraid of becoming embroiled in the arguments, so that he swears each time henceforth to let the traps smash to pieces where the sea tosses them with no interference on his part.

This storm did not abate after a day's blow, but grew worse and continued for a week. Before it was over the shores of the Island were lined with hundreds of new lobster-pots and buoys, the traps smashed to uselessness and the new rope snarled about them and amongst the kelp and rock-weed also tossed up by the storm. There was scarcely a foot of the six-mile shore-line around the Island that hadn't its huge tangle of traps and buoys and ropes awash in the tattered seaweed. The loss in material (and the time and work that had gone into the making of the gear) was tremendous. Some of the men salvaged what little they could of their smashed traps and buoys, but this was a very small fraction of what they had put in the water a week before. While that was the greatest damage we have seen follow a storm, scarcely a winter passes without some losses. Many of the fishermen think it would be better to have no winter season, but as prices are usually high at that time of year, most of them prefer to gamble on good weather.

The severity of our winters have varied greatly. The first five winters were very mild, practically all our precipitation fell as rain, and the pools in the fields barely caught overnight. Ashford's remark that here we had no winter, only a wet season, seemed true. Then following the mildest winter we had yet experienced came our coldest, one of the bitterest ever known along this shore, and we learned what it meant to be really isolated for long stretches of time. Betty June was only a few months old, but fortunately she kept in the best of health (as we all did) and thrived amazingly.

That year the weather turned cold early in November and by the end of the month there was salt water ice all around us, a full month earlier than usual. Just before Christmas a south-west wind cleared the ice from the sound and harbour temporarily and Morrill was able to reach Shag Harbour and get our Christmas mail. Then the ice shut in around us again, and weeks elapsed before we again contacted the outside world.

As far as the eye could reach not a speck of blue water showed, only huge cakes of ragged drift ice stretched in every direction. Not a sea made and broke along the shore, the silence was almost frightening after the customary throaty rumble of the running surf and was scarcely lessened in its intensity by the intermittent faint hiss and whisper of ice-cakes and slush rising and falling with the tide among the rocks. All the can-buoys and harbour markers were broken from their moorings and drifted back and forth with the ice that encircled them as it surged in and out of the Sound and swung in a wide circle past the Point.

The weather stayed perfectly clear and fine, the sky a deep unclouded blue, except on the rare occasions when for a day or two the wind blew from the southerly quarters and the ice was opened and carried miles away to the warmer sea and dissolution. Then we saw open water again, and its sullen greyness seemed more hostile than the dazzling white ice that had fettered the Island. These breaks were few and of short duration, almost immediately the wind would haul in to the opposite direction and the cold northerlies again formed the heavy shore ice and moved it along the coast to fill all Lobster Bay with closely-packed sheets of frozen brine. This ice never congealed into a solid mass, always the cakes moved with the tide as in a slow stream, and many of them were not large enough to bear a man's weight. The government steamer, I believe, could have forced her way through the ice to us; during a similarly hard winter the wife and children of a former lightkeeper were taken from here on a boat sent by the Department.

All through December, January, February and most of March the ice lay thick and white around us, and in May there were still high walls of ice-cakes and frozen spray along the western side, especially in the Kelp Cove where they towered above my head as I walked the beach before them one lovely May morning. But by the middle of March Morrill was able to resume his boat-trips to Shag Harbour, although ice still lingered along the shores.

The following winters were progressively milder and although since then there have been spells during January or February of each year when salt water ice closes Shag Harbour and makes travelling impossible for a week or two, we have never again seen the quantities of ice that encircled us during what we call, "That Hard Winter."

Only one day of that coldest winter were we unable to keep the living-room comfortably warm, but all winter the kitchen was too cold to be of much use to us, and it was difficult even to cook our meals in its draughty frigidity.

By last winter we considered ourselves veterans in circumventing the weather or adapting ourselves to its vagaries, but we let ourselves be fooled like any greenhorns. Our friend Ethren arrived to cut some pot-bows and to spend a few days with Morrill. The January weather was pleasant and mild and when Sunday developed into one of those perfect days we occasionally have in mid-winter, Morrill and Ethren decided to take the boat to Bear Point in hopes of persuading Ethren's wife to return with them to share the visit. Anne begged permission to go and stay with her chum, the daughter of the house, while the mother should be here. Ethren's wife decided against returning in the boat, but Anne stayed for her visit regardless. Almost immediately after the boat's return a storm blew up and soon the salt water ice made it impossible for Morrill to take Ethren to the mainland and to get Anne. For almost two weeks we were ice-bound here while Anne was forced to remain on the mainland. Ethren left in our dory one threatening afternoon, with a rising easterly wind that was pushing the ice from our shores but still blocked the harbours, and we anxiously watched him working his way through and around the thick lines of ice that still remained in the Sound, until we judged he had reached the shelter of Emerald Isle, whence we believed he would be safe. A few days later Morrill was able to bring Anne home. We resolved anew to take no chances on winter weather; as we had known, but foolishly ignored, a change in wind or temperature might prevent for months anyone leaving or reaching the Island.

Early in the winter Morrill begins to cut his firewood and he hauls it out of the woods by ox-sled whenever one of our infrequent snows allows him to do so. Our wood consists almost entirely of soft wood and much of it is gnarled and twisted. The better pieces are sawed short and split for the kitchen range, but the heavy, knotty wood is burnt unsplit in our big drum-like heat stove in the living-room. This wood makes an excellent fire and some of the black-spruce pieces are nearly as solid and give off as much heat as hardwood.

At least once or twice during the wood-cutting season we have a picnic in the woods. The children and I pack a lunch and join Morrill wherever he is chopping, generally not too far from the lighthouse. Most often for lunch we take buttered bread, cake or a pie, milk and cream, with bacon and eggs to fry and coffee to boil over the fire. The cheerful snap and crackle of the fire as we pile on spruce boughs and watch the flames leap is a big part of the outing —and so are wood-smoke and tree spills in our bacon and coffee! Frequently the children's enthusiasm for a roaring fire offers difficulties to the cook and I threaten to take the "grub" and make myself a little cooking fire off in a corner somewhere if they do not curb their zeal until the bacon and eggs are done. We pile slices of fried bacon and an egg on a thick slice of home-made bread and pour mugs of fragrant coffee. Laurie and Betty June are now allowed weak coffee on picnics, but Anne remains loyal to her glass of milk. The sandwiches are enormous but good, our sugar-cured bacon has a flavour all its own, and we consume huge quantities of it before we turn our attention to the pie or cake.

If Morrill and I miss the hardwood trees at many times, in midwinter we realize the crowding fir and spruce present an unsurpassed picture, their branches laden with rounded cushions of snow and their blue shadows slicing across the drifted whiteness. After lunch is over we relax, our backs against a snug pile of spruce boughs and our faces towards the red glow of the fire. It always requires considerable effort on my part to gather the dishes and collect my offspring preparatory for a return to home and awaiting lessons and housework.

The children love to ride on the empty wood-sleds (what child doesn't?) and when the bright sun on the snow and trees is not to be resisted I have one ride back with Morrill to drink in the beauty of the woods and to break briefly for him the monotony of chopping and hauling all day alone, as he has been forced to do lately because the short winter days are almost over before Laurie is through his schoolwork.

At Bedford I often went for long tramps through the deep woods on my showshoes; I brought them with me but there is seldom sufficient snow on which to use them. Betty June loves to wear the moccasins and snowshoes and to tramp over the odd drifts, but only once in the fifteen years here do I remember good snowshoeing along the path. Then I put on my webbed shoes and broke the way for the others to walk to the boathouse, and we spent a hilarious afternoon in the deep drifts. The wind swirls across the Island so viciously that most of the snow that falls during a storm is blown into the sea and what remains is piled into drifts, leaving alternate stretches of bare ground. This state of things not only spoils my snow-shoeing, but is a great hindrance to Morrill when he is trying to haul his firewood.

The same inconsiderate behaviour on the part of the wind prevents good coasting, and added to the lack of suitable snow is the disadvantage of our only hill being neither steep nor long. Nevertheless, the children spent many happy days with their sleds on the hillside when they were small. Sometimes when the moon came up round and bright in the early evenings, Morrill and I have gone coasting with them for an hour or so, partly because we remember the added pleasure we felt when our parents joined in our pastimes, and partly because we are both "a little childish" as Morrill says and cannot resist the fun of coasting in the moonlight, remembering the joyous evenings spent on the steep hills of Bedford years ago.

The pond by the lighthouse would make an excellent place for skating, but all too often it freezes with a rough surface from the high wind or a soft snow spoils it when we have hopes of good ice. All the children learned to skate when they were small, and some winters we have had many enjoyable hours skating and playing "hockey." Other winters Morrill and I have not had our skates on, and the children have fared little better. When Morrill and I took an hour or so at noon to skate with the children we all played what we called hockey, the children and I against Daddy. As the youngsters had never even seen a game played and I had never taken part in one, you can imagine we played with more enthusiasm than skill. Stones on the ice took the place of goal-posts, and although all the family have skates and hockey-sticks, when Mike played he wore his rubber boots and kept goal with an oar! Betty June said only a few days ago, "You know, Mummy, I used to be terrible when we were playing hockey. I never knew what I should do to stop Daddy when he had the puck and I couldn't skate much. I used to slide in front of him and then fall down. That was the only thing I could think to do."

In any family where there are children the day about which the whole year revolves is, of course, Christmas, and so it has been with us. We have never possessed nearly as much money as we should wish to spend for gifts, but everything else to make a perfect Christmas we have had.

When I was teaching, always about the first of December I began to develop phases of each subject that stressed the coming holiday season: we read Christmas stories, we made Christmas decorations in drawing periods and learned Christmas songs in music time. As soon as my children were old enough for lessons we followed much the same procedure. As they could see no store windows and took no part in a school or church tree or entertainment I tried other ways of bringing the Christmas season vividly before them. I saved all my cards and so did the children's grandparents; these were passed on to the children the following year, and from them they cut out lovely designs and made cards to send away and also little cloth scrap-books for younger cousins and friends. But most of all the cards were looked at over and over again and the pictures (some of them really lovely) revealed new beauties and a fresh aspect of Christmas at each inspection. We made transparencies for the windows and while the children were still too small to do other hand-work we made chains of brightly-coloured paper links to festoon all our rooms. They were no works of art, perhaps, but the young eyes were not critical and it was not hard for me to see beauty in them. When the children were big enough to "sew" they did weird and wonderful embroidery on tea-towels for Grandma and the numerous aunts—both the real and the "courtesy" ones.

When they reached the age to enjoy "cooking," and that was still while they needed a chair to reach the table-top, they cut out cookies in various Christmas designs, baked and then frosted them with coloured icings. Some of these went to Grandma and Grandpa who loved the awkward shapes and often slightly bilious effects with the frosting, because of the affection and Christmas spirit that went into the making; and a big cookie-can of these were part of our own Christmas cheer.

Our stores were the Eaton's and Simpson's mail-order catalogues and by the time December arrived the big books were already worn and marked at the pages of cheaper toys and Christmas assortments. The lists that were made and re-made! And the multifarious calculations to divide the costs of the larger gifts among the three children in a correct ratio to the weekly allowances (naturally Betty June with only four cents a week, say, couldn't be expected to bear the same share of expenses as Lo and Anne with their munificent eight and nine cents) filled reams of paper and hours of Lo's and Anne's time. I was always amazed at how much they were able to purchase with their tiny savings and how suitably they remembered their little friends and each other—and, with the greatest love and thoughtfulness, Mummy and Daddy. I would make out the order of Christmas supplies (Daddy adding the gift for Mummy) and it went off in the mail early in December. Then came the long wait until a suitable day arrived for Daddy to go off and get the bulging parcel. Unpacking this and distributing the purchases was almost as much fun as unwrapping one's gifts on Christmas Day.

The gifts for folks not on the Island must be wrapped and ready for the mail early in the month and if December seemed to be shaping up as stormy or unsettled we got our parcels to Shag Harbour beforetimes, often asking the Post-mistress to hold them until a suitable mailing date.

Although I could perhaps have improved on their attempts, I always encouraged the children to do their own wrappings with the festive papers and cords and certainly the "doing up" of gifts remains one of the greatest pleasures of Christmas. Once the gifts for those outside the family were wrapped and away we turned our attention to the family preparations.

A week before Christmas Day we put up the chains of coloured paper and placed the wreaths and transparencies in the windows so that the lighthouse began to take on a festive appearance. Most of our friends and relatives, knowing the infrequency of our trips to the mainland and the uncertainty of the weather this time of year, sent their parcels to us early. These soon added another touch foretelling Christmas, and were put in our bedroom for safekeeping. No one would have *thought* of peeking at a Christmas gift, but it was most interesting to turn a parcel over and about and to conjecture what lovely joys it might contain! And those that disclosed a rattle or tinkle were the most maddeningly intriguing things! I have said how good our friends and relatives were in remembering us generously at Christmas time and the contents of the parcels never belied their promising exteriors.

Because our little ones saw no trees in store windows or in the homes of friends, and because we never put our tree up until Christmas Eve and they preferred to take no part in trimming it, we early inaugurated the Doll's Tree. It was chosen and cut by Anne and Laurie on an afternoon walk and carried home in triumph; it was always symmetrical although no taller than would bring the upper branches within easy reach of chubby arms. About the middle of December it was installed in the same place that the family tree later occupied. Each year as I put away the Christmas decorations I placed in a special box any short ends of tinsel, slightly-broken ornaments, scraps of gay paper and cellophane and these were saved for the Doll's Tree. All three children spent hours happily making decorations, trimming the tree and tying up gifts for the dolls and Teddy bears. The Doll's Tree was kept up until we began to clean house preparatory for Christmas Day, when it was dismantled and taken outdoors to make way for the big tree.

Getting the Christmas tree was the occasion for a family outing. We all bundled up in warm clothing and went along the path and through the woods, stopping at every likely copse of spruce and fir, and passing judgment on the individual trees. At last we would all agree on a likely conifer and Morrill would begin to chop it down, while we stood breathless until he should have taken that first decisive cut and then watched every step of the felling with mounting excitement. Our trees are large, from six to eight feet tall and with amply spreading branches; while Laurie was too small and no hired man was with us to take one end, Morrill pulled the tree, still vibrant and resilient, on Laurie's sled, over snow or bare ground as conditions dictated, along the path, over the hill and home to the shed. While he prepared the base, we hastened to move things in the kitchen and living-room so as to clear a place before the western window.

Then came the bustling and squeezing and pushing to get the tree through the doors and upended, while the crisp cold perfume of its branches filled the room with awakened memories of all the Christmas Eves we ever knew, all the tremulous thrill of being about to touch briefly something too lovely, too sweet, too good and heavenly to bear touching, of becoming for a few hours part of the miracle and sensing in our own hearts, tight with joy and love, the birth of a new world of peace and good will to all men. Once the tree was in its place we all fell quieter momentarily, as if it brought the calmer joys of Christmas with it and its submissive branches spoke to us for a few fleeting seconds of the sacrifices that buy us happiness. After the tree had been decked with its ornaments we forgot the hush that had fallen upon us when we first beheld it upright and beautiful in its appointed place.

I always tried to keep Christmas Eve as quiet as was possible with three little ones almost bursting with joy and excitement. After the supper dishes were put away and everyone was scrubbed and shining, came story-time, and the stories that had come to be regarded as the special ones for Christmas were rather an odd collection and are now gradually being outgrown. First the Christmas story of the Bible so full of beauty and wonder; then The Night Before Christmas, jolly and rollicking, and next a rhymed tale of three orphans who lived on an Island off the coast of Maine and whose Christmas dinner was lost when their boat capsized but who made out marvellously with a baked cod. (It is not hard to understand why this jingle appealed to our three little Islanders.) Another favourite was a *Family Herald* story about a poor little girl whose Christmas had to be postponed till New Year's and then was of the scantiest. I don't know why this became a favourite except that it aroused their pity and Christmas should be, as Dickens says, a charitable time when we remember those less fortunate than ourselves. Finally I finished by telling a story I remembered from my teaching days, a tale of how Santa sprained his ankle and Mrs. Claus substituted for him. This was greatly beloved and when it was done three sleepy youngsters hung up their stockings, previously selected and marked with vari-coloured strings for quick identification, and were ready to go to bed. Though many years have passed since the first Christmas on Bon Portage we keep the Christmas preparations as

little unchanged as we can with the growth and develop-
ment that the years bring to the three youngest members
of the family.

Every parent who has filled a stocking or trimmed a
tree knows how we spend the remainder of the evening;
the happiness with which we place each gift upon the tree,
seeing in imagination the light across the beloved little
faces as the Christmas joys shall unfold for them in the
morning.  If we have a hired man with us he takes part
with us in trimming the tree and placing the gifts, and
shares as much as lies in our powers and his the family
spirit of Christmas; and it is part of the fun to keep the
children's awkwardly tied gifts to him out of sight as he
works about the tree.

Often we are able to get lovely Christmas music over
the radio and its poignant beauty fills the cosy lamp-lit
room where the tree sparkles in its tinsel and flashing balls.
Like all the world, of late years our hearts have been saddened particularly at the Christmas season for the plight
of unhappy millions, but we feel we can do no good by
curtailing the happiness of our children; although we
pare to a minimum the money we spend, so much of our
Christmas cheer costs nothing but time and love.  The
uncertainty of the winter weather makes it impossible for
us to share our Christmas with young service men away
from home as we have so often wished we might.

No modern silver and blue or other chastely restrained
colour schemes are found on the Bon Portage trees.  Like
the ones I remember from my childhood our trees are as
gaudily and glitteringly bedight as we can manage and I
even have some of the crimson balls that enthralled me
as a child, passed on to me when the family tree at Bedford
graduated to electric lights.  We often use candles as we
feel the fire hazard is small when we remember the green
wet tree so recently cut.

At last when the final ornament and gaily-wrapped gift is placed and the stockings bulging, Morrill and I pause for a moment to enjoy the scintillating sight before our weary but happy eyes. We never tarry long as we know the hours are few before the fun begins.

Long before the lazy winter sun is up we hear voices, tense with excitement and happiness, in the rooms above us and the steep stairway creaking under eager feet; then whispers and happy squeals and indrawn breaths of pure delight come from between our open bedroom door and where we know the tree stands, half revealing, half conceal-ing its treasures in the gleam of Laurie's flashlight. But the gifts on the tree are for later, so a dash is made for the stockings behind the stove. We call out, "Merry Christ-mas, kids!" to let them know we are ready to join in the mirth. Then comes a mad rush for our bed and three pairs of icy feet are thrust into the erstwhile warmth between our blankets as three bathrobed youngsters range themselves against the footboards and pull the lower ends of the bedclothes over them. They suffer the illusion that we are all covered and warm under this arrangement and we listen to the happy chatter as they unpack their stock-ings and strew our covers with the contents.

The year that Betty June was three the other two tried in vain to arouse her to the same pitch of excitement they were experiencing. Betty June just couldn't remember anything about Christmas and wasn't greatly interested; even hanging the stockings seemed not to impress her and Anne and Laurie were in a terrible state of impatience and frustration and tried to arouse her interest with detailed accounts of all Christmas held. She remained maddeningly imperturbable. But on Christmas morning it was quite a different story—she arrived in our room, blue eyes aglow and tousled curls perky with excitement. She took her place at the foot of the bed and proceeded to unpack her stocking. Viewing each item with surprised glee and mounting ecstasy, she placed it near her, as she enumerated:

"I told you Santa would bring me a dolly."
"I told you Santa would bring me candy."
"I told you Santa would bring me grapes."

and so on through the dates, nuts, figs and raisins to the orange in the toe. Then in one long-drawn sigh of satisfaction she looked around at the circle of our amused faces and announced in triumphant conclusion, "*I* told you!" And such is the power of the Christmas spirit that even Laurie forebore to say, "You never said a word," though I saw him stop it on the tip of his tongue.

We never dare to leave a fire overnight because the flues are none too safe and because of the tremendous draughts when the wind breezes up, so on Christmas as on all other winter mornings the rooms are chill and Morrill gets up first to make the fires. Soon the living-room is cosy and the little ones depart for its warmth with their treasures to re-examine them between attempts at getting dressed.

The rule is nothing from the stockings except grapes or an orange to be eaten before breakfast, so they all eat a fairly hearty meal and this is a great help in preventing upsets later.

After the necessary morning chores are done, we spin out the opening of the gifts as long as possible. Morrill takes the presents from the tree and Betty June as youngest distributes them. Then each of us takes a turn at opening a gift while the others watch and admire. This system possessed great advantages when the children were too small to remember which kind friend or relative had sent which of the many gifts unwrapped, as it enabled me to keep a list for future acknowledgments.

Unwrapping the gifts takes most of the morning and then I must hasten to the kitchen to prepare dinner. We have never had turkey nor do we miss it. Goose, both wild and domestic, ducks, also of both kinds, and chicken have all at various times provided us with our Christmas dinner. For dessert we have a steamed carrot pudding (the recipe for which has been in our family for generations) served with whipped cream, and, of course, the usual extras that go with Christmas.

Seldom do we have a white Christmas but always if the weather does not absolutely forbid, and I remember only one such Christmas Day, we go for a skate or a long walk after dinner; this makes a welcome break in the surfeit of goodies and excitement and we arrive home hungry enough to do justice to a supper of cold meat and a bottle of extra special preserves, as well as the time-honoured fruit cake.

After supper we light the candles on the tree, then play some of the new games or read one of the books invariably found among our gifts. We all go early to bed, perfectly happy from a day that has brought us many welcome gifts and assurances of love and care from friends and dear ones, a knowledge that though we are apart from them and cannot join in their Christmas cheer we hold a place in their minds and hearts, and this is the best part of Christmas. It was at Christmas time during our first years here that I missed most keenly the fun and companionship of a large boisterous family and the friendships and social gatherings of pre-marriage days.

We keep the tree up till New Year's, then we reluctantly dismantle it. The children were allowed when very small to take a part in this, they prefer not to share in decorating the tree but to see it first in all its glory in the early hours of Christmas morning, but they admire each ornament as it is taken from the tree, gently wrapped and tucked away for another year. We are by no means weary of the happy glitter and spicy perfume of our tree, but school lessons must be resumed immediately after New Year's Day and the tree and greenery must be put away to welcome a clean and busy New Year.

When I started to write I thought I would like to pass on to the many young Canadian couples of the post-war years, who will, I hope, be building their lives along the northern frontiers and other isolated spots, much good advice on how to be happy and to find compensations for the isolation, the lack of companions and of many amenities that have made life easy and interesting. That must have been the schoolteacher in me cropping up again. After all, only the same main ingredients go to making a happy marriage and a full and contented life wherever circumstances place a young couple, everything is included in these two—hard work and love.